FROM INQUIRY TO ACADEMIC WRITING

A Practical Guide

FROM INQUIRY TO ACADEMIC WRITING
A Practical Guide

Stuart Greene
University of Notre Dame

April Lidinsky
Indiana University South Bend

Bedford/St. Martin's   BOSTON ■ NEW YORK

For Bedford/St. Martin's

Executive Editors: Leasa Burton and Stephen A. Scipione
Senior Production Editor: Lori Chong Roncka
Senior Production Supervisor: Nancy Myers
Senior Marketing Manager: Karita dos Santos
Editorial Assistant: Marisa Feinstein
Production Assistants: Lidia MacDonald-Carr and Lindsay DiGianvittorio
Copyeditor: Barbara Bell
Text Design: Linda M. Robertson
Art Director: Donna Lee Dennison
Cover Art: Lucio del Pezzo, *Casellario*, 1988. Painted wood.
        © Berardinelli Arte, Verona, Italy.
Composition: Stratford/TexTech
Printing and Binding: R. R. Donnelley & Sons Company

President: Joan E. Feinberg
Editorial Director: Denise B. Wydra
Editor in Chief: Karen S. Henry
Director of Marketing: Karen Melton Soeltz
Director of Editing, Design, and Production: Marcia Cohen
Managing Editor: Elizabeth M. Schaaf

Library of Congress Control Number: 2007934302

Manufactured in the United States of America.

2   1   0   9   8
f   e   d   c   b

For information, write: Bedford/St. Martin's, 75 Arlington Street, Boston, MA 02116 (617–399–4000)

ISBN-10: 0–312–45166–0   ISBN-13: 978–0–312–45166–0

Acknowledgments

Jean Anyon. "The Economic Is Political." From *Radical Possibilities: Public Policy, Urban Education and a New Social Movement* by Jean Anyon. Copyright © 2005 by Taylor & Francis Group LLC. Reprinted by permission of Routledge, an imprint of Taylor & Francis Group.

Acknowledgments and copyrights are continued at the back of the book on page 272, which constitute an extension of the copyright page. It is a violation of the law to reproduce these selections by any means whatsoever without the written permission of the copyright holder.

9 From Introductions to Conclusions: Drafting an Essay   201

10 From Revising to Editing: Working with Peer Groups   227

Preface for Instructors

From *Inquiry to Academic Writing: A Practical Guide* is a rhetoric that introduces students to college-level reading, thinking, inquiry, analysis, and argument. It is based on a first-year composition course that we have taught over the years in which we guide students through the writing process to produce essays that use evidence and sources in increasingly complex ways. Throughout, we present academic writing as conversational — as a collegial exchange of ideas, undertaken in a spirit of collaboration in the pursuit of new knowledge. On the one hand, we want students to see that academic writing is a social act in which they are expected to work responsibly with the ideas of others. On the other hand, we encourage students to see themselves as makers of knowledge — as writers who use sources in a variety of ways to develop and advance arguments that make new contributions to ongoing conversations about ideas and issues.

We aim to demystify cross-curricular thinking, reading, and writing by breaking down their processes into a series of manageable habits and skills that students can learn and practice. Because academic writing involves complex and overlapping skills, we use a sequenced "step-by-step" pedagogy to clarify (without oversimplifying) the various skills involved in developing academic arguments. For example, we explain that students must learn to make inquiries (by asking questions to discover and explore issues) and value complexity (by avoiding binary thinking and engaging with multiple perspectives); and then we also provide activities to help students practice and develop those habits of mind.

■ The Book's Organization

Although you can teach the chapters in any order, adapting them to suit the needs of your course and your students, the arc of the text follows an incremental and cumulative sequence that begins with academic thinking and proceeds to academic reading, academic research, and finally to academic writing. That said, we hasten to add that we constantly emphasize the recursive and overlapping nature of these skills (especially the connection between reading and writing) and the centrality of the writing process. Indeed, we assume students will be writing throughout the semester, and so punctuate every chapter with short readings and activities designed to get students to pause and try out the kinds of writing they will need to practice through the various stages of developing their papers.

We begin with an introduction for students, in which we explain what academic writing is, and how the book is designed to help them develop as academic thinkers, readers, and writers. Then, in Part One, Chapter 1 presents an overview of academic writing as a process motivated by inquiry, and is followed by chapters that offer strategies for reading critically and working with other writers' ideas. Inevitably, reading and writing processes are intertwined. Thus in Chapter 2 we encourage students to practice "writerly reading" — reading texts as writers who can analyze critically the decisions other writers make (whether those writers are professional scholars or college peers) — so that they can implement the most appropriate strategies given their own purpose for writing. While Chapters 2 through 5 address the nuts and bolts of getting started on writing, from how to mark a text to forming questions and developing a working thesis, we recognize that this process is rarely linear and that it benefits from conversation with invested readers. Chapters 6 and 7 help students develop and support their theses by providing a range of strategies for finding and working with sources — for example, showing students the ways they can use summary, paraphrase, and synthesis in the service of their purpose as writers. In Chapters 8 and 9 we link writerly reading with the ability to practice "readerly writing," or writing that is self-conscious about the needs of real readers.

Chapter 10 presents revision in the context of peer groups. The responses of classmates can help students determine when they might need to read additional material before shaping more effective research questions, for example, or when a draft indicates that more evidence-gathering will be needed to support a student's argument. Our supporting materials for peer workshops foster productive group interaction at every stage of writing, including reading, collecting, planning, developing, researching (for some assignments), and revising. These materials emphasize the spirit of inquiry that guides effective responses to peer writing and the conversational aspect of writing that occurs during workshops and on the page as a writer engages the ideas of others. Finally, in Chapter 11, we provide students with strategies for conducting original research that build upon earlier chapters on using personal experience or writing a researched argument.

As we noted earlier, although the process of developing an academic argument can be messy and unruly at times, the structured step-by-step pedagogy in Part One should support students during each stage of the process. Most readings are followed by "For Analysis and Discussion" questions that send students back into the reading to identify and internalize the rhetorical moves writers make. In every chapter, "Steps to . . ." boxes summarize the major points about each stage of thinking, reading, and writing, offering quick references that bring the most salient information into focus for student review and practice. "Practice Sequences" in each chapter ask students to try out and build on the strategies we have explained or demonstrated. We also provide intermittent templates, formulas, and worksheets that students may use as heuristics or to organize information as they read and write. Your students should feel further supported and encouraged by seeing the abundance of student writing we use as examples in Part One, side by side with the examples of professional writing we include.

■ The Text Is Available Combined with a Reader

From Inquiry to Academic Writing: A Text and Reader features the text chapters in this book, plus a reader that focuses on cross-disciplinary conversations inside (and outside) of the academy. The substantial readings are by well-known academic writers and public intellectuals, and the themes address issues of education, globalization, race, class, gender, and popular culture. You can view the table of contents and request a copy at **www.bedfordstmartins.com**.

■ Additional Resources

An instructor's manual, *Resources for Teaching FROM INQUIRY TO ACADEMIC WRITING* can be downloaded from the companion Web site, **www.bedford stmartins.com/frominquiry**. The manual addresses every step of the process of academic writing we set forth in the text, with additional comments on the readings integrated in the text chapters. Not only do we discuss many of the issues involved in taking our rhetorical approach to academic argument — problems and questions students and instructors may have — we also suggest background readings on the research informing our approach.

Additional resources on the Web site include downloadable templates, worksheets, and summary boxes for students; TopLinks that supplement the readings in the book; and connections to the suite of online resources offered by Bedford/St. Martin's, including *Re: Writing*.

▪ Acknowledgments

We would first like to thank the many reviewers who commented on the proposal and the manuscript. Their comments were invariably useful, and frequently cheering as well. The list of reviewers includes Angela Adams, Loyola University Chicago; Steve Adkison, Idaho State University; Teresa Fernandez Arab, University of Kansas; Yesho Atil, Asheville-Buncombe Technical Community College; Paula Bacon, Pace University–Pleasantville; Susan Bailor, Front Range Community College; Mary Ellen Bertolini, Middlebury College; Laurel Bollinger, University of Alabama–Huntsville; Margaret Bonesteel, Syracuse University; Laurie Britt-Smith, St. Louis University; Lise Buranen, California State University, Los Angeles; Marie Coffey, San Antonio College; Carolyn Cole, Oklahoma Baptist University; Tami Comstock-Peavy, Arapahoe Community College; Emily Cosper, Delgado Community College; Ryan Crider, Missouri State University; Calum Cunningham, Fanshawe College–London; J. Madison Davis, University of Oklahoma–Norman; Erin Denney, Community College of San Francisco; Jason DePolo, North Carolina A&T State University; Brock Dethier, Utah State University; Lisa Egan, Brown University; Ed Eleazer, Francis Marion University; Elaine Fredericksen, University of Texas–El Paso; Rhoda Greenstone, Long Beach City College; Rima Gulshan, George Mason University; Sinceree Gunn, University of Alabama–Huntsville; Ann Hartney, Fort Lewis College; Virginia Scott Hendrickson, Missouri State University; Zachery Hickman, University of Miami; Monica Hogan, Johnson County Community College; Karen Keaton Jackson, North Carolina Central University; Margaret Johnson, Idaho State University; Laura Katsaros, Monmouth University; Howard Kerner, Polk Community College; Jeff Klausman, Whatcom Community College; Tamara Kuzmenkov, Tacoma Community College; Erin Lebacqz, University of New Mexico; Lindsay Lewan, Arapahoe Community College; April Lewandowski, Front Range Community College–Westminster; Renee Major, Louisiana State University; Mark McBeth, John Jay College; Timothy McGinn, Northwest Arkansas Community College; Erica Messenger, Bowling Green State University–Main; Alyce Miller, Indiana University; Whitney Myers, University of New Mexico; Teddy Norris, St. Charles Community College; Lolly J. Ockerstrom, Park University; Jill Onega, University of Alabama–Huntsville; Robert Peltier, Trinity College; Jeanette Pierce, San Antonio College; Mary Jo Reiff, University of Tennessee; Mary Roma, New York University; David Ryan, University of San Francisco; Daniel Schenker, University of Alabama–Huntsville; Roy Stamper, North Carolina State University; Scott Stevens, Western Washington University; Sarah Stone, University of California–Berkeley; Joseph Sullivan, Marietta College; Gretchen Treadwell, Fort Lewis College; Charles Warren, Salem State College; Patricia Webb, Arizona State University; Susan Garrett Weiss, Goucher College; Worth Weller, Indiana University–Purdue University Fort Wayne; and Jackie White, Lewis University.

We are also grateful to many people at Bedford/St. Martin's, starting with president Joan E. Feinberg, editorial director Denise B. Wydra, and editor-in-chief Karen S. Henry. We would especially like to thank executive editor Leasa Burton, who believed in this project early on and told us to be prepared to revise — revise a lot. (And we have!) Steve Scipione has been a terrific editor: he read our work carefully and offered sage advice at every stage of the process. We could not have completed this project without Leasa and Steve and their tireless assistants, Sarah Guariglia and Marisa Feinstein. In the marketing department, we thank marketing director Karen M. Soeltz, and are especially grateful to marketing manager Karita dos Santos and her assistant Jessica Chesnutt. The talented production department conscientiously steered the manuscript through a demanding schedule to create the book you hold. We thank managing editor Elizabeth M. Schaaf; assistant managing editor John Amburg; Lori Chong Roncka, the book's patient and scrupulous production editor; and their assistant Lidia McDonald-Carr. Barbara Bell provided exceptionally alert and constructive copyediting, while Sandy Schechter and Warren Drabek negotiated the complicated process of acquiring permissions. Anna Palchik oversaw the design of the book, and Donna Dennison designed the cover.

A note from Stuart Greene: I want to thank the many students and faculty with whom I've worked over the years. Specifically, I would like to thank Kelly Kinney, Stephen Fox, Rebecca Nowacek, and Katherine Weese, who served as my assistant directors in the past and who taught me a great deal about the teaching of writing. I also would like to thank Robert Kachur, who made important contributions to early iterations of this book. And I will always appreciate the many discussions I have had with John Duffy over these many years and with Connie Mick, a tireless and innovative teacher of writing. A special thanks to Mike Palmquist with whom I taught writing as "conversation" more than twenty years ago and who gave this book direction. Finally, very special thanks to Denise Della Rossa, who has listened to me rehearse these ideas for years. I dedicate this book to her.

A note from April Lidinsky: I am grateful for the superb pedagogical training I received from Lou Kelly at the University of Iowa and Kurt Spellmeyer and Hugh English at Rutgers, the State University of New Jersey, who demonstrated the deep pleasures of theorizing and practicing a hermeneutical approach to writing. Ron Christ, also at Rutgers, taught me the ropes of classical rhetoric and the connected delights of close reading and "close writing." My colleagues and graduate student instructors at the University of Notre Dame, especially Julie Bruneau, Connie Mick, Marion C. Rohrleitner, Misty Schieberle, and Scott T. Smith, inspired me with their energy and vision. Without students to test and sharpen our ideas, this book would not be possible; my teaching has deepened through interactions with many wonderful students over the years. More personally, I am indebted to JoElla Hunter and Tom Lidinsky, my parents, for their model of lifelong reading and learning, and to Ken Smith for his talent for crafting sentences as well as a life of meaning. My thinking, writing, and daily life are immeasurably richer for his partnership.

Contents

FROM INQUIRY TO ACADEMIC WRITING
A Practical Guide

Introduction:
What Is Academic Writing?

In the strictest sense, *academic writing* is what scholars do to communicate with other scholars in their fields of study, their disciplines. It's the research report a biologist writes, the interpretive essay a literary scholar composes, the media analysis a film scholar produces. At the same time, *academic writing* is what you have to learn so that you can participate in the different disciplinary conversations that take place in your courses. You have to learn to *think* like an academic, *read* like an academic, *do research* like an academic, and *write* like an academic — even if you have no plans to continue your education and become a scholar yourself. Learning these skills is what this book is about.

Fair warning: It isn't easy. In fact, initially you may well be perplexed by the vocabulary and sentence structure of many of the academic essays you read. Scholars often use specialized language to capture the complexity of an issue or to introduce specific ideas from their discipline. Every discipline has its own vocabulary. You probably can think of words and phrases that are not used every day but that are necessary, nevertheless, to express certain ideas precisely. For example, consider the terms *centrifugal force, Oedipus complex,* and *onomatopoeia.* These terms carry with them a history of study; when you learn to use them, you also are learning to use the ideas they represent. Terms like these help us describe the world specifically rather than generally; they help us better understand how things work and how to make better decisions about what matters to us.

Sentence structure presents another challenge. The sentences in academic writing are often longer and more intricate than the sentences in popular magazines. Academics want to go beyond what is quick, obvious, and general. They want to ask questions based on studying a subject from multiple points of view, to make surprising, interesting connections that would not occur to someone who has not analyzed the subject carefully. It follows that academic writers are accustomed to extensive reading that prepares them to examine an issue, knowledgeably, from many different perspectives, and to make interesting intellectual use of what they discover in their research. To become an adept academic writer, you have to learn these practices as well.

Academic writing will challenge you, no doubt. But hang in there. Any initial difficulty you have with academic writing will pay off when you discover new ways of looking at the world and of making sense of it. Moreover, the habits of mind and core skills of academic writing are highly valued in the world outside the academy.

At base, academic writing entails making an **argument** — text crafted to persuade an audience — often in the service of changing people's minds and behaviors. When you write an academic essay, then, you have to

- define a situation that calls for some response in writing;
- demonstrate the timeliness of your argument;
- establish a personal investment;
- appeal to readers whose minds you want to change by understanding what they think, believe, and value;
- support your argument with good reasons;
- anticipate and address readers' reasons for disagreeing with you, while encouraging them to adopt your position.

From this list you can see that an academic argument is not about shouting down an opponent. Instead, it is the careful expression of an idea or perspective based on reasoning and the insights garnered from a close examination of the arguments others have made on the issue.

MOVING FROM INQUIRY TO ACADEMIC WRITING

The chapters in the first part of this book introduce you to the habits of mind and core skills of academic writing. By **habits of mind**, we mean the patterns of thought that lead you to question assumptions and opinions, explore alternative opinions, anticipate opposing arguments, compare one type of experience to another, and identify the causes and consequences of ideas and events. These forms of **critical thinking** demand an inquiring mind that welcomes complexities and seeks out and weighs many different points of view, a mind willing to enter complex conversations both in and out of the academy. We discuss academic habits of mind in Chapter 1 and refer to them throughout the rest of the text.

Core skills are the specific steps and strategies needed to develop habits of mind into strong, persuasive writing. The core skills of academic writers manifest in specific reading, writing, and research practices. Many students fantasize about having a "Eureka!" moment, a sudden flash of insight that allows them to write a brilliant paper at a blazing pace in a single draft — and just in time to turn in the assignment. In fact, good academic writing has far less to do with a writer's luck or brilliance than it does with the effective practice of specific core skills that anyone can learn. To help you develop those core skills, we include many opportunities to practice them throughout this book. Chapter by chapter, you will hone your abilities to

- read as a writer and write as a reader;
- analyze arguments;
- discover issues;
- develop an academic thesis;
- use sources;
- write an academic essay.

Read as a writer, and write as a reader.   Writers read to gather ideas; they also read to discover the strategies other writers use to persuade (and even entertain) readers. In other words, writers analyze not only *what* other writers say but also *how* they say it. When you study how writers influence readers through language, you are analyzing the **rhetoric** (the available means of persuasion) of what you read. In practice, this means you consider how the writer's choices are shaped by his or her perspectives, motives, and values, and then infer the effect these choices have on how the issue is presented. As you read, think about the strategies that are most persuasive: lively language, detailed descriptions, clear organization, occasional humor, provocative examples, a passion for the issue. Then, use those strategies in your own writing.

Reading is also the first step in the writing process. When you mark up a text as you read — an activity we see as essential — you begin to put your own ideas on paper. The passages you underline, the comments you scribble in the margins, the connections you make to other texts you have read are the sketchy prelude to the argument you will eventually make in your essay. We focus on the connection between reading and writing in Chapter 2.

Analyze arguments.   When you read an academic essay, you need to understand the argument the writer is making, what the writer wants to persuade you to believe. To a great extent, an argument is a chain of **claims** — assertions, some supported by evidence, some not, that advance the argument. To evaluate an argument, then, you need to recognize and analyze the kinds of claims the writer is making. We show you how to do this in Chapter 3.

Discover issues.   All academic writing begins with curiosity about an issue. An **issue** is a question that presents a fundamental tension within a topic that can be explored and debated. A writer makes an inquiry into a topic, reading what others have said until a particular issue becomes apparent. Consider, for example, the topic of homelessness. At issue for some is that not enough is being done to address the roots of the problem (What can city governments do to remedy the causes of homelessness?). For others, the issue is economic (Where do cities find the money to build adequate shelters?). For still others, the issue is that solutions can generate problems for other groups (What effect will a new homeless shelter have on nearby businesses?). In Chapter 4 we discuss the process of exploring a topic to identify an issue and then shape it into a question that can be debated.

Develop an academic thesis.   A **thesis** is a writer's main claim, the assertion that crystallizes the writer's argument on a given issue. The thesis in an effective piece of academic writing is a central argument that is evident at the beginning of the essay and threads through every paragraph thereafter. As you read more and more academic writing in your classes, you will discover many different strategies for building an argument. In fact, you may be surprised to find that the thesis in a piece of academic writing often does not fit tidily into a single sentence that always appears at the end of a single introductory paragraph. In Chapter 5, we discuss how you can develop an academic thesis that acknowledges the conversation in which you are participating, recognizes the needs and assumptions of your readers, and advances your own fresh perspective on an issue.

Use sources.   All academic writing responds to **sources** — texts that convey the ideas of others — even if the sources are not quoted in the body of the essay. Academic writers do more than gather and repeat the ideas of others. They use sources in a variety of ways but always to advance an argument that contributes to the ongoing conversation about an issue. That is, academic writing is researched; it makes use of sources to advance the writer's own argument. In Chapters 6 and 7, we show you how to find and evaluate sources and then use them effectively in your writing.

Write an academic essay.   In your own essays, you need to present yourself and your argument in a way that will win your readers' minds and hearts. In Chapter 8 we examine the kinds of appeals that can help you do that. You also need to structure your essays so that they lead your readers where you want to them to be: in agreement with, or at least respectful of, your point of view on an issue. Chapter 9 shows you a number of ways to shape your essays to these ends. And because the academic writing process is inherently collaborative, and because it is enormously useful to develop your ideas within the context of peer review, we devote Chapter 10 to describing strategies for working with your classmates to improve your writing and theirs. Finally, in Chapter 11, we discuss another kind of research — primary, or field, research — and the methods that can help you explore an issue beyond the pages of texts.

WRITING IN AND OUT OF THE ACADEMY: ENTERING THE CONVERSATION OF IDEAS

Earlier we claimed that the habits of mind and core skills of academic writing are highly valued in the world outside the academy. In fact, if we count as "academic" any argument that draws on the habits of mind and core skills we present throughout this book, academic writing is commonplace outside the academy — to disseminate and debate ideas, to help people look at the world differently and, perhaps, to change their lives. This kind of writing can alter the way issues are discussed in the culture at large and even the direction of events in that culture.

One example is Martin Luther King Jr.'s famous "Letter from Birmingham Jail," a text that has become an icon of American culture and the civil rights movement. (If you haven't read "Letter from Birmingham Jail," you can easily find a copy on a number of Web sites.) King composed the letter on April 16, 1963, writing in the margins of the *Birmingham News* and on paper that a sympathetic jailer gave him. In prison because he had dared to challenge the status quo, King was critical of "liberal-minded" people who failed to act on behalf of social justice. A jailhouse is certainly not a place where academic writing would be expected to occur, and King did not cite the sources he alludes to in his letter, as he would were he writing for publication in an academic journal. Still, the habits of mind and rhetorical strategies of one trained in academic thinking and writing (King earned a doctorate in theology from Boston University) are very much in evidence in "Letter from Birmingham Jail."

King's letter is characteristically academic in its questioning of conventional assumptions and opinions, in its exploration of alternative opinions, in its anticipation of opposing arguments, and in its use of what he had read in the service of making an argument. Responding to a recently published statement, "White Clergymen Urge Local Negroes to Withdraw from Demonstrations," King's letter sharply criticizes those who argue that his protests against segregation are misplaced and ill timed, interweaving ideas about justice and moral action from a wide range of sources with which educated readers would be familiar. His assertion is clear and focused, and he uses evidence to support his argument that nonviolent protest that challenges unjust laws is both timely and necessary. He is appealing to an audience of white moderates who are sympathetic to his cause but not his actions. To help them see the need for civil disobedience, he draws a parallel between the blacks' struggle for civil rights and the American patriots' struggle for independence from Britain.

In his effort to distinguish between just and unjust laws, King was in conversation with historical and contemporary thinkers; and, like an academic, he drew on his knowledge of different disciplines — specifically, law, philosophy, and theology — to advance his argument about ethics, justice, and moral action. In doing so, he attributed his definitions of justice to venerated thinkers and writers, among them Socrates, St. Augustine, Thomas Aquinas, Martin Buber, and Reinhold Niebuhr. In this way, King used what he had read to explain how many different thinkers in history thought and acted in ways consistent with what he argues in his letter.

It's probably safe to say you are not (yet) at the center of a major conversation of ideas, as Martin Luther King Jr. was. Still, our assumption is that you will have to participate in any number of such conversations during your college career, and, indeed, that you may find yourself compelled and even eager to enter such conversations — either as a trained academic or an educated citizen — when college is behind you. The examples we present in Part One of the book and the readings we have compiled in Part Two give you the flavor of the conversations taking place in and out of the academy. The readings, which range widely in subject and style, have been chosen because they explore ideas that capture the imaginations and consciences of our students as well as those of the larger reading public. Many of the selections here originally appeared in academic journals, but many others have spent weeks on the *New York Times* best-sellers' list. They have been required reading for incoming students on many campuses, but they also have intrigued and engaged general readers. In fact, you may have encountered some of these texts on tables at the front of your local bookstore or been exposed to the writers themselves on talk radio or television. Writers like Jared Diamond, Barbara Ehrenreich, Thomas Friedman, and Malcolm Gladwell are intellectuals who use their academic research and analytical skills to write texts that take on big ideas, to frame them in interesting new ways, and to offer striking examples that make readers think outside the box.

The big ideas the readings explore — what we think is important to learn, the individual's place in a shrinking world, the slippery categories of social identity, the social effects of gender, the intersections of technology and popular culture, for example — raise questions that resist easy answers. Some of the readings grapple with frustrating classroom dynamics or examine the commercial and political contexts of educational institutions. Some take on the marketing of children's toys or Disney films. Others inquire into the ways cyber technologies shape our communication with one another, our understanding of the astounding success of the Harry Potter series or other cultural events, or the tipping point of some behaviors or products that turn mundane practices or objects into social epidemics.

Although all of these selections are researched essays, they do not read like dry research papers. Instead their authors employ a wide range of rhetorical styles to interest their readers. Some take a journalistic approach that may remind you of in-depth news analysis. Some make use of autobiographical details, the authors sharing personal anecdotes to explain their interest in an issue or offer an example. Others employ a more formal tone, relying on research and expertise to build their arguments. Like your own writing, then, these readings use many different strategies to make many different kinds of connections — from the personal to the scholarly, from the individual experience to a larger social pattern. This multileveled inquiry is at the heart of the thinking and writing we invite you to try throughout this book.

All the readings we have included in Part Two are substantial, and many are quite challenging; they are not skim-it-once-and-you've-got-it pieces. You will need to return to them more than once, probably more than twice, with your pen in hand, asking questions in the margins and forging links to other readings and ideas. These readings are also typical of other texts you will read in college that embrace complexity rather than shy away from it. The premise of most of the college-level writing you will read and write yourself is this: "Things are more complex and interesting than you may think: Let me teach you how."

We do not ask you to face the challenging readings in Part Two without guidance. The headnotes that introduce each reading suggest some of the rhetorical and thematic features you should look for as you read. The questions that follow every reading will help you focus on specific aspects of the text, to help you gain the fullest understanding of the reading through different perspectives. Reading Rhetorically questions ask you to look at the stylistic decisions a writer makes in crafting an essay. Inquiring Further questions use each essay as a launching point for further thinking, research, and discovery about an issue raised in the text. Framing Conversations questions provide the starting point for writing your own essays in response to two or three readings. All of these questions are meant to help you increase your mastery of the habits of mind and core skills we present in Part One.

Finally, the assignment sequences at the end of the book define a subject for extended inquiry, offering a sequential path through the readings via writing assignments that build on one another. Topics for these sequences include media representations of American education, the challenges of researching other people, and the tensions between individual and group identities. Instead of asking you to write an essay and then move on to a new topic, we present each essay as an opportunity to develop a frame or lens through which to consider subsequent readings. As you draw on different combinations of resources over a series of compositions, and contribute your own research from the library and from data you've gathered in the field, your ideas about the issues you write

about will become richer and more complex. You will be reading, researching, and writing like an academic writer, taking part in conversations with
other academic writers. Furthermore, these assignments may help you see
the world around you — from everyday happenings to special events — in
unexpected and illuminating ways.

PART ONE

A Text for Moving from Inquiry to Academic Writing

1

Starting with Inquiry: Habits of Mind of Academic Writers

At the center of all academic writing is a curiosity about how the world works and a desire to understand it in its full complexity. To discover and make sense of that complexity, academic writers apply rigorous **habits of mind**, patterns of thought that lead them to question assumptions, explore alternatives, anticipate opposing arguments, compare experiences, and identify the causes and consequences of ideas and events. Habits of mind are especially important today, when we are bombarded with appeals to buy this or that product and with information that may or may not be true. For example, in "106 Science Claims and a Truckful of Baloney" (*The Best American Science and Nature Writing*, 2005), William Speed Weed illustrates the extent to which the claims of science vie for our attention alongside the claims of advertising. He notes that advertisers often package their claims as science, but wonders whether a box of Cheerios really can reduce cholesterol. As readers we have a responsibility to test the claims of both science and advertising in order to decide what to believe and act upon. Weed found that "very few of the 100 claims" he evaluated "proved completely true" and that "a good number were patently false." Testing the truth of claims — learning to consider information carefully and critically, and to weigh competing points of view before making our own judgments — gives us power over our own lives.

The habits of mind and practices valued by academic writers are probably ones you already share. You are behaving "academically" when you comparison-shop, a process that entails learning about the product in magazines and on the Internet and then looking at the choices firsthand before you decide which one you will purchase. You employ these same habits of mind when you deliberate over casting a vote in an election. You inform yourself about the issues that are most pressing; you learn about the candidates' positions on these issues; you consider other arguments for and against both issues and candidates; and you weigh those arguments and your own understanding to determine which candidate you will support.

Fundamentally, academic habits of mind are analytical. When you consider a variety of factors — the quality and functionality of the item you plan to buy, how it meets your needs, how it compares to similar items before making a shopping choice, you are conducting an **analysis**. That is, you are pausing to examine the reasons why you should buy something, instead of simply handing over your cash and saying, "I want one of those." To a certain extent, analysis involves breaking something down into its various parts and reflecting on how the parts do or don't work together. For example, when you deliberate over your vote, you may consult one of those charts that newspapers often run around election time: A list of candidates appears across the top of the chart, and a list of issues appears on the side. You can scan the columns to see where each candidate stands on the issues, and you can scan the rows to see how the candidates compare on a particular issue. The newspaper editors have performed a preliminary analysis for you. They've asked, "Who are the candidates?" "What are the issues?" and "Where does each candidate stand on the issues?"; and they have presented the answers to you in a format that can help you make your decision. But you still have to perform your own analysis of the information before you cast your ballot. Suppose no candidate holds your position on every issue. Who do you vote for? Which issues are most important to you? Or suppose two candidates hold your position on every issue. Which one do you vote for? What characteristics or experience are you looking for in an elected official? And you may want to investigate further by visiting the candidates' Web sites or by talking with your friends to gather their thoughts on the election.

As you can see, analysis involves more than simply disassembling or dissecting something. It is a process of continually asking questions and looking for answers. Analysis reflects, in the best sense of the word, a *skeptical* habit of mind, an unwillingness to settle for obvious answers in the quest to understand why things are the way they are and how they might be different.

This book will help you develop the questioning, evaluating, and conversational skills you already have into strategies that will improve your ability to make careful, informed judgments about the often conflicting and confusing information you are confronted with every day in your classes, in the news, in advertising, in all of your interactions. With these strategies, you will be in a position to use your writing skills to create change where you feel it is most needed.

The first steps in developing these skills are to recognize the key academic habits of mind and then to refine your practice of them. We explore four key habits of mind in the rest of this chapter: (1) inquiring, (2) seeking and valuing complexity, (3) understanding that academic writing is a conversation, and (4) understanding that writing is a process.

ACADEMIC WRITERS MAKE INQUIRIES

Academic writers usually study a body of information so closely and from so many different perspectives that they can ask questions that may not occur to people who are just scanning the information. That is, academic writers learn to make **inquiries**. Every piece of academic writing begins with a question about the way the world works, and the best questions lead to rich, complex insights that others can learn from and build on. You will find that the ability to ask good questions is equally valuable in your daily life. Asking thoughtful questions about politics, popular culture, work, or anything else — questions like How has violence become so commonplace in our schools? What exactly did that candidate mean by "Family values are values for all of us," anyway? What is lost and gained by bringing Tolkien's *Lord of the Rings* trilogy to the screen? What does it take to move ahead in this company? Are those practices ethical? — is the first step in understanding how the world works and how it can be changed.

Inquiry typically begins with **observation**, a careful noting of phenomena or behaviors that puzzle you or challenge your beliefs and values (in a text or in the real world), which prompts an attempt to understand them by **asking questions** (Why does this exist? Why is this happening? Do things have to be this way?) and **examining alternatives** (Maybe this doesn't need to exist. Maybe this could happen another way instead.). For example, Mark Edmundson, a professor of English at the University of Virginia, *observes* that his students seem to prefer classes they consider "fun" over those that push them to work hard. This prompts him to *ask* how the consumer culture — especially the entertainment culture — has altered the college experience. In his essay "On the Uses of a Liberal Education," he wonders what it means that colleges increasingly see students as customers they need to please with Club Med–style exercise facilities that look "like a retirement spread for the young" more than as minds to be educated. He further *asks* what will happen if we don't change course — if entertaining students and making them feel good about themselves continue to be higher priorities than challenging students to stretch themselves with difficult ideas. Finally, he considers alternatives to entertainment-style education and *examines those alternatives* to see what they would offer students.

In her reading on the American civil rights movement of the 1950s and 1960s, one of our students *observed* that the difficulties many immigrant groups experienced when they first arrived in the United States are not acknowledged as struggles for civil rights. This student of Asian descent *wondered why* the difficulties Asians faced in assimilating into American culture are not seen as analogous to the efforts of African Americans to gain civil rights (Why are things this way?). In doing so, she *asked* a number of relevant questions: What do we leave out when we tell stories about ourselves? Why reduce the struggle for civil rights to black-and-white terms? How can we represent the multiple struggles of people who have contributed to building our nation? Then she *examined alternatives* — different ways of presenting the history of a nation that prides itself on justice and the protection of its people's civil rights (Maybe this doesn't need to exist. Maybe this could happen another way.). The academic writing you will read — and write yourself — starts with questions and seeks to find rich answers.

Steps to Inquiry

1 **Observe.** Note phenomena or behaviors that puzzle you or challenge your beliefs and values.

2 **Ask questions.** Consider why things are the way they are.

3 **Examine alternatives.** Explore how things could be different.

A Practice Sequence: Inquiring

The activities below will help you practice the strategies of observing, asking questions, and examining alternatives.

1 Find an advertisement for a political campaign (you can find many political ads on the Internet), and write down anything about what you observe in the ad that puzzles you or that challenges your beliefs and values. Next, write down questions you might have (Do things have to be this way?). Finally, write down other ways you think the ad could persuade you to vote for this particular candidate (Maybe this could happen another way instead.).

2 Locate and analyze data about the students at your school. For example, you might research the available majors and determine which departments have the highest and lowest enrollments. (Some schools have fact books that can be accessed online; and typically the registrar maintains a database with this information.) Is there anything that puzzles you? Write down any questions you have (Why are things the way they are?). What alternative explanations can you provide to account for differences in the popularity of the subjects students major in?

3 Read the following passage about school choice that appeared on the Civil Rights Project Web site in 2002. The Civil Rights Project is a leading research center on civil rights, with a particular interest in education reform. Since its founding in 1996, the project has

convened dozens of national conferences and roundtables, commissioned more than 400 new research and policy studies; and
produced major reports on desegregation, student diversity, school
discipline, special education, dropouts, and Title I programs.

After you read the passage, write down what puzzles you or
challenges your beliefs and values. Next, write down any questions
you might have. Finally, write down what you see as alternative ways
to look at the problem the writer identifies. When you complete this
exercise, share your responses with one of your classmates.

> School choice has been viewed as a remedy to improve the quality of
> local schools and empower inner-city and lower-income parents by
> offering parents the freedom to choose the kind of education their
> children would receive.
>
> In the realm of public school education, school choice has taken
> the form of magnet schools, charter schools, and other test-based or
> specially tracked schools. Parents and students have the option to
> choose schools other than neighborhood schools that generally have a
> similar racial, ethnic, and socio-economic makeup to their local area.
> Private school choice, on the other hand, is a measure that some states
> have adopted to give lower-income students the opportunity to attend
> private schools they otherwise could not afford. This comes in the form
> of a voucher that parents can use toward the cost of private or religious
> school tuition for their children.
>
> Though advocates of school choice claim that it is the best way
> to enable students in failing public schools to get a better education,
> the issue of school choice raises some troubling questions about the
> impacts of individual "choice" on a society that aims to provide all of
> its citizens with equal access to educational opportunities.
>
> Educators have found that choice programs are likely to increase
> the segregation of students by race, social class, and educational
> background. Greater choice in public education is also unlikely, on
> its own, to increase either the number of programs offered or the
> overall performance of schools.
>
> While school choice may allow such *informed* families and commu-
> nities to make significant decisions about their children's education,
> it is important to understand that not all families are equally informed.
> Better-educated parents who are more likely to be involved closely with
> their children's schooling, for example, have consistently been prone to
> participate in choice programs. While those children in families that
> are aware of school options and have the means to actively choose them
> may benefit from a greater range of opportunities, those that are not
> aware of options will not. The lack of resources and information for
> families living in largely minority areas of high poverty means that
> not everyone will benefit equally from school choice. Those students
> that are able to make informed school decisions will leave those that
> are not in their neighborhood schools. Thus, school choice will
> further segregate schools along racial, ethnic, socio-economic, and
> educational backgrounds.

ACADEMIC WRITERS SEEK
AND VALUE COMPLEXITY

Seeking and valuing complexity are what inquiry is all about. As you read academic arguments (for example, about school choice), observe how the media work to influence your opinions (for example, in political ads), or analyze data (for example, about major subjects), you will explore reasons why things are the way they are and how they might be different. When you do so, we encourage you not to settle for simple either/or reasons. Instead, look for multiple explanations.

When we rely on **binary thinking** — imagining there are only two sides to an issue — we tend to ignore information that does not fall tidily into one side or the other. Think of the sound-bite assertions you hear bandied about on talk shows on the pretext of "discussing" a hot-button issue like stem-cell research or abortion: "It's just wrong/right because it is!" Real-world questions — How has the Internet changed our sense of what it means to be an author? What are the global repercussions of fast food? How do we make sense of terrorism? — don't have easy for-or-against answers. Remember that an **issue** is a subject that can be explored and debated. Issue-based questions, then, need to be approached with a mind open to complex possibilities. (We say more about identifying issues and formulating issue-based questions in Chapter 4.)

If we take as an example the issue of terrorism, we would discover that scholars of religion, economics, ethics, and politics tend to ask very differ-ent questions about terrorism, and to propose very different approaches for addressing this worldwide problem. This doesn't mean that one approach is right and the others are wrong; it means that complex issues are likely to have multiple explanations, rather than a simple choice between A and B.

In her attempt to explain the popularity of the Harry Potter books and movies, Elizabeth Teare, a professor of English, provides a window on the steps we can take to examine the complexity of a topic. She begins her essay "Harry Potter and the Technology of Magic" with the observations that author J. K. Rowling is one of the ten most influential people in pub-lishing, and that her books have "transformed both the technologies of reading and the way we understand those technologies." Motivated by a sense of curiosity, if not puzzlement, Teare formulates a guiding question: "What is it that makes these books — about a lonely boy whose first act on learning he is a wizard is to go shopping for a wand — not only an interna-tional phenomenon among children and parents and teachers but also a topic of compelling interest to literary, social, and cultural critics?" Notice that in doing so, she indicates that she will examine this question from the multiple perspectives of literary, social, and cultural critics. To find answers to this question, Teare explores a range of perspectives from a variety of sources, including publishers' Web sites, trade journals, aca-demic studies, and works of fiction for young readers.

One of our students was curious about why a well-known musician, Eminem, was at once so widely popular and so bitterly reviled, a phenomenon he observed in discussions with friends and in reviews of Eminem's music. He set out to understand these conflicting responses by examining the differing perspectives of music critics, politicians, religious evangelists, and his peers; and then he formulated an issue-based question: "How can we explain Eminem's popularity given the ways people criticize Eminem personally and his music?" In looking at this issue, the student opened himself to complexity by resisting simple answers to his question about why Eminem and his music evoked such different and conflicting responses.

Steps to Seeking and Valuing Complexity

1 **Reflect on what you observe.** Clarify your initial interest in a phenomenon or behavior by focusing on its particular details. Then reflect on what is most interesting and least interesting to you about these details, and why.

2 **Examine issues from multiple points of view.** Imagine more than two sides to the issue, and recognize that there may well be other points of view too.

3 **Ask issue-based questions.** Try to put into words questions that will help you explore why things are the way they are.

A Practice Sequence: Seeking and Valuing Complexity

These activities build on the previous exercises we asked you to complete.

1 Look again at the political ad. Think about other perspectives that would complicate your understanding of how the ad might persuade voters.

2 Imagine other perspectives on the data you found on the students in your school. Let's say, for example, that you've looked at data on student majors. How did you explain the popularity of certain majors and the unpopularity of others? How do you think other students would explain these discrepancies? What explanations would faculty members offer?

3 Consider your responses to the excerpt on school choice that you shared with one of your classmates. In addition to the explanations each of you provided, what are some other ways you could look at the issue of school choice? What would parents argue? What about administrators? Teachers? Students?

ACADEMIC WRITERS SEE WRITING
AS A CONVERSATION

Another habit of mind at the heart of academic writing is the understanding that ideas always build on and respond to other ideas, just as they do in the best kind of conversations. Of course, conversations in academic writing happen on the page; they are not spoken. Still, these conversations are quite similar to the conversations you have through e-mail and instant messaging: You are responding to something someone else has written (or said) and are writing back in anticipation of future responses. Academic writing also places a high value on the belief that good, thoughtful ideas come from conversations with others, *many* others. As your exposure to other viewpoints increases, as you take more and different points of view into consideration and build on them, your own ideas will develop more fully and fairly. You already know that to get a full picture of something, often you have to ask for multiple perspectives. When you want to find out what "really" happened at an event when your friends are telling you different stories, you listen to all of them and then evaluate the evidence to draw conclusions you can stand behind — just as academic writers do.

Theologian Martin Marty starts a conversation about hospitality in his book *When Faiths Collide* (2004). *Hospitality* is a word he uses to describe a human behavior that has the potential to bring about real understanding among people who do not share a common faith or culture. As Marty points out, finding common ground is an especially important and timely concern "in a world where strangers meet strangers with gunfire, barrier walls, spiritually land-mined paths, and the spirit of revenge." He believes that people need opportunities to share their stories, their values, and their beliefs; in doing so, they feel less threatened by ideas they do not understand or identify with.

Yet Marty anticipates the possibility that the notion of hospitality will be met with skepticism or incomprehension by those who find the term "dainty." After all, he observes, that there are hospitality suites and hospitality industries suggests current usage of the term is different from historical usage, particularly in the Bible. To counter the incredulity or incomprehension of those who do not immediately understand his use of the term *hospitality*, Marty gives his readers entré to a conversation with other scholars who understand the complexity and power of the kind of hospitality shown by people who welcome a stranger into their world. The stranger he has in mind may simply be the person who moves in next door; but that person could also be an immigrant, an exile, or a refugee. Marty brings another scholar, Darrell Fasching, into the conversation to explain that hospitality entails welcoming "the stranger . . . [which] inevitably involves us in a sympathetic passing over into the other's life and stories" (cited in Marty, p. 132). And John Koenig, another scholar Marty cites, traces the biblical sources of the term in an effort to show the value of understanding those we fear. That understanding, Marty argues, might lead to peace among warring factions. The conversation Marty begins on the page helps us see that his views on bringing about peace have their source in other people's ideas. In turn, the fact that he draws on multiple sources gives strength to Marty's argument.

The characteristics that make for effective oral conversation are also in play in effective academic conversation: empathy, respect, and a willingness to exchange and revise ideas. **Empathy** is the ability to understand the perspectives that shape what people think, believe, and value. To express both empathy and respect for the positions of all people involved in the conversation, academic writers try to understand the conditions under which each opinion might be true and then to represent the strengths of that position accurately. For example, imagine that your firm commitment to protecting the environment is challenged by those who see the value of developing land rich with oil and other resources. In challenging their position, it would serve you well to understand their motives, both economic (lower gas prices, new jobs that will create a demand for new houses) and political (less dependence on foreign oil). If you can demonstrate your knowledge of these factors, those committed to developing resources in protected areas will listen to you. To convey empathy and respect while presenting your own point of view, you might introduce your argument by saying:

> Although it is important to develop untapped resources in remote areas of the United States both to lower gas prices and create new jobs, and to eliminate our dependence on other countries' resources, it is in everyone's interest to use alternative sources of power and protect our natural resources.

As you demonstrate your knowledge and a sense of shared values, you could also describe the conditions under which you might change your own position.

People engaging in productive conversation try to create change by listening and responding to one another rather than dominating one another. Instead of trying to win an argument, they focus on reaching a mutual understanding. This does not mean that effective communicators do not take strong positions; more often than not they do. However, they are more likely to achieve their goals by persuading others instead of ignoring them and their points of view. Similarly, writers come to every issue with an agenda. But they realize that they may have to compromise on certain points to carry those that mean the most to them. More important, they understand that their perceptions and opinions may be flawed or limited, and they are willing to revise them when valid new perspectives are introduced.

In an academic community, ideas develop through give-and-take, through a conversation that builds on what has come before and grows stronger from multiple perspectives. You will find this dynamic at work in your classes, when you discuss your ideas: You will build on other people's insights, and they will build on yours. As a habit of mind, paying attention to academic conversations can improve the thinking and writing you do in every class you take.

Steps to Joining an Academic Conversation

1 **Be receptive to the ideas of others.** Listen carefully and empathetically to what others have to say.

2 **Be respectful of the ideas of others.** When you refer to the opinions of others, be respectful.

3 **Engage with the ideas of others.** Try to understand how people have arrived at their feelings and beliefs.

4 **Be flexible in your thinking about the ideas of others.** Be willing to exchange ideas and to revise your own opinions.

A Practice Sequence: Joining an Academic Conversation

The following excerpt is taken from Thomas Patterson's *The Vanishing Voter* (2002), an examination of voter apathy. Read the excerpt and then complete the exercises that follow.

> Does a diminished appetite for voting affect the health of American politics? Is society harmed when the voting rate is low or in decline? As the *Chicago Tribune* said in an editorial, it may be "humiliating" that the United States, the oldest continuous democracy, has nearly the lowest voting rate in the world. But does it have any practical significance? . . .
>
> The increasing number of nonvoters could be a danger to democracy. Although high participation by itself does not trigger radical change, a flood of new voters into the electorate could possibly do it. It's difficult to imagine a crisis big and divisive enough to prompt millions of new voters to suddenly flock to the polls, especially in light of Americans' aversion to political extremism. Nevertheless, citizens who are outside the electorate are less attached to the existing system. As the sociologist Seymour Martin Lipset observed, a society of nonvoters "is potentially more explosive than one in which most citizens are *regularly* involved in activities which give them some sense of participation in decisions which affect their lives."
>
> Voting can strengthen citizenship in other ways, too. When people vote, they are more attentive to politics and are better informed about issues affecting them. Voting also deepens community involvement, as the philosopher John Stuart Mill theorized a century ago. Studies indicate that voters are more active in community affairs than nonvoters are. Of course, this association says more about the type of person who votes as opposed to the effect of voting. But recent evidence, as Harvard University's Robert Putnam notes, "suggests that the act of voting itself encourages volunteering and other forms of government citizenship."

1 In this excerpt, Patterson presents two arguments: that increasing voter apathy is a danger to democracy and that voting strengthens citizenship. With which of these arguments do you sympathize more? Why? Can you imagine reasons that another person might not agree with you? Write them down. Now do the same exercise with the argument you find less compelling.

2 Your instructor will divide the class into four groups and assign each group a position — pro or con — on one of Patterson's arguments. Brainstorm with the members of your group to come up with examples or reasons why your group's position is valid. Make a list of those examples or reasons, and be prepared to present them to the class.

3 Your instructor will now break up the groups into new groups, each with at least one representative of the original groups. In turn with the other members of your new group, take a few moments to articulate your position and the reasons for it. Remember to be civil and as persuasive as possible.

4 Finally, with the other members of your new group, talk about the merits of the various points of view. Try to find common ground ("I understand what you are saying; in fact, it's not unlike the point I was making about . . ."). The point of this discussion is not to pronounce a winner (who made the best case for his or her perspective) but to explore common ground, exchange and revise ideas, and imagine compromises.

ACADEMIC WRITERS UNDERSTAND THAT WRITING IS A PROCESS

Academic writing is a process of defining issues, formulating questions, and developing sound arguments. This view of writing counters a number of popular myths: that writing depends on inspiration, that writing should happen quickly, that learning to write in one context prepares you to write in other contexts, and that revision is the same as editing. The writing process addresses these myths. First, choosing an idea that matters to you is one way to make your writing matter. And, there's a better chance that writing you care about will contribute in a meaningful way to the conversation going on about a given issue in the academic community. Second, writers who invest time in developing and revising their ideas will improve both the quality of their ideas and their language — their ability to be specific and express complexity.

There are three main stages to the writing process: collecting information, drafting, and revising. We introduce them here and expand on them throughout this book.

■ Collect Information and Material

Always begin the process of writing an essay by collecting *in writing* the material — the information, ideas, and evidence — from which you will shape your own argument. Once you have read and marked the pages of a text, you have begun the process of building your own argument. The important point here is that you start to put your ideas on paper. Good writing comes from returning to your ideas on your own and with your classmates, reconsidering them, and revising them as your thinking develops. This is not something you can do with any specificity unless you have written down your ideas. The box below shows the steps for gathering information from your reading, the first stage in the process of writing an academic essay. (In Chapter 2, these steps are illustrated and discussed in more detail.)

Steps to Collecting Information and Material

1 **Mark your texts as you read.** Note key terms; ask questions in the margins; indicate connections to other texts.

2 **List quotations you find interesting and provocative.** You might even write short notes to yourself about what you find significant about the quotes.

3 **List your own ideas in response to the reading or readings.** Include what you've observed about the way the author or authors make their arguments.

4 **Sketch out the similarities and differences among the authors whose work you plan to use in your essay.** Where would they agree or disagree? How would each respond to the others' arguments and evidence?

■ Draft, and Draft Again

The next stage in the writing process begins when you are ready to think about your focus and how to arrange the ideas you have gathered in the collecting stage. Writers often find that writing a first draft is an act of discovery, that their ultimate focus emerges during this initial drafting process. Sometimes it is only at the end of a four-page draft that a writer says, "Aha! This is what I really want to talk about in this essay!" Later revisions of an essay, then, are not simply editing or cleaning up the grammar of a first draft. Instead, they truly involve *re*vision, seeing the first draft again to establish the clearest possible argument and the most persuasive evidence. This means that you do not have to stick with the way a draft turns out the first time. You can — and must! — be willing to rewrite a substantial amount of a first draft if the focus of the argument changes, or if in the process of writing new ideas emerge that enrich the essay. This is why it's important not to agonize over wording in a first draft: It's difficult to toss out a paragraph you've sweated over for hours. Use the first draft to get your ideas down on paper so that you and your peers can discuss what you see there, with the knowledge that you (like your peers) will need to stay open to the possibility of changing an aspect of your focus or argument.

Steps to Drafting

1 **Look through the materials** you have collected to see what interests you most and what you have the most to say about.

2 **Identify what is at issue,** what is open to dispute.

3 **Formulate a question** that your essay will respond to.

4 **Select the material you will include**, and decide what is outside your focus.

5 **Consider the types of readers** who might be most interested in what you have to say.

6 **Gather more material** once you've decided on your purpose — what you want to teach your readers.

7 **Formulate a working thesis** that conveys the point you want to make.

8 **Consider possible arguments** against your position and your response to them.

■ Revise Significantly

The final stage, revising, might involve several different drafts as you continue to sharpen your insights and the organization of what you have written. As we discuss in Chapter 10, you and your peers will be reading one another's drafts, offering feedback as you move from the larger issues to the smaller ones. It should be clear by now that academic writing is done in a community of thinkers: That is, people read other people's drafts and make suggestions for further clarification, further development of ideas, and sometimes further research. This is quite different from simply editing someone's writing for grammatical errors and typos. Instead, drafting and revising with real readers, as we discuss in Chapter 7, allow you to participate in the collaborative spirit of the academy, in which knowledge making is a group activity that comes out of the conversation of ideas. Importantly, this process approach to writing in the company of real readers mirrors the conversation of ideas carried on in the pages of academic books and journals.

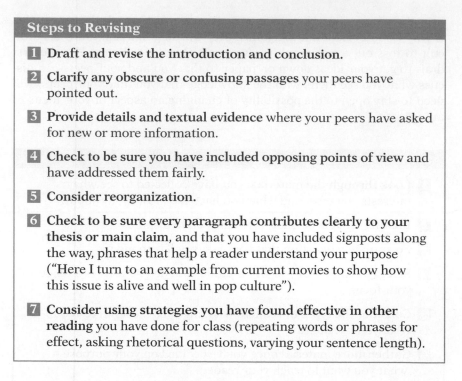

The four academic habits of mind we have discussed throughout this chapter — making inquiries, seeking and valuing complexity, understanding writing as a conversation, and understanding writing as a process — are fundamental patterns of thought you will need to cultivate as an academic writer. The core skills we discuss through the rest of the book build on these habits of mind.

2

From Reading as a Writer
to Writing as a Reader

R eading for class and then writing an essay might seem to be separate
tasks, but reading is actually the first step in the writing process. In
this chapter we present the small steps and specific practices that will help
you read more effectively and move from reading to writing strategies
as you compose your own college essays. These steps and practices will
lead you to understand a writer's purpose in responding to a situation, the
motivation for asserting a claim in an essay and entering a particular conversation with a particular audience.

READING AS AN ACT OF COMPOSING:
ANNOTATING

Leaving your mark on the page — **annotating** — is your first act of composing. When you mark up the pages of a text, you are reading critically,
engaging with the ideas of others, questioning and testing those ideas, and
inquiring into their significance. **Critical reading** is sometimes called
active reading to distinguish it from memorization, when you just read
for the main idea so that you can "spit it back out on a test." When you
read actively and critically, you bring your knowledge, experiences, and
interests to a text, so that you can respond to the writer, continuing the
conversation the writer has begun.

Experienced college readers don't try to memorize a text or assume
they must understand it completely before they respond to it. Instead they
read strategically, looking for the writer's claims, for the writer's key ideas

and terms, and for connections with key ideas and terms in other texts they have read. They also read to discern what conversation the writer has entered, and how the writer's own argument is connected to those he or she makes reference to.

When you annotate a text, your notes in the margins might address the following questions:

- What arguments is this author responding to?
- Is the issue relevant or significant?
- How do I know that what the author says is true?
- Is the author's evidence legitimate? Sufficient?
- Can I think of an exception to the author's argument?
- What would the counterarguments be?

Good readers ask the same kinds of questions of every text they read, considering not just *what* a writer says (the content), but *how* he or she says it given the writer's purpose and audience.

The marks you leave on a page might indicate your own ideas and questions, patterns you see emerging, links to other texts, even your gut response to the writer's argument — agreement, disgust, enthusiasm, confusion. They reveal your own thought processes as you read and signal that you are entering the conversation. In effect, they are traces of your own responding voice.

Developing your own system of marking or annotating pages can help you feel confident when you sit down with a new reading for your classes. Based on our students' experiences, we offer this practical tip: Although wide-tipped highlighters have their place in some classes, it is more useful to read with a pen or pencil in your hand, so that you can do more than draw a bar of color through words or sentences you find important. Experienced readers write their responses to a text in the margins, using personal codes (boxing key words, for example), writing out definitions of words they have looked up, drawing lines to connect ideas on facing pages, or writing notes to themselves ("Connect this to Scholes on video texts"; "Hirsch would disagree big time — see his ideas on memorization in primary grades"; "You call THIS evidence?!"). These notes will help you get started on your own writing assignments, and you cannot make them with a highlighter.

Marking or annotating your readings benefits you twice. First, it is easier to participate in class discussions if you have already noted passages that are important, confusing, or linked to specific passages in other texts you have read. It's a sure way to avoid that sinking feeling you get when you return to pages you read the night before but now can't remember at all. Second, by marking key ideas in a text, noting your ideas about them, and making connections to key ideas in other texts, you have begun the process of writing an essay. When you start writing the first draft of your essay, you can quote the passages you have already marked and explain what you find significant about them based on the notes you have already made to yourself. You can make the connections to other texts in the paragraphs of your own essay that you have already begun to make on the pages of your textbook. If you mark your texts effectively, you'll never be at a loss when you sit down to write the first draft of an essay.

Let's take a look at how one of our students marked several paragraphs of Douglas Massey and Nancy Denton's *American Apartheid: Segregation and the Making of the Underclass* (1993). In the excerpt below, the student underlines what she believes is important information and begins to create an outline of the authors' main points.

1. racist attitudes

2. private behaviors

3. & institutional practices
lead to ghettos
(authors' claim?)

Ghetto = multi-story, high-density housing projects.
Post-1950

I remember this happening where I grew up, but I didn't know the government was responsible. Is this what happened in There Are No Children Here?

The spatial isolation of black Americans was achieved by   *1*
a conjunction of <u>racist attitudes</u>, <u>private behaviors</u>, and <u>institutional practices</u> that disenfranchised blacks from urban housing markets and led to the creation of the <u>ghetto</u>. Discrimination in employment exacerbated black poverty and limited the economic potential for integration, and black residential mobility was systematically blocked by pervasive discrimination and white avoidance of neighborhoods containing blacks. <u>The walls of the ghetto were buttressed after 1950</u> by government programs that promoted slum clearance and <u>relocated displaced ghetto residents into multi-story, high-density housing projects</u>.

Authors say situation of "spatial isolation" remains despite court decisions. Does it?

In theory, this self-reinforcing cycle of prejudice,   *2*
discrimination, and segregation was broken during the 1960s by a growing rejection of racist sentiments by whites and a series of court decisions and federal laws that banned discrimination in public life. (1) <u>The Civil Rights Act of 1964 outlawed racial discrimination in employment</u>, (2) the <u>Fair Housing Act of 1968 banned discrimination in housing</u>, and (3) the <u>*Gautreaux* and *Shannon* court decisions prohibited public authorities from placing housing projects</u> exclusively in black neighborhoods. Despite these changes, however, the <u>nation's largest black communities remained as segregated as ever in 1980</u>. Indeed, many urban areas displayed a pattern of intense racial isolation that could only be described as <u>hypersegregation</u>.

Subtler racism, not on public record.

Although the racial climate of the United States improved outwardly during the 1970s, <u>racism still restricted the residential freedom of black Americans</u>; it just did so in less blatant ways. In the aftermath of the civil rights revolution, few whites voiced openly racist sentiments; realtors no longer refused outright to rent or sell to blacks; and few

*Lack of enforcement
of Civil Rights Act?
Fair Housing Act?
Gautreaux and
Shannon? Why?
Why not?*

local governments went on record to oppose public housing projects because they would contain blacks. This lack of overt racism, however, did not mean that prejudice and discrimination had ended.

Notice that this student underlines information that helps her understand the argument the authors make. In her annotations, she numbers the three key factors (racist attitudes, private behaviors, and institutional practices) that influenced the formation of ghettos in the United States. She also identifies the situation that motivates the authors' analysis: the extent to which "the spatial isolation of black Americans" still exists despite laws and court decisions designed to end residential segregation. And she makes connections to her own experience and to another book she has read. By understanding the authors' arguments and making these connections, she begins the writing process. She also sets the stage for her own research, for examining the authors' claim that residential segregation still exists.

A Practice Sequence: Annotating

1 Take a few minutes to read and mark what you find significant in the paragraph below from Massey and Denton's *American Apartheid*. Notice how many different kinds of marks you make (circling, boxing, underlining, asking questions, noting your responses and connections to other texts you've read, and the like).

> Economic arguments can be invoked to explain why levels of black-white segregation changed so little during the 1970s. After decades of steady improvement, black economic progress stalled in 1973, bringing about a rise in black poverty and an increase in income inequality. As the black income distribution bifurcated, middle-class families experienced downward mobility and fewer households possessed the socio-economic resources necessary to sustain residential mobility and, hence, integration. If the economic progress of the 1950s and 1960s had been sustained into the 1970s, segregation levels might have fallen more significantly. William Clark estimates that 30%–70% of racial segregation is attributable to economic factors, which, together with urban structure and neighborhood preferences, "bear much of the explanatory weight for present residential patterns."

2 Now, move into a small group with three or four other students and compare your annotated texts. What do you make of the similarities and differences you see? What strategies can you borrow from one another?

READING AS A WRITER: ANALYZING A TEXT RHETORICALLY

When you identify a writer's purpose for responding to a situation by composing an essay that puts forth claims meant to sway a particular audience, you are performing **rhetorical analysis** — separating out the parts of an argument to better understand how the argument works as a whole. We discuss each of these elements — situation, purpose, claims, and audience — as we analyze the following preface from E. D. Hirsch's book *Cultural Literacy: What Every American Needs to Know* (1987). Formerly a professor of English, Hirsch has long been interested in educational reform. That interest developed from his (and others') perception that today's students do not know as much as students did in the past. Although he wrote this book more than twenty years ago, many observers still believe that the contemporary problems of illiteracy and poverty can be traced to a lack of cultural literacy. Read the preface. You may want to mark it up with your own questions and responses, and then consider them in light of our analysis (following the preface) of Hirsch's rhetorical situation, purpose, claims, and audience.

ABOUT THE READING

E. D. Hirsch Jr., a retired English professor, is the author of many acclaimed books, including *The Schools We Need and Why We Don't Have Them* (1996) and *The Knowledge Deficit* (2006). His book *Cultural Literacy* was a best seller in 1987 and had a profound effect on the focus of education in the late 1980s and 1990s.

E. D. HIRSCH JR.

Preface to *Cultural Literacy*

Rousseau points out the facility with which children lend themselves to our false methods: . . . "The apparent ease with which children learn is their ruin."

—JOHN DEWEY

There is no matter what children should learn first, any more than what leg you should put into your breeches first. Sir, you may stand disputing which is best to put in first, but in the meantime your backside is bare. Sir, while you stand considering which of two things you should teach your child first, another boy has learn't 'em both.

—SAMUEL JOHNSON

To be culturally literate is to possess the basic information needed to thrive in the modern world. The breadth of that information is great, extending over the major domains of human activity from sports

1

to science. It is by no means confined to "culture" narrowly understood as an acquaintance with the arts. Nor is it confined to one social class. Quite the contrary. Cultural literacy constitutes the only sure avenue of opportunity for disadvantaged children, the only reliable way of combating the social determinism that now condemns them to remain in the same social and educational condition as their parents. That children from poor and illiterate homes tend to remain poor and illiterate is an unacceptable failure of our schools, one which has occurred not because our teachers are inept but chiefly because they are compelled to teach a fragmented curriculum based on faulty educational theories. Some say that our schools by themselves are powerless to change the cycle of poverty and illiteracy. I do not agree. They *can* break the cycle, but only if they themselves break fundamentally with some of the theories and practices that education professors and school administrators have followed over the past fifty years.

Although the chief beneficiaries of the educational reforms advocated in this book will be disadvantaged children, these same reforms will also enhance the literacy of children from middle-class homes. The educational goal advocated is that of mature literacy for *all* our citizens.   2

The connection between mature literacy and cultural literacy may already be familiar to those who have closely followed recent discussions of education. Shortly after the publication of my essay "Cultural Literacy," Dr. William Bennett, then chairman of the National Endowment for the Humanities and subsequently secretary of education in President Ronald Reagan's second administration, championed its ideas. This endorsement from an influential person of conservative views gave my ideas some currency, but such an endorsement was not likely to recommend the concept to liberal thinkers, and in fact the idea of cultural literacy has been attacked by some liberals on the assumption that I must be advocating a list of great books that every child in the land should be forced to read.   3

But those who examine the Appendix to this book will be able to judge for themselves how thoroughly mistaken such an assumption is. Very few specific titles appear on the list, and they usually appear as words, not works, because they represent writings that culturally literate people have read about but haven't read. *Das Kapital* is a good example. Cultural literacy is represented not by a *prescriptive* list of books but rather by a *descriptive* list of the information actually possessed by literate Americans. My aim in this book is to contribute to making that information the possession of all Americans.   4

The importance of such widely shared information can best be understood if I explain briefly how the idea of cultural literacy relates to currently prevailing theories of education. The theories that have dominated American education for the past fifty years stem ultimately from   5

Jean Jacques Rousseau, who believed that we should encourage the natural development of young children and not impose adult ideas upon them before they can truly understand them. Rousseau's conception of education as a process of natural development was an abstract generalization meant to apply to all children in any time or place: to French children of the eighteenth century or to Japanese or American children of the twentieth century. He thought that a child's intellectual and social skills would develop naturally without regard to the specific content of education. His content-neutral conception of educational development has long been triumphant in American schools of education and has long dominated the "developmental," content-neutral curricula of our elementary schools.

In the first decades of this century, Rousseau's ideas powerfully influenced the educational conceptions of John Dewey, the writer who has the most deeply affected modern American educational theory and practice. Dewey's clearest and, in his time, most widely read book on education, *Schools of Tomorrow*, acknowledges Rousseau as the chief source of his educational principles. The first chapter of Dewey's book carries the telling title "Education as Natural Development" and is sprinkled with quotations from Rousseau. In it Dewey strongly seconds Rousseau's opposition to the mere accumulation of information.   6

> Development emphasizes the need of intimate and extensive personal acquaintance with a small number of typical situations with a view to mastering the way of dealing with the problems of experience, not the piling up of information.

Believing that a few direct experiences would suffice to develop the skills that children require, Dewey assumed that early education need not be tied to specific content. He mistook a half-truth for the whole. He placed too much faith in children's ability to learn general skills from a few typical experiences and too hastily rejected "the piling up of information." Only by piling up specific, communally shared information can children learn to participate in complex cooperative activities with other members of their community.   7

This old truth, recently rediscovered, requires a countervailing theory of education that once again stresses the importance of specific information in early and late schooling. The corrective theory might be described as an anthropological theory of education, because it is based on the anthropological observation that all human communities are founded upon specific shared information. Americans are different from Germans, who in turn are different from Japanese, because each group possesses specifically different cultural knowledge. In an anthropological perspective, the basic goal of education in a human community is acculturation, the transmission to children of the specific information shared by the adults of the group or polis.   8

Plato, that other great educational theorist, believed that the specific   9
contents transmitted to children are by far the most important elements
of education. In *The Republic* he makes Socrates ask rhetorically, "Shall
we carelessly allow children to hear any casual tales which may be
devised by casual persons, and to receive into their minds ideas for the
most part the very opposite of those which we shall wish them to have
when they are grown up?" Plato offered good reasons for being concerned with the specific contents of schooling, one of them ethical: "For
great is the issue at stake, greater than appears — whether a person is to
be good or bad."

Time has shown that there is much truth in the durable educational   10
theories of both Rousseau and Plato. But even the greatest thinkers, being
human, see mainly in one direction at a time, and no thinkers, however
profound, can foresee the future implications of their ideas when they are
translated into social policy. The great test of social ideas is the crucible of
history, which, after a time, usually discloses a one-sidedness in the best
of human generalizations. History, not superior wisdom, shows us that
neither the content-neutral curriculum of Rousseau and Dewey nor the
narrowly specified curriculum of Plato is adequate to the needs of a modern nation.

Plato rightly believed that it is natural for children to learn an adult   11
culture, but too confidently assumed that philosophy could devise the
one best culture. (Nonetheless, we should concede to Plato that within
our culture we have an obligation to choose and promote our best traditions.) On the other side, Rousseau and Dewey wrongly believed that
adult culture is "unnatural" to young children. Rousseau, Dewey, and
their present-day disciples have not shown an adequate appreciation of
the need for transmission of specific cultural information.

In contrast to the theories of Plato and Rousseau, an anthropological   12
theory of education accepts the naturalness as well as the relativity of
human cultures. It deems it neither wrong nor unnatural to teach young
children adult information before they fully understand it. The anthropological view stresses the universal fact that a human group must have
effective communications to function effectively, that effective communications require shared culture, and that shared culture requires transmission of specific information to children. Literacy, an essential aim of
education in the modern world, is no autonomous, empty skill but
depends upon literate culture. Like any other aspect of acculturation, literacy requires the early and continued transmission of specific information. Dewey was deeply mistaken to disdain "accumulating information
in the form of symbols." Only by accumulating shared symbols, and the
shared information that the symbols represent, can we learn to communicate effectively with one another in our national community.

■ Identify the Situation

The **situation** is what motivates you to write. Suppose you want to respond to the government's attempts to limit music downloads from the Internet. The *situation* is that the music industry has long believed it has been losing sales of CDs and other music products because of downloading, so industry leaders lobbied lawmakers in Washington, D.C., and persuaded them to restrict people's ability to take what the industry argues is its property. Discovering the range of perspectives here — for instance, of the music industry and its lobbyists, of legislators, of copyright lawyers, of consumer groups, of consumers who download music — will take some research, which is why we call writing a form of inquiry — it often begins with learning to identify the situation. Learning to identify the situation in a piece of writing, the conversations and issues that motivated the author to respond in writing, will help you figure out how to respond in your own writing.

To understand what motivated Hirsch to write, we need look no further than the situation he identifies in the first paragraph of the preface: "the social determinism that now condemns [disadvantaged children] to remain in the same social and educational condition as their parents." Hirsch wants to make sure his readers are aware of the problem so that they will be motivated to read his argument (and take action). He presents as an urgent problem the situation of disadvantaged children, an indication of what is at stake for the writer and for the readers of the argument. For Hirsch, this situation needs to change.

The urgency of a writer's argument is not always triggered by a single situation; often it is multifaceted. Again in the first paragraph, Hirsch identifies a second concern when he states that poverty and illiteracy reflect "an unacceptable failure of our schools, one which has occurred not because our teachers are inept but chiefly because they are compelled to teach a fragmented curriculum based on faulty educational theories." When he introduces a second problem, Hirsch helps us see the interconnected and complex nature of the situations authors confront in academic writing.

■ Identify the Writer's Purpose

The **purpose** for writing an essay may be to respond to a particular situation; it also can be what a writer is trying to accomplish. Specifically, what does the writer want readers to do? Does the writer want us to think about an issue, to change our opinions? Does the writer want to make us aware of a problem that we may not have recognized? Does the writer advocate for some type of change? Or is some combination of all three at work?

Hirsch's overall purpose is to promote educational reforms that will produce a higher degree of literacy for all citizens. He begins his argument with a broad statement about the importance of cultural literacy: "Cultural literacy constitutes the only sure avenue of opportunity for disadvantaged children, the only reliable way of combating the social determinism that now condemns them to remain in the same social and educational condition as their parents" (para. 1). As his argument unfolds, his purpose continues to unfold as well. He identifies the schools as a source of the problem and suggests how they must change to promote literacy:

> Some say that our schools by themselves are powerless to change the cycle of poverty and illiteracy. I do not agree. They *can* break the cycle, but only if they themselves break fundamentally with some of the theories and practices that education professors and school administrators have followed over the past fifty years. (para. 1)

The "educational goal," Hirsch says at the end of paragraph 2, is "mature literacy for *all* our citizens." To reach that goal, he insists, education must break with the past. In paragraphs 5 through 11, he cites the influence of Jean-Jacques Rousseau, John Dewey, and Plato, tracing what he sees as the educational legacies of the past. Finally, in the last paragraph of the excerpt, Hirsch describes an "anthropological view, . . . the universal fact that a human group must have effective communications to function effectively, that effective communications require shared culture, and that shared culture requires transmission of specific information to children." It is here, Hirsch argues, in the "transmission of specific information" to children, that schools must do a better job.

■ Identify the Writer's Claims

Claims are assertions that authors must justify and support with evidence and good reasons. The **thesis**, or **main claim**, is the controlling idea that crystallizes a writer's main point, helping readers track the idea as it develops throughout the essay. A writer's purpose clearly influences the way he or she crafts the main claim of an argument, the way he or she presents all assertions and evidence.

Hirsch's main claim is that "cultural literacy constitutes the only sure avenue of opportunity for disadvantaged children, the only reliable way of combating the social determinism that now condemns them to remain in the same social and educational condition as their parents" (para. 1). Notice that his thesis also points to a solution: making cultural literacy the core of public school curricula. Here we distinguish the main claim, or thesis, from the other claims or assertions that Hirsch makes. For example, at the very outset, Hirsch states that "to be culturally literate is to possess the basic information needed to thrive in the modern world." Although this is an assertion that requires support, it is a **minor claim**; it does not shape what Hirsch writes in the remainder of his essay. His main claim, or thesis, is really his call for reform.

■ Identify the Writer's Audience

A writer's language can help us identify his or her **audience**, the readers whose opinions and actions the writer hopes to influence or change. In

Hirsch's text, words and phrases like *social determinism, cycle of poverty and illiteracy, educational reforms, prescriptive,* and *anthropological* indicate that Hirsch believes his audience is well educated. References to Plato, Socrates, Rousseau, and Dewey also indicate the level of knowledge Hirsch expects of his readers. Finally, the way the preface unfolds suggests that Hirsch is writing for an audience that is familiar with a certain **genre**, or type, of writing: the formal argument. Notice how the author begins with a statement of the situation and then asserts his position. The very fact that he includes a preface speaks to the formality of his argument. Hirsch's language, his references, the structure of the document, all suggest that he is very much in conversation with people who are experienced and well-educated readers.

More specifically, the audience Hirsch invokes is made up of people who are concerned about illiteracy in the United States and the kind of social determinism that appears to condemn the educationally disadvantaged to poverty. Hirsch also acknowledges directly "those who have closely followed recent discussions of education," including the conservative William Bennett and liberal thinkers who might be provoked by Bennett's advocacy of Hirsch's ideas (para. 3). Moreover, he appears to assume his readers have achieved "mature literacy," even if they are not actually "culturally literate." He is writing for an audience that not only is well educated but also is deeply interested in issues of education as they relate to social policy.

Steps to Analyzing a Text Rhetorically

1 **Identify the situation.** What motivates the writer to write?

2 **Identify the writer's purpose.** What does the writer want readers to do or think about?

3 **Identify the writer's claims.** What is the writer's main claim? What minor claims does he or she make?

4 **Identify the writer's audience.** What do you know about the writer's audience? What does the writer's language imply about the readers? What about the writer's references? The structure of the essay?

A Practice Sequence: Reading Rhetorically

This exercise asks you to work your way through a series of paragraphs, identifying in turn the key elements of rhetorical analysis: situation, purpose, claim, and audience.

1 Begin by identifying the situation. Read the following passage from a student essay titled "Overcoming Social Stratification in

America." As you read, identify the specific words and phrases that suggest the situation that motivated the writer to compose the essay. Then describe the situation in one or two sentences.

> The social stratification encompassing American society today has placed African Americans and other minority groups at a disadvantage: Limited social mobility is preventing them from achieving higher social status. In his article "What Every American Needs to Know," E. D. Hirsch suggests that minority groups are disadvantaged as a result of a major decline in communication among Americans caused by the current educational system's failure to teach "cultural literacy." Hirsch contends that cultural literacy acts as a social equalizer, creating an American identity based on shared knowledge among all individuals independent of their social stratum. However, Hirsch's theory ignores race's inherent ability to define all social constructions in America. JanMohamed and Lloyd, in their article "Toward a Theory of Minority Discourse: What Is to Be Done?" propose that a schism separating minorities from the majority has been evolving since the colonial period. E. B. Higginbotham alludes to the effect of this deep separation and a broad antagonism toward the majority, claiming they have turned the idea of race into what she calls in her article "African-American Women's History and the Metalanguage of Race," a "metalanguage." Because of race, Hirsch's notion of cultural literacy has little relevance to attempts to eradicate social stratification in America. For minorities to achieve higher status, they must overcome the metalanguage, which has turned the term *minority* into a reference to a person of inferior political status instead of a group of people comprising a smaller population in society.

2 Identify the writer's purpose. Read the passage below from a student essay titled "Education Today: From Cultural Literacy to Multicultural Contact." What words and phrases suggest the student's purpose for writing? In a few sentences, describe the writer's purpose.

> The telephone as we know it today was invented exactly 125 years ago. The first wireless telephone was first used some 45 years later. The development of the Internet took place in the late sixties. Today, handheld devices can transmit real-time video via satellite. These and other technological advances have allowed the world to expand at an ever-increasing pace. Nowadays, the world is a place of continuous progress, a constantly changing environment in which adaptation is the only key to success. While some sectors of society were able to perform a smooth transition from the national to the global level of thinking, others had a more difficult time. One particular component that failed to adapt properly is the educational system. The emphasis on test taking and short-term memorization, which was introduced during the early 1900s, is outdated but still maintained in the teaching style today. I propose that education should be more multifaceted.

3 Identify the writer's claim. Read the passage below from a student essay titled "'Writing' the Wrong: The Dilemma of the Minority Author." Identify and write down the writer's main claim, or thesis.

> Literature, because of its ability to convey a set of values and ideals to a particular audience, has been a significant medium for shaping revolutionary events in America. For minority authors of various ethnic backgrounds, literature is a means by which they can encourage an end to the subordination of minority groups. Yet the goal of minority literature goes beyond achieving reform. Minority authors also hope to convey a piece of their own unique identity through the text that fills their pages. Unfortunately, however, because of the marginalization of minority texts by Western culture, many minority authors have found it difficult to achieve the twofold purpose of their writing. To move their works toward the forefront of society and so disseminate their message of societal reform to a larger audience that includes European Americans, minority authors have found that they must risk a portion of their own unique identity. An unwillingness to do so, in fact, can leave them powerless to effect any form of societal revolution that could end the overshadowing of minorities by the dominant culture. Although it is unfortunate that minority authors must initially sacrifice a piece of their identity to reach a larger audience, doing so gives them "insider" status and thus greater influence on societal change.

4 Identify the writer's audience. Read the following excerpt from "The Problems and Dangers of Assimilatory Policies." Admittedly, the essay was written in response to a classroom assignment, so the student's instructor and classmates would be part of the writer's audience. But what sort of generalizations can you make about the audience that would read this essay outside the classroom environment?

> American society considers itself to be in an age of enlightenment. Racism has been denounced, and cultural colorblindness in all things is encouraged. Economic opportunities are available for everyone, and equal consideration before the law is provided for each citizen. American society considers itself the embodiment of liberty, equality, and justice for all.
>
> In a society like the one described, it follows that one's background and culture [do] not have any influence on one's socioeconomic status; theoretically, the two should be completely disconnected. Yet, as we all know, this is not the case. The people of the highest status in America are almost uniformly white males. Sadly, America, the place of equality and liberty, is still very much a stratified society, not only by socioeconomic class/status, but minority cultures much more often fill the ranks of the lower classes. Fortunately for those of minority cultures, the country's policymakers now accept, at least in

speech, the basic equality and potential of all cultures to rise out of poverty; unfortunately, they still refuse to recognize the validity of differences in these cultures from what they, the policymakers, view as American.

5 Share your analysis. Working with two or three of your classmates, come to a consensus on the (1) situation, (2) purpose, (3) main claim, and (4) audience of the excerpts. Then choose a spokesperson to report your group's thoughts to the rest of the class.

WRITING AS A READER: COMPOSING A RHETORICAL ANALYSIS

One of our favorite exercises is to ask our students to choose a single paragraph from a text they have read and to write a rhetorical analysis of it. Once you are able to identify how writers make their arguments, you are better able to make use of their strategies in your own writing. You may be amazed by how much you can say or write about a single paragraph in an essay once you begin to consider such factors as purpose and audience.

For example, one of our students wrote a rhetorical analysis of the third paragraph of Ada María Isasi-Díaz's essay "Hispanic in America: Starting Points." Here is the paragraph from Isasi-Díaz's work:

> A preliminary note about terminology. What to call ourselves is an issue hotly debated in some segments of our communities. I use the term "Hispanic" because the majority of the communities I deal with include themselves in that term, though each and every one of us refers to ourselves according to our country of origin: Cubans, Puerto Ricans, Mexican Americans, etc. What I do wish to emphasize is that "Latina/o" does not have a more politicized or radical connotation than "Hispanic" among the majority of our communities. In my experience it is most often those outside our communities who insist on giving Latina/o such a connotation. The contrary, however, is true of the appellation "Chicana/o," which does indicate a certain consciousness and political stance different from but not necessarily contrary to those who call themselves Mexican Americans.

Now here is the student's analysis of the paragraph, which she wrote after she read Isasi-Díaz's whole essay and identified (1) the situation that Isasi-Díaz responded to, (2) her purpose, (3) her claim, and (4) her intended audience (through the use of language). Our annotations highlight some of the rhetorical strategies the student made use of in her analysis.

The student focuses on the author's language as a way to grasp the situation.

The student notes that the author uses personal experience as evidence.

The student also considers how what she reads might apply to her own writing. The student identifies those parts of the essay that could affect readers, using her own response as an example.

The student makes a connection to other essays she has read.

Isasi-Díaz is obviously concerned about the words she uses to set   *1* out her argument: She begins this early paragraph with "a preliminary note about terminology." She wants us to know that there is an argument about the label *Hispanic* within Hispanic communities, and she uses *our* repeatedly in this paragraph to remind us that she is part of those communities. She assumes that we might be outside those communities and that we need this terminology clarified (in my case, she's right!). Isasi-Díaz uses personal experience to show us that she knows what she is talking about: "In my experience it is most often those outside our communities who insist . . ." She walks us through the different terms (*Latina/o, Chicana/o, Mexican American*) and offers not exactly definitions but connotations, telling us which label indicates what kind of political position. I like the way she wants to clear up all these different terms, and I think I might try in my own essay to have a paragraph early on that clarifies the definitions and connotations of the key words I am using.

It is interesting that Isasi-Díaz makes a big deal of being   *2* inside her communities, and blames those "outside" her communities for "insist[ing]" on giving what she sees as the wrong connotation to words. As an outsider myself, this might have turned me off a bit, but she does make clear that there is a wide range of experiences (suggested by her long list of countries of origin) and opinions within "our communities" (the fact that *communities* is plural rather than singular suggests this, too), so she is doing something more complicated than "us versus them" here. It makes me think of Gloria Anzaldúa's essay, where she also shows how many different perspectives are embedded in the very words a person uses, particularly on the border between Mexico and the United States. It also reminded me of Mary Louise Pratt's idea of "transculturation," where people struggle to retain and adapt their cultural identities in "contact zones."

■ Write a Rhetorical Analysis of a Paragraph

Now we'd like you to try the same exercise. First, read the excerpt from Ada María Isasi-Díaz's essay that follows. As you read, underline where the writer makes the following points explicit:

- The situation to which she is responding
- The purpose of her essay
- Her main claim, or thesis
- Words and phrases that suggest who she believes is her audience

ABOUT THE READING

Ada María Isasi-Díaz is a professor of theology and ethics at the Theological School, Drew University. A political refugee from Cuba, she came to the United States in 1960 and entered an Ursuline convent. She later spent three years as a missionary in Lima, Peru, where she worked with the poor and the oppressed, joining them in their struggle for justice. In her book *Mujerista Theology* (1996), she provides what she calls a comprehensive introduction to Hispanic feminist theology, which seeks to create a valid voice for Latinas and challenges theological understandings, church teachings, and religious practices that oppress Latinas. "Hispanic in America: Starting Points" was originally published in the May 13, 1991, issue of *Christianity in Crisis*.

ADA MARÍA ISASI-DÍAZ

Hispanic in America: Starting Points

The twenty-first century is rapidly approaching and with it comes a *1* definitive increase in the Hispanic population of the United States. We will soon be the most numerous ethnic "minority" — a minority that seems greatly problematic because a significant number of us, some of us would say the majority, behave differently from other immigrant groups in the United States.

Our unwillingness to jump into the melting pot; our insistence on *2* maintaining our own language; our ongoing links with our countries of origin — due mostly to their geographic proximity and to the continuous flow of more Hispanics into the United States; and the fact that the largest groups of Hispanics, Mexican Americans and Puerto Ricans are geographically and politically an integral part of this country: These factors, among others, make us different. And the acceptance of that difference, which does not make us better or worse than other groups but simply different, has to be the starting point for understanding us. What follows is a kind of working paper, a guide toward reaching that starting point.

A preliminary note about terminology. What to call ourselves is an *3* issue hotly debated in some segments of our communities. I use the term "Hispanic" because the majority of the communities I deal with include themselves in that term, though each and every one of us refers to ourselves according to our country of origin: Cubans, Puerto Ricans, Mexican Americans, etc. What I do wish to emphasize is that "Latina/o" does not have a more politicized or radical connotation than "Hispanic" among the majority of our communities. In my experience it is most often those outside our communities who insist on giving Latina/o such a connotation. The contrary, however, is true of the appellation "Chicana/o," which does indicate a certain consciousness and political stance different from but not necessarily contrary to those who call themselves Mexican Americans.

The way Hispanics participate in this society has to do not only with us, but also with U.S. history, economics, politics, and society. Hispanics are in this country to begin with mostly because of U.S. policies and interests. Great numbers of Mexican Americans never moved to the United States. Instead, the border crossed *them* in 1846 when Mexico had to give up today's Southwest in the Treaty of Guadalupe-Hidalgo. The spoils of the Spanish American War at the end of the nineteenth century included Puerto Rico, where the United States had both military and economic interests. Without having any say, that nation was annexed by the United States.

Cuba suffered a somewhat similar fate. The United States sent troops to Cuba in the midst of its War of Independence against Spain. When Spain surrendered, the United States occupied Cuba as a military protectorate. And though Cuba became a free republic in 1902, the United States continued to maintain economic control and repeatedly intervened in Cuba's political affairs. It was, therefore, only reasonable that when Cubans had to leave their country, they felt they could and should find refuge here. The United States government accepted the Cuban refugees of the Castro regime, giving them economic aid and passing a special law making it easy for them to become residents and citizens.

As for more recent Hispanic immigrants, what can be said in a few lines about the constant manipulation by the United States of the economies and political processes of the different countries of Central America? The United States, therefore, has the moral responsibility to accept Salvadorans, Guatemalans, Hondurans, and other Central Americans who have to leave their countries because of political persecution or hunger. In short, the reasons Hispanics are in the United States are different from those of the earlier European immigrants, and the responsibility the United States has for our being here is vastly greater.

In spite of this difference, many people believe we Hispanics could have become as successful as the European immigrants. So why haven't we? For one thing, by the time Hispanics grew in numbers in the United States, the economy was no longer labor-intensive. Hispanics have lacked not "a strong back and a willingness to work," but the opportunity to capitalize on them. Then, unlike the European immigrants who went west and were able to buy land, Hispanics arrived here after homesteading had passed. But a more fundamental reason exists: racism. Hispanics are considered a nonwhite race, regardless of the fact that many of us are of the white race. Our ethnic difference has been officially construed as a racial difference: In government, businesses, and school forms, "Hispanic" is one of the choices under the category *race*.

No possibility exists of understanding Hispanics and being in dialogue   *8*
with us unless the short exposition presented is studied and analyzed.
The starting point for all dialogue is a profound respect for the other, and
respect cannot flourish if the other is not known. A commitment to study
the history of Hispanics in the United States — from the perspective of
Hispanics and not only from the perspective presented in the standard
textbooks of American history — must be the starting point in any
attempt to understand Hispanics.

A second obstacle to dialogue is the prevalent insistence in this coun-   *9*
try that one American Way of Life exists, and it is the best way of life for
everybody in the world. The melting pot concept has provided a frame-
work in which assimilation is a must, and plurality of cultures an impos-
sibility. Hispanic culture is not seen as an enrichment but as a threat. Few
understand that Hispanic culture provides for us, as other cultures do for
other peoples, guidelines for conduct and relationships, a system of values, and institutions and power structures that allow us to function at our
best. Our culture has been formed and will continue to be shaped by the
historical happenings and the constant actions of our communities —
communities in the United States that are influenced by what happens
here as well as in our countries of origin.

It is only within our own culture that Hispanics can acquire a sense of   *10*
belonging, of security, of dignity, and of participation. The ongoing
attempts to minimize or to make our culture disappear will only create
problems for the United States. They engender a low sense of identity that
can lead us to nonhealthy extremes in our search for some self-esteem.
For us, language is the main means of identification here in the United
States. To speak Spanish, in public as well as in private, is a political act, a
means of asserting who we are, an important way of struggling against
assimilation. The different state laws that forbid speaking Spanish in official situations, or militate against bilingual education, function as an
oppressive internal colonialism that ends up hurting U.S. society.

A Practice Sequence: Rhetorically Analyzing a Paragraph

1 Review your annotations and write a paragraph in which you
describe the rhetorical situation and the writer's purpose, main
claim, and audience.

2 Now write an analysis of a paragraph in Isasi-Díaz's essay. Choose
a substantial paragraph (not paragraph 3!) that you find especially
interesting either for what the author writes or how she writes it.
Using quotations from the text, write a one-page essay in which
you consider the situation Isasi-Díaz is responding to, her purpose
as a writer, or her audience.

■ Write a Rhetorical Analysis of an Essay

By now you should be developing a strong sense of what is involved in analyzing a paragraph rhetorically. You should be ready to take the next steps: performing a rhetorical analysis of a complete text and then sharing your analysis and the strategies you've learned with your classmates.

Read the next text, "Cultural Baggage" by Barbara Ehrenreich, annotating it to help you identify her situation, purpose, thesis, and audience. As you read, also make a separate set of annotations — possibly with a different color pen or pencil, circled, or keyed with asterisks — in which you comment on or evaluate the effectiveness of her essay. What do you like or dislike about it? Why? Does Ehrenreich persuade you to accept her point of view? What impressions do you have of her as a person? Would you like to be in a conversation with her?

ABOUT THE READING

Barbara Ehrenreich is a social critic, activist, and political essayist. Her book *Nickel and Dimed: On (Not) Getting By in America* (2001) describes her attempt to live on low-wage jobs; it became a national best seller in the United States. Her most recent book, *Bait and Switch: The (Futile) Pursuit of the American Dream* (2005), explores the shadowy world of the white-collar unemployed. Ehrenreich has also written for *Mother Jones, The Atlantic, Ms., The New Republic, In These Times,* Salon.com, and other publications. "Cultural Baggage" was originally published in the *New York Times Magazine* in 1992.

BARBARA EHRENREICH

Cultural Baggage

An acquaintance was telling me about the joys of rediscovering her *1* ethnic and religious heritage. "I know exactly what my ancestors were doing 2,000 years ago," she said, eyes gleaming with enthusiasm, "and *I can do the same things now.*" Then she leaned forward and inquired politely, "And what is your ethnic background, if I may ask?"

"None," I said, that being the first word in line to get out of my mouth. *2* Well, not "none," I backtracked. Scottish, English, Irish — that was something, I supposed. Too much Irish to qualify as a WASP; too much of the hated English to warrant a "Kiss Me, I'm Irish" button; plus there are a number of dead ends in the family tree due to adoptions, missing records, failing memories and the like. I was blushing by this time. Did "none" mean I was rejecting my heritage out of Anglo-Celtic self-hate? Or was I revealing a hidden ethnic chauvinism in which the Britannically derived serve as a kind of neutral standard compared with the ethnic "others"?

Throughout the 1960s and 70s, I watched one group after another — 3
African Americans, Latinos, Native Americans — stand up and proudly
reclaim their roots while I just sank back ever deeper into my seat. All this
excitement over ethnicity stemmed, I uneasily sensed, from a past in
which *their* ancestors had been trampled upon by *my* ancestors, or at
least by people who looked very much like them. In addition, it had begun
to seem almost un-American not to have some sort of hyphen at hand,
linking one to more venerable times and locales.

But the truth is, I was raised with none. We'd eaten ethnic foods in my 4
childhood home, but these were all borrowed, like the pasties, or Cornish
meat pies, my father had picked up from his fellow miners in Butte,
Montana. If my mother had one rule, it was militant ecumenism in all
manners of food and experience. "Try new things," she would say, meaning anything from sweetbreads to clams, with an emphasis on the "new."

As a child, I briefly nourished a craving for tradition and roots. 5
I immersed myself in the works of Sir Walter Scott. I pretended to believe
that the bagpipe was a musical instrument. I was fascinated to learn from
a grandmother that we were descended from certain Highland clans and
longed for a pleated skirt in one of their distinctive tartans.

But in *Ivanhoe*, it was the dark-eyed "Jewess" Rebecca I identified 6
with, not the flaxen-haired bimbo Rowena. As for clans: Why not call
them "tribes," those bands of half-clad peasants and warriors whose idea
of cuisine was stuffed sheep gut washed down with whiskey? And then
there was the sting of Disraeli's remark — which I came across in my
early teens — to the effect that his ancestors had been leading orderly,
literate lives when my ancestors were still rampaging through the Highlands daubing themselves with blue paint.

Motherhood put the screws on me, ethnicity-wise. I had hoped that by 7
marrying a man of Eastern European Jewish ancestry I would acquire for
my descendants the ethnic genes that my own forebears so sadly lacked.
At one point, I even subjected the children to a seder of my own design,
including a little talk about the flight from Egypt and its relevance to
modern social issues. But the kids insisted on buttering their matzos and
snickering through my talk. "Give me a break, Mom," the older one said.
"You don't even believe in God."

After the tiny pagans had been put to bed, I sat down to brood over 8
Elijah's wine. What had I been thinking? The kids knew that their Jewish
grandparents were secular folks who didn't hold seders themselves. And
if ethnicity eluded me, how could I expect it to take root in my children,
who are not only Scottish English Irish, but Hungarian Polish Russian
to boot?

But, then, on the fumes of Manischewitz, a great insight took form in 9
my mind. It was true, as the kids said, that I didn't "believe in God." But

this could be taken as something very different from an accusation — a reminder of a genuine heritage. My parents had not believed in God either, nor had my grandparents or any other progenitors going back to the great-great level. They had become disillusioned with Christianity generations ago — just as, on the in-law side, my children's other ancestors had shaken their Orthodox Judaism. This insight did not exactly furnish me with an "identity," but it was at least something to work with: We are the kind of people, I realized — whatever our distant ancestors' religions — who do *not* believe, who do not carry on traditions, who do not do things just because someone has done them before.

The epiphany went on: I recalled that my mother never introduced a   10
procedure for cooking or cleaning by telling me, "Grandma did it this way." What did Grandma know, living in the days before vacuum cleaners and disposable toilet mops? In my parents' general view, new things were better than old, and the very fact that some ritual had been performed in the past was a good reason for abandoning it now. Because what was the past, as our forebears knew it? Nothing but poverty, superstition and grief. "Think for yourself," Dad used to say. "Always ask why."

In fact, this may have been the ideal cultural heritage for my particular   11
ethnic strain — bounced as it was from the Highlands of Scotland across the sea, out to the Rockies, down into the mines and finally spewed out into high-tech, suburban America. What better philosophy, for a race of migrants, than "Think for yourself"? What better maxim, for a people whose whole world was rudely inverted every thirty years or so, than "Try new things"?

The more tradition-minded, the newly enthusiastic celebrants of   12
Purim and Kwanzaa and Solstice, may see little point to survival if the survivors carry no cultural freight — religion, for example, or ethnic tradition. To which I would say that skepticism, curiosity and wide-eyed ecumenical tolerance are also worthy elements of the human tradition and are at least as old as such notions as "Serbian" or "Croatian," "Scottish" or "Jewish." I make no claims for my personal line of progenitors except that they remained loyal to the values that may have induced all of our ancestors, long, long ago, to climb down from the trees and make their way into the open plains.

A few weeks ago, I cleared my throat and asked the children, now   13
mostly grown and fearsomely smart, whether they felt any stirrings of ethnic or religious identity, etc., which might have been, ahem, insufficiently nourished at home. "None," they said, adding firmly, "and the world would be a better place if nobody else did, either." My chest swelled with pride, as would my mother's, to know that the race of "none" marches on.

A Practice Sequence: Rhetorically Analyzing an Essay

1 Write a brief rhetorical analysis of Barbara Ehrenreich's essay, referring to your notes and citing passages where she indicates her situation, purpose, main claim, and audience.

2 An option for group work: As a class, divide into three or more groups. Each group should answer the following questions in response to their reading of Ehrenreich's essay "Cultural Baggage":

> *Group 1:* Identify the situation(s) motivating Ehrenreich to write. Then evaluate: How well does her argument function as a conversation with other authors who have written on the same topic?
>
> *Group 2:* Analyze the audience's identity, perspectives, and conventional expectations. Then evaluate: How well does the argument function as a conversation with the audience?
>
> *Group 3:* Analyze the writer's purpose. Then evaluate: Do you believe Ehrenreich achieves her purpose in this essay? Why or why not?

Then, as a class, share your observations:

- To what extent does the author's ability as a conversationalist — that is, her ability to enter into a conversation with other authors and her audience — affect your evaluation of whether she achieves her purpose in this essay?
- If you were to meet this writer, what suggestions or advice would you give her for making her argument more persuasive?

Much if not all of the writing you do in college will be based on what you have read. This is the case, for example, when you summarize a philosopher's theory, analyze the significance of an experiment in psychology, or, perhaps, synthesize different and conflicting points of view in making an argument about race and academic achievement in sociology. As we maintain throughout this book, writing and reading are inextricably linked to each other. Good academic writers are also good critical readers: They leave their mark on what they read, identifying issues, making judgments about the truth of what writers tell them, and evaluating the adequacy of the evidence in support of an argument. This is where writing and inquiry begin: understanding our own position relative to the scholarly conversations that we want to enter. Moreover, critical readers try to understand the strategies that writers use to persuade them to agree with them. At times, these are strategies that we can adapt in advancing our arguments. In the next chapter, we provide some strategies for identifying and evaluating the adequacy of a writer's claims.

3

From Identifying Claims to Analyzing Arguments

A **claim** is an assertion of fact or belief that needs to be supported with **evidence** — the information that backs up a claim. A main claim, or thesis, summarizes the writer's position on a situation and answers the question(s) the writer addresses. It also encompasses all of the minor claims and their supporting evidence that the writer makes throughout the argument. As readers, we need to identify a writer's main claim because it helps us organize our own understanding of the writer's argument. It acts as a signpost that tells us, "This is what the essay is about," "This is what I want you to pay attention to," and "This is how I want you to think, change, or act." When you evaluate a claim, whether it is an argument's main claim or a minor claim, it is helpful to identify the type of claim it is: a claim of fact, a claim of value, or a claim of policy. You also need to evaluate the reasons for and the evidence that supports the claim. Because academic argument should acknowledge multiple points of view, you also should be prepared to identify what, if any, concessions a writer offers his or her readers, and what counterarguments he or she anticipates from others in the conversation.

IDENTIFYING TYPES OF CLAIMS

To illustrate how to identify a writer's claims, let's take a look at a text by educators Myra and David Sadker that examines gender bias in schools. The text is followed by our analyses of the types of claims (fact, value, and policy) and then, in the next section, of the nature of the arguments (evidence, concessions, and counterarguments) the authors present.

ABOUT THE READING

Myra Sadker was a professor of education at American University until 1995, the year she died. Dr. Sadker coauthored *Sexism in School and Society*, the first book on gender bias in America's schools in 1973, and became a leading advocate for equal educational opportunities.

David Sadker is a professor at American University and has taught at the elementary, middle school, and high school levels. David Sadker and his late wife earned a national reputation for their groundbreaking work in confronting gender bias and sexual harassment. "Hidden Lessons" is an excerpt from their book *Failing at Fairness: How Our Schools Cheat Girls* (1994).

MYRA SADKER AND DAVID SADKER

Hidden Lessons

Sitting in the same classroom, reading the same textbook, listening to the same teacher, boys and girls receive very different educations. From grade school through graduate school female students are more likely to be invisible members of classrooms. Teachers interact with males more frequently, ask them better questions, and give them more precise and helpful feedback. Over the course of years the uneven distribution of teacher time, energy, attention, and talent, with boys getting the lion's share, takes its toll on girls. Since gender bias is not a noisy problem, most people are unaware of the secret sexist lessons and the quiet losses they engender.   *1*

Girls are the majority of our nation's schoolchildren, yet they are second-class educational citizens. The problems they face — loss of self-esteem, decline in achievement, and elimination of career options — are at the heart of the educational process. Until educational sexism is eradicated, more than half our children will be shortchanged and their gifts lost to society.   *2*

Award-winning author Susan Faludi discovered that backlash "is most powerful when it goes private, when it lodges inside a woman's mind and turns her vision inward, until she imagines the pressure is all in her head, until she begins to enforce the backlash too — on herself."* Psychological backlash internalized by adult women is a frightening concept, but what is even more terrifying is a curriculum of sexist school lessons becoming secret mind games played against female children, our daughters, and tomorrow's women.   *3*

---

*Editor's note: Journalist Faludi's book *Backlash: The Undeclared War Against American Women* (1991) was a response to the antifeminist backlash against the women's movement.

After almost two decades of research grants and thousands of hours of classroom observation, we remain amazed at the stubborn persistence of these hidden sexist lessons. When we began our investigation of gender bias, we looked first in the classrooms of one of Washington, D.C.'s elite and expensive private schools. Uncertain of exactly what to look for, we wrote nothing down; we just observed. The classroom was a whirlwind of activity so fast paced we could easily miss the quick but vital phrase or gesture, the insidious incident, the tiny inequity that held a world of meaning. As we watched, we had to push ourselves beyond the blind spots of socialization and gradually focus on the nature of the interaction between teacher and student. On the second day we saw our first example of sexism, a quick, jarring flash within the hectic pace of the school day:

> Two second-graders are kneeling beside a large box. They whisper excitedly to each other as they pull out wooden blocks, colored balls, counting sticks. So absorbed are these two small children in examining and sorting the materials, they are visibly startled by the teacher's impatient voice as she hovers over them. "Ann! Julia! Get your cottonpickin' hands out of the math box. Move over so the boys can get in there and do their work."

Isolated here on the page of a book, this incident is not difficult to interpret. It becomes even more disturbing if you think of it with the teacher making a racial distinction. Picture Ann and Julia as African-American children moved away so white children can gain access to the math materials. If Ann and Julia's parents had observed this exchange, they might justifiably wonder whether their tuition dollars were well spent. But few parents actually watch teachers in action, and fewer still have learned to interpret the meaning behind fast-paced classroom events.

The incident unsettles, but it must be considered within the context of numerous interactions this harried teacher had that day. While she talked to the two girls, she was also keeping a wary eye on fourteen other active children. Unless you actually shadowed the teacher, stood right next to her as we did, you might not have seen or heard the event. After all, it lasted only a few seconds.

It took us almost a year to develop an observation system that would register the hundreds of daily classroom interactions, teasing out the gender bias embedded in them. Trained raters coded classrooms in math, reading, English, and social studies. They observed students from different racial and ethnic backgrounds. They saw lessons taught by women and by men, by teachers of different races. In short, they analyzed America's classrooms. By the end of the year we had thousands of observation sheets, and after another year of statistical analysis, we discovered a syntax of sexism so elusive that most teachers and students were completely unaware of its influence.

Recently a producer of NBC's *Dateline* contacted us to learn more about our discovery that girls don't receive their fair share of education. Jane Pauley, the show's anchorwoman, wanted to visit classrooms, capture these covert sexist lessons on videotape, and expose them before a television audience. The task was to extricate sound bites of sexism from a fifth-grade classroom where the teacher, chosen to be the subject of the exposé, was aware she was being scrutinized for sex bias.

Dateline had been taping in her class for two days when we received a   9
concerned phone call. "This is a fair teacher," the producer said. "How can we show sexism on our show when there's no gender bias in this teacher's class?" We drove to the NBC studio in Washington, D.C., and found two *Dateline* staffers, intelligent women concerned about fair treatment in school, sitting on the floor in a darkened room staring at the videotape of a fifth-grade class. "We've been playing this over and over. The teacher is terrific. There's no bias in her teaching. Come watch."

After about twenty minutes of viewing, we realized it was a case of déjà   10
vu: The episodal sexist themes and recurring incidents were all too familiar. The teacher was terrific, but she was more effective for half of the students than she was for the other. She was, in fact, a classic example of the hundreds of skillful well-intentioned professionals we have seen who inadvertently teach boys better than girls.

We had forgotten how difficult it was to recognize subtle sexism before   11
you learn how to look. It was as if the *Dateline* staff members were wearing blinders. We halted the tape, pointed out the sexist behaviors, related them to incidents in our research, and played the tape again. There is a classic "aha!" effect in education when people finally "get it." Once the hidden lessons of unconscious bias are understood, classrooms never look the same again to the trained observer.

Much of the unintentional gender bias in that fifth-grade class could   12
not be shown in the short time allowed by television, but the sound bites of sexism were also there. *Dateline* chose to show a segregated math group: boys sitting on the teacher's right side and girls on her left. After giving the math book to a girl to hold open at the page of examples, the teacher turned her back to the girls and focused on the boys, teaching them actively and directly. Occasionally she turned to the girls' side, but only to read the examples in the book. This teacher, although aware that she was being observed for sexism, had unwittingly transformed the girls into passive spectators, an audience for the boys. All but one, that is: The girl holding the math book had become a prop.

Dateline also showed a lively discussion in the school library. With both   13
girls' hands and boys' hands waving for attention, the librarian chose boy after boy to speak. In one interaction she peered through the forest of girls' hands waving directly in front of her to acknowledge the raised hand of a boy in the back of the room. Startled by the teacher's attention, the boy muttered, "I was just stretching."

The next day we discussed the show with future teachers, our students   14
at The American University. They were bewildered. "Those teachers really were sexist. They didn't mean to be, but they were. How could that

happen — with the cameras and everyone watching?" When we took those students into classrooms to discover the hidden lessons for themselves, they began to understand. It is difficult to detect sexism unless you know precisely how to observe. And if a lifetime of socialization makes it difficult to spot gender bias even when you're looking for it, how much harder it is to avoid the traps when you are the one doing the teaching.

■ Identify Claims of Fact

Claims of fact are assertions (or arguments) that a condition has existed, exists, or will exist. Claims of fact are made by individuals who believe that something is true; but claims are never simply facts, and some claims are more objective, and so easier to verify, than others. For example, "It's raining in Boston today" is a "factual" claim of fact; it's easily verified. But consider the argument some make that the steel and automotive industries in the United States have depleted our natural resources and left us at a crisis point. This is an assertion that a condition exists. A careful reader must examine the basis for this kind of claim: Are we truly facing a crisis? And if so, are the steel and automotive industries truly responsible? A number of politicians counter this claim of fact by insisting that if the government would harness the vast natural resources in Alaska, there would be no "crisis." This is also a claim of fact, in this case an assertion that a condition will exist in the future. Again, it is based on evidence, evidence gathered from various sources that indicates sufficient resources in Alaska to keep up with our increasing demands for resources and to allay a potential crisis.

Our point is that most claims of fact are debatable. They may be based on factual information, but they are not necessarily true. Most claims of fact present **interpretations** of evidence derived from **inferences**. That is, a writer will examine evidence (for example, about the quantity of natural resources in Alaska and the rate that industries harness those resources and process them into goods), draw a conclusion based on reasoning (an inference), and offer an explanation based on that conclusion (an interpretation). So, for example, an academic writer will study the evidence on the quantity of natural resources in Alaska and the rate that industries harness those resources and process them into goods; only after the writer makes an informed decision on whether Alaska's resources are sufficient to keep pace with the demand for them will he or she take a position on the issue.

In the first paragraph of their essay, the Sadkers make the claims of fact that female students are "more likely to be invisible members of classrooms," and that teachers interact differently with female students than they do with male students. The careful reader will want to see how the Sadkers support these claims of fact throughout the essay. Can they convincingly present their argument about "the secret sexist lessons and the quiet losses they engender" in the paragraphs that follow?

■ Identify Claims of Value

A claim of fact is different from a **claim of value**, which expresses an evaluation of a condition that has existed, exists, or will exist. Is a condition good or bad? Is it important or inconsequential? An argument that developing the wilderness in Alaska would irreversibly mar the beauty of the land indicates that the writer values the beauty of the land over the possible benefits of development. A claim of value presents a judgment, which is sometimes signaled by a value-laden word like *ugly, beautiful,* or *immoral,* but may also be conveyed more subtly by the writer's tone and attitude.

Sadker and Sadker make a claim of value when they suggest that a "majority of our nation's schoolchildren" have become "second-class educational citizens" and point out that the consequences of treating girls differently from boys in school has resulted in a "loss of self-esteem, decline in achievement, and elimination of career options" for girls (para. 2). Of course, the critical reader's task is to question these evaluations: Does gender bias in the classroom affect self-esteem, achievement, and career options? Both of these statements are minor claims, but they make assertions that require support. After all, how do the Sadkers know these things? Whether or not readers are persuaded by these claims depends on the evidence or reasons that the authors use to support them. We discuss the nature of evidence and what constitutes "good reasons" later in this chapter.

■ Identify Claims of Policy

A **claim of policy** is an argument for what should be the case; it is a call for change. Two recent controversies on college campuses center on claims of policy. One has activists arguing that universities and colleges should have a policy that all workers on campus earn a living wage. The other has activists arguing that universities and colleges should have a policy that prevents them from investing in countries where the government ignores human rights. Claims of policy are often signaled by words like *should* and *must*: "For public universities to live up to their democratic mission, they *must* provide all their workers with a living wage." Myra and David Sadker make a claim of policy when they assert that "educational sexism" must be eradicated; otherwise, they point out, "more than half our children will be shortchanged and their gifts lost to society" (para. 2).

Not all writers make their claims as explicitly as the Sadkers do; nor does every argument include all three types of claims. But you should be able to identify the three different types of claims. Moreover, you should keep in mind what the situation is and what kind of argument can best address what you see as a problem. Ask yourself: Does the situation involve a question of fact? Does the situation involve a question of value? Does the situation require a change in policy? Or is some combination at work?

Steps to Identifying Claims

1 **Ask:** Does the argument assert that a condition has existed, exists, or will exist? If so, it's a claim of fact.

2 **Ask:** Does the argument express an evaluation of a condition that has existed, exists, or will exist? If so, it's a claim of value.

3 **Ask:** Does the argument call for change, and is it directed at some future action? If so, it's a claim of policy.

A Practice Sequence: Identifying Claims

What follows is a series of claims. Identify each one as a claim of fact, value, or policy. Be prepared to justify your categorizations.

1 Taxing the use of fossil fuels will end the energy crisis.

2 We should reform the welfare system to ensure that people who receive support from the government also work.

3 Images of violence in the media create a culture of violence in schools.

4 The increase in homelessness is a deplorable situation that contradicts the whole idea of democracy.

5 Distributing property taxes is the one sure way to end poverty and illiteracy.

6 Individual votes don't really count.

7 Despite the 20 percent increase in the number of females in the workforce over the past forty years, women are still not treated equitably.

8 Affirmative action is a policy that has outlived its usefulness.

9 There are a disproportionate number of black males in American prisons.

10 The media are biased, which means we cannot count on newspapers or television news for the truth.

ANALYZING ARGUMENTS

Analyzing an argument involves identifying the writer's main and minor claims and then examining (1) the reasons and evidence given in support of each claim, (2) the writer's concessions, and (3) the writer's attempts to handle counterarguments.

▪ Analyze the Reasons Used to Support a Claim

Stating a claim is one thing; supporting that claim is another. As a critical reader, you need to evaluate whether a writer has provided *good reasons* to support his or her position. Specifically, you will need to decide whether the support for a claim is recent, relevant, reliable, and accurate. As a writer, you will need to use the same criteria when you support your claims.

Is the source recent?   Knowledgeable readers of your written arguments not only will be aware of classic studies that you should cite as "intellectual touchstones"; they will also expect you to cite recent evidence, evidence published within five years of when you are writing. Of course, older research can be valuable. For example, in a paper about molecular biology, you might very well cite James Watson and Francis Crick's groundbreaking 1953 study in which they describe the structure of DNA. That study is an intellectual touchstone that changed the life sciences in a fundamental way, much as Einstein's theory of relativity changed how physicists think about the universe. Or if you were writing about educational reform, you might very well mention Hirsch's 1987 book *Cultural Literacy*. Hirsch's book did not change the way people think about curricular reform as profoundly as Watson and Crick's study changed the way scientists think about biology, but his term *cultural literacy* continues to serve as useful shorthand for a particular way of thinking about curricular reform that remains influential to this day.

Although citing Hirsch is an effective way to suggest you have studied the history of an educational problem, it will not convince your readers that there is a crisis in education today. To establish that, you would need to use as evidence studies published over the past few years to show, for example, that there has been a steady decline in test scores since Hirsch wrote his book. And you would need to support your claim that curricular reform is the one sure way to bring an end to illiteracy and poverty with data that are much more current than those available to Hirsch in the 1980s. No one would accept the judgment that our schools are in crisis if your most recent citation is more than twenty years old.

Is the source relevant?   Evidence that is relevant must have real bearing on your issue and also depends greatly on what your readers expect. Suppose two of your friends complain that they were unable to sell their condominiums for the price they asked. You can claim there is a crisis in the housing market, but your argument won't convince most readers if your only evidence is personal anecdote. Such anecdotal evidence may alert you to a possible topic and help you connect with your readers, but you will need to test the **relevance** of your friends' experience — Is it pertinent? Is it typical of a larger situation or condition? — if you want your readers to take your argument seriously. At the very least, you should scan real estate listings to see what the asking prices are for properties comparable to your friends' properties. By comparing listings, you are defining the grounds for your argument. If your friends are disappointed that their one-bedroom condominiums sold for less than a three-bedroom condominium with deeded parking in the same neighborhood, it may will be that their expectations were too high. If you aren't comparing like things, your argument is going to be seriously flawed. If your friends' definition of what constitutes a "reasonable price" differs dramatically from everyone else's, their experience is probably irrelevant to the larger question of whether the local housing market is depressed.

Is the source reliable?   You also need to evaluate whether the data you are using to support your argument are reliable. After all, some researchers present findings based on a very small sample of people that can also be rather selective. For example, a researcher might argue that 67 percent of the people he cited believe that school and residential integration are important concerns. But how many people did this person interview? More important, who responded to the researcher's questions? A reliable claim cannot be based on a few of the researcher's friends.

Let's return to the real estate example. You have confirmed that your friends listed their condominiums at prices that were not out of line with the market. Now what? You need to seek out reliable sources to continue testing your argument. For example, you might search the real estate or business section of your local newspaper to see if there are any recent stories about a softening of the market; and you might talk with several local real estate agents to get their opinions on the subject. In consulting your local newspapers and local agents, you are looking for **authoritative sources** against which to test your anecdotal evidence — the confirmation of experts who report on, study, evaluate, and have an informed opinion on local real estate. Local real estate agents are a source of **expert testimony**, firsthand confirmation of the information you have discovered. You would probably not want to rely on the testimony of a single real estate agent, who may have a bias; instead, talk with several agents to see if a consensus emerges.

Is the source accurate?   To determine the accuracy of a study that you want to use to support your argument, you have to do a little digging to find out who else has made a similar claim. For instance, if you want to cite authoritative research that compares the dropout rate for white students with the rate for students of color, you could look at research conducted by the Civil Rights Project. Of course, you don't need to stop your search there. You could also check the resources available through the National Center for Education Statistics. You want to show your readers that you have done a relatively thorough search to make your argument as persuasive as possible.

The accuracy of **statistics** — factual information presented numerically or graphically (for example, in a pie or bar chart) — is difficult to verify. To a certain extent, then, their veracity has to be taken on faith. Often the best you can do is assure yourself that the source of your statistical information is authoritative and reliable — government and major research universities generally are "safe" sources — and that whoever is interpreting the statistical information is not distorting it. Returning again to our real estate example, let's say you've read a newspaper article that cites statistical information about the condition of the local real estate market (for example, the average price of property and volume of sales this year in comparison to last year). Presumably the author of the article is an expert, but he or she may be interpreting rather than simply reporting on the statistics. To reassure yourself one way or the other, you may want to check the sources of the author's statistics — go right to your source's sources — which a responsible author will cite. That will allow you to look over the raw data and come to your own conclusions. A further step you could take would be to discuss the article with other experts — local real estate agents — to find out what they think of the article and the information it presents.

Now, let's go back to Myra and David Sadker's essay. How do they develop their assertion that girls are treated differently from boys in classrooms from "grade school through graduate school"? First, they tell us (in paragraph 4) that they have been conducting research continuously for "almost two decades" and that they have accumulated "thousands of hours of classroom observation." This information suggests that their research is both recent and relevant. But are their studies reliable and accurate? That their research meets the reliability criterion is confirmed by the grants they received over the years: Granting institutions (experts) have assessed their work and determined that it deserved to be funded. Grants confer authority on research. In addition, the Sadkers explain that they observed and refined their analyses over time to achieve accuracy: "As we watched, we had to push ourselves beyond the blind spots of socialization and gradually focus on the nature of the interaction between teacher and student."

In paragraph 7, the authors provide more evidence that the observations that support their claim are accurate. Not only have they observed many instances of gender bias in classrooms; so have trained "raters." The raters add objectivity to the findings because they did not share the Sadkers' interest in drawing a specific conclusion about whether gender bias exists in classrooms. Also the raters observed a wide cross-section of students and teachers from "different racial and ethnic backgrounds." At the end of their study, the Sadkers had collected thousands of pieces of data and could feel quite confident about their conclusion — that they had "discovered a syntax of sexism so elusive that most teachers and students were completely unaware of its influence."

■ Identify Concessions

Part of the strategy of developing a main claim supported with good reasons is to offer a **concession**, an acknowledgment that readers may not agree with every point the writer is making. A concession is a writer's way of saying, "Okay, I can see that there may be another way of looking at the issue or another way to interpret the evidence used to support the argument I am making." For example, you may not want your energy costs to go up, but after examining the reasons why it may be necessary to increase taxes on gasoline — to lower usage and conserve fossil fuels — you might concede that a tax increase on gasoline could be useful. The willingness to make concessions is valued in academic writing because it acknowledges both complexity and the importance of multiple perspectives. It also acknowledges the fact that information can always be interpreted in different ways.

The Sadkers make a concession when they acknowledge in the last paragraph of the excerpt that "it is difficult to detect sexism unless you know precisely how to observe." And, they explain, "if a lifetime of socialization makes it difficult to spot gender bias even when you're looking for it, how much harder it is to avoid the traps when you are the one doing the teaching." Notice that these concessions do not weaken their argument. The authors' evidence appears overwhelmingly to support their thesis. The lesson here is that conceding a point in your argument shows that you have acknowledged there are other ways of seeing things, other interpretations. This is an important part of what it means to enter a conversation of ideas.

Often a writer will signal a concession with a variation of the phrase "It is true that . . ." (for example, "I agree with X that Y is an important factor to consider" or "Some studies have convincingly shown that . . ."). Generally, the writer will then go on to address the concession, explaining how it needs to be modified or abandoned in the light of new evidence or the writer's perspective on the issue.

■ Identify Counterarguments

As the term suggests, a **counterargument** is an argument raised in response to another argument. You want to be aware of and acknowledge what your readers may object to in your argument. Anticipating readers' objections is an important part of developing a conversational argument. For example, if you were arguing in support of universal health care, you would have to acknowledge that the approach departs dramatically from the traditional role the federal government has played in providing health insurance. That is, most people's access to health insurance has depended on their individual ability to afford and purchase this kind of insurance. You would have to anticipate how readers would respond to your proposal, especially readers who do not feel that the federal government should ever play a role in what has heretofore been an individual responsibility. Anticipating readers' objections demonstrates that you understand the complexity of the issue and are willing at least to entertain different and conflicting opinions.

In the excerpt from "Hidden Lessons," the Sadkers describe the initial response of *Dateline* staffers to what they observed in the classroom they were videotaping: "This is a fair teacher. . . . [T]here's no gender bias in this teacher's class." Two women whom the Sadkers describe as "intelligent" and "concerned about fair treatment in school" agreed: "We've been playing this over and over. The teacher is terrific. There's no bias in her teaching. Come watch" (para. 9).

Notice the Sadkers' acknowledgment that even intelligent, concerned people may not see the problems that the Sadkers spent more than twenty years studying. In addressing the counterargument — that sexism does not exist — the authors are both empathetic to and respectful of what any reasonable person might or might not see. This is in keeping with what we would call a conversational argument: that writers listen to different points of view, that they respect arguments that diverge from their own, and that they be willing to exchange ideas and revise their own points of view.

In an argument that is more conversational than confrontational, writers often establish areas of common ground, both to convey to readers that they are understood and to acknowledge the conditions under which readers' views are valid. Writers do this by making concessions and anticipating and responding to counterarguments. This conversational approach is what many people call a **Rogerian approach to argument**, based on psychologist Carl Rogers's approach to psychotherapy. The objective of a Rogerian strategy is to reduce listeners' sense of threat so that they are open to alternatives. For academic writers, it involves four steps:

1. Conveying to readers that they are understood
2. Acknowledging conditions under which readers' views are valid
3. Helping readers see that the writer shares common ground with them
4. Creating mutually acceptable solutions to agreed-on problems

The structure of an argument, according to the Rogerian approach, grows out of the give-and-take of conversation between two people and the topic under discussion. In a written conversation, the give-and-take of face-to-face conversation takes the form of anticipating readers' counterarguments and uses language that is both empathetic and respectful to put the readers at ease.

Steps to Analyzing an Argument

1 **Identify the type of claim.** A claim of fact? Value? Policy?

2 **Analyze the reasons used to support the claim.** Are they recent? Relevant? Reliable? Accurate?

3 **Identify concessions.** Is there another argument that even the author acknowledges is legitimate?

4 **Identify counterarguments.** What arguments contradict or challenge the author's position?

■ Analyze a Sample Student Argument

Read the excerpt from a student essay that follows with pen or pencil in hand, noting the writer's claims, reasons, concessions, and responses to counterarguments. The essay is an example of a **researched argument**: The writer uses evidence to advance an argument that contributes to the ongoing conversation about an issue. (Notice how the author cites and documents his research; we have more to say about citation and documentation in Chapter 7.) The author, Ryan Metheny, was writing at a time when anti-immigrant attitudes in the United States were running high. In this essay, which was selected from a pool of exceptional student essays to be published in a campus magazine that was required reading for all first-year students at his school, Metheny addresses what he sees as a fundamental tension between democratic principles of equality and the exclusionary nature of the English-only movement. Specifically, he responds to the marginalization of Ebonics (also known as African American Vernacular English) in schools. His purpose is to make policymakers and educators aware of the problem. He also explains to a broader audience the ways in which race and power, not grammatical correctness, determine which language practices gain legitimacy and which do not.

Metheny 1

Ryan Metheny
Professor Klein
English 1020
May 16, 20--

The Problems and Dangers of Assimilatory Policies

American society considers itself to be in an age of enlighten- *1*
ment. Racism has been denounced and cultural colorblindness in all things is encouraged. Economic opportunities are available for everyone, and equal consideration before the law is provided for each citizen. American society considers itself the embodiment of liberty, equality, and justice for all.

In a society such as the one described, it follows that one's *2*
background and culture do not have any influence on one's socioeconomic status; theoretically, the two should be completely disconnected. Yet, as we all know, this is not the case. The people of the highest status in America are almost uniformly white males. Sadly, America, the place of equality and liberty, is still very much a

Metheny 2

stratified society, not only by socioeconomic class/status, but because minority cultures much more often fill the ranks of the lower classes. Fortunately for those of minority cultures, the country's policymakers now accept, at least in speech, the basic equality and potential of all cultures to rise out of poverty; unfortunately, they still refuse to recognize the validity of differences in these cultures from what they, the policymakers, view as American (Labov i–iii).

The most obvious example of this is the stubborn grasp the country holds on what it calls "standard English" — the dialect used by the intellectual and social elite of America. Standard English is considered to be the one and only conduit through which people of status exchange information — and therefore the one and only conduit through which power can be attained. It is seen as the American method of communication. Historically, the various groups that come to America have had to adopt this method as their own in order to receive their piece of the American socioeconomic pie — and, indeed, many groups have — Germans, Irish, Italians. These groups, however, are white. Assimilation for non-white groups has been agonizingly slow, especially for historically oppressed peoples such as African Americans (Smitherman 167–200). We consider adoption of standard English to be the price one pays for entrance into the all-inclusive society. But, of course, this is not only contradictory (an inclusive society should accept all cultural differences as valid), but it is also an unfair policy for non-white groups. We have set up standard English as the holy grail of communication. If we wish to avoid hypocrisy, we should live up to the virtues of inclusiveness we claim to have.

Implementation of more inclusiveness should begin by decreasing our fervor in support of standard English. The reasons for this are many. On the technical, linguistic level, standard English should certainly not be esteemed so highly because it is a superior language — it is not. Standard English is just as flexible and changing as any other language. It is ironic that the cultural dialects that many minorities utilize, such as Ebonics, have a heavy hand in changing the standard English that we demand they adopt. Even the slaves brought to America, the lowest of the low socioeconomically during the period in which they were enslaved, had a heavy hand in changing American standard English. Joseph Holloway and Winifred

3

4

Voss pointed out in 1993 that nearly 200 place names in nine Southern states are of African origin. They also [point] out the African origins of many other terms now used in standard English — even the beloved name "Bambi" of Walt Disney's cartoon has its origins in the Bantu word "mubambi," a word which means "one who lies down in order to hide" (Holloway and Voss 57, 227–229). This flexibility of standard English seems to point toward another hypocrisy of America — we play down the importance of the non-standard Ebonics dialect, while accepting parts of that dialect as our own. Certainly this suggests that standard English is not inherently more "civilized" than other dialects.

Conversely, is Ebonics then not accepted because it is inherently "uncivilized"? No. Ebonics can be just as expressive and meaningful, if not more so, than standard English (Smitherman 167–200). Ebonics as a language fosters important verbal reasoning and logical skills, just as any language does. Its nuances of grammar and intonation are highly communicative combinations of English vocabulary and grammar with African mechanics. Anyone who has ever heard a bout of the "dozens" will readily admit that Ebonics can indeed be a fast-paced, inventive dialect that requires quick thinking. The ability to express an impromptu "yo mama" joke on the spur of the moment is a kind of genius all its own. Such verbal skills should not be discouraged. To do so invalidates the experiences of African Americans. A people's experiences cannot be denied, especially in the land of equality and justice. If Ebonics remains unrecognized despite its clear validity as a mode of communication, and despite standard English's lack of any kind of superiority to it, what ideologies are truly behind its continuing lack of recognition? Actually, the lack of recognition of Ebonics may well be rooted in mere class-related bigotry (Smitherman). The upper class views such a mode of speech as unintelligent, a mockery of the "true" language. What such a view is in fact indicative of is not only a blatant case of ethnocentrism . . . but also a feeling of superiority that native standard English speakers feel over the lower classes. This sense of superiority fuels the demand that speakers of other dialects and languages adopt standard English in order to join the successful mainstream. Such an attitude supports the dominance of the upper classes. This must surely be considered wrong in a land

5

Metheny 4

where every person, regardless of income and status, is equal before the law.

Ebonics is not inferior: oppression of Ebonics could well be a case of bigotry. Therefore, acceptance of Ebonics as a valid form of communication should be strongly considered. To implement such an acceptance, we must begin with the schools, for that is where society first exerts influence upon the individual. So far, any kind of acceptance here has been rare, and when present, it has often been implemented inappropriately. Baugh pointed out in 1999 several cases in which Ebonics and Ebonics-related problems were not addressed appropriately. In one case, two native Ebonics speakers were placed in special education based on verbal aptitude tests given in standard English — a dialect they were not familiar with. In another case, a math teacher gave his inner-city students word problems that he thought were being culturally sensitive, but which in fact could be considered racist. One problem asked, "If you were a pimp and had knocked up seven hos, and had twenty-three hos total, how many hos would still need to be knocked up?" while another asked, "If you had a half-pound of heroin, and want to make twenty percent more profit, how much cut would you need?" These are extreme examples, true, but they illustrate the lack of success that many educators have had when it comes to addressing the problems inherent in educating Ebonics speakers.

Such problems are further frustrated by the aforementioned stratified nature of American society. Baugh illustrates this using a graph in which five theoretical socioeconomic groups, and their corresponding dialects, are arrayed vertically from upper to lower classes. The children in the uppermost group are capable of going even higher socioeconomically than their parents, shown by a line slanting up, or slightly lower, shown by a line slanting down. The next group down is similarly capable of a certain amount of increase or decrease in status.

This graph shows two things: first, that each socioeconomic group is normally only capable of a certain range of change in status; and second, that there is very little overlap in range between groups. This implies that the lower classes most minorities are still a part of cannot advance their status very quickly in succeeding generations. Baugh goes on to claim that this is due to the manner in which

6

7

8

children are educated from a very early age, both in schools and at home. Inner-city schools are often poorly funded and fail to teach their students adequately. Similarly, the home life of poorer students often does not foster learning in important ways, such as the reading of parents to children at an early age. Which is not to say, of course, that Ebonics as a language does not support learning — rather, low socioeconomic status often does not support learning. Ebonics speakers, since they more often fill lower socioeconomic groups, are often at an unfair disadvantage when compared to native standard English speakers.

As the inclusive society, we must address this economic unfairness. Arguments in favor of using standard English as the only valid form of communication in the United States have not done this. E. D. Hirsch argues that cultural literacy focused around a single standard dialect is necessary for a society to operate efficiently. Complementing Hirsch's ideas, Richard Rodriguez argues that knowing the "public language" is needed for one to have a public identity. These scholars make logical points in support of the efficiency of having one language per society. Efficiency, however, should not come at the expense of the marginalization of economically disadvantaged nonstandard English speakers. Standard English proponents have no solution to the problem of assimilation other than telling the marginalized to bite the bullet and join the mainstream, so to speak. What ever happened to equality and inclusiveness? Assimilation should not even be necessary — rather, differences should be accepted. Pragmatists may respond that joining the mainstream is vital in order to advance economically, whether doing so at the expense of one's identity is right or not. Of course, in the current state of American society, they are largely correct. I propose, however, that living up to reasonable standards of inclusiveness as a country will correct the join-the-mainstream-or-fail dilemma. We should not simply accept the hard reality, but rather work to change.

9

Metheny 6

Works Cited

Baugh, John. Out of the Mouths of Slaves: African American Language and Educational Malpractice. Austin: University of Texas Press, 1999. 1–39.

Hirsch, E. D. Cultural Literacy: What Every American Needs to Know. New York: Vintage Books, 1988. 1–32.

Holloway, Joseph E., and Winifred K. Voss. The African Heritage of American English. Bloomington: Indiana University Press, 1993.

Labov, William. Foreword. In Out of the Mouths of Slaves: African American Language and Educational Malpractice by John Baugh, i–iii. Austin: University of Texas Press, 1999.

Rodriguez, Richard. Hunger of Memory: The Education of Richard Rodriguez. New York: Bantam Books, 1983.

Smitherman, Geneva. Talkin and Testifyin: The Language of Black America. Detroit: Wayne State University Press, 1977. 167–200.

A Practice Sequence: Analyzing an Argument

Now that you have annotated Ryan Metheny's essay, we would like you to work in four groups to consider the strategies this writer uses to advance his argument. That is, analyze the way the writer states his main claim and develops his argument in drawing the conclusions he does.

Group 1: What type of claim does Metheny make? What reasons does he use to support his argument?

Group 2: To what extent are you persuaded by the reasons the writer gives to support his argument that Ebonics should be given legitimacy? Point to specific words and phrases you found persuasive.

Group 3: How effective is the writer in anticipating his readers' responses? Does he make any concessions to readers or anticipate possible counterarguments?

Group 4: Make an outline in which you include your own counterargument to this writer's position.

4

From Identifying Issues
to Forming Questions

Remember that inquiry is central to the process of composing. As you read and begin to write an essay, you will find that the real work of writing is figuring out the answers to the following questions:

- What have these authors been talking about?
- What are the relevant concerns of those whose work I have been reading?
- What are the situations motivating these people to write?
- What frames do these writers use to construct their arguments?
- Who will be interested in reading what I have to say?
- How can I connect with readers who may be both sympathetic and antagonistic toward my argument?
- What is at stake in my own argument? (What if things change? What if things stay the same?) For whom?
- What kinds of evidence might persuade my readers?
- What objections are my readers likely to raise?

To answer these questions, you must read in the role of writer, with an eye toward *identifying an issue* (an idea or statement that is open to dispute) that compels you to respond in writing, *understanding the situation* (the factors that give rise to the issue and shape your response), and *formulating a question* (what you intend to answer in response to the issue). In Table 4.1, we identify a series of situations and one of the issues and questions that derive from each of them. Notice that the question you ask is a tool that defines the area of inquiry as you read; it also can help you

TABLE 4.1   A Series of Situations with Related Issues and Questions

SITUATION	ISSUE	QUESTION
Congress plans to pass legislation that prohibits music downloads.	You feel that this piece of legislation would challenge your freedom as a consumer.	To what extent can Congress pass legislation that compromises the freedoms of individual consumers?
Different state legislatures are passing legislation to prevent Spanish-speaking students from using their own language in schools.	Your understanding of research on learning contradicts the idea that students should be prevented from using their own language in the process of learning a new language.	Under what conditions should students be allowed to use their own language while they learn English?
A manufacturing company has plans to move to your city with the promise of creating new jobs in a period of high unemployment.	You feel that this company will compromise the quality of life for the surrounding community because the manufacturing process will pollute the air.	What would persuade the city to prevent this company from moving in even though the company will provide much-needed jobs?
Your school has made an agreement with a local company to supply vending machines that sell drinks and food. The school plans to use its share of the profit to improve the library and purchase a new scoreboard for the football field.	You see that the school has much to gain from this arrangement, but you also know that obesity is a growing problem at the school.	Is there another way for the school to generate needed revenue without putting students' health at risk?
An increasing number of homeless people are seeking shelter on your college campus.	Campus security has stepped up its efforts to remove the homeless even though the shelters off campus are overcrowded.	How can you persuade the school to shelter the homeless and to provide funds to support the needs of the homeless in your city?

formulate your working thesis, the statement that answers your question. (We say more about developing a thesis in Chapter 5.) In this chapter, in addition to further discussing the importance of situation, we look at how you can identify issues and formulate questions to guide your reading and writing.

IDENTIFYING ISSUES

Below we present several steps to identifying an issue. You don't have to follow them in this particular order, of course; in fact, you may find yourself going back and forth among them as you try to bring an issue into focus. Keep in mind that issues do not simply exist in the world well formed. Instead, writers construct what they see as issues from the situations they observe. For example, consider legislation to limit music downloads from the Internet. If this kind of law conflicts with your own practices and sense of freedom, you may have begun to identify an issue: the clash of values over what constitutes fair use and what does not. Be aware that others may not understand your issue, and that in your writing you will have to explain carefully what is at stake.

■ Draw on Your Personal Experience

Writing begins with critical reading, identifying what is at issue for *you*. After all, the issue typically is what motivates people to write. You may have been taught that formal writing is objective, that you must keep a dispassionate distance from your subject, and that you should not use *I* in a college-level paper. The fact is, however, that our personal experiences influence how we read, what we pay attention to, and what inferences we draw. It makes sense, then, to begin with you — where you are and what you think and believe. We all use personal experience to make arguments in our everyday lives, to urge the people around us to act or think in certain ways. In an academic context, the challenge is to use personal experience to argue a point, to illustrate something, or to illuminate a connection between theories and the sense we make of our daily experience. You don't want simply to tell your story; but you do want your story to strengthen your argument.

In his book *Cultural Literacy*, E. D. Hirsch personalizes his interest in reversing the cycle of illiteracy in America's cities. To establish the nature of the problem in the situation he describes, he cites research showing that student performance on standardized tests in the United States is falling. But he also reflects on his own teaching in the 1970s, when he first perceived "the widening knowledge gap [that] caused me to recognize the connection between specific background knowledge and mature literacy." And he injects anecdotal evidence from conversations with his son, a teacher. Those stories heighten readers' awareness that school-aged children do not know much about literature, history, or government. (For example, his son mentions a student who challenged his claim that Latin is a "dead language" by demanding, "What do they speak in Latin America?") Hirsch's use of his son's testimony makes him vulnerable to criticism, as readers might question whether Hirsch can legitimately use his son's experience to make generalizations about education. But in fact, Hirsch is using personal testimony — his own and his son's — to augment and put a human face on the research he cites. He presents his issue, that schools must teach cultural literacy, both as something personal and as something with which we should all be concerned. The personal note helps readers see Hirsch as someone who has long been concerned with education and who has even raised a son who is an educator.

In "Dyes and Dolls: Multicultural Barbie and the Merchandising of Difference," author Ann duCille reveals how a personal experience drives her argument about the cultural significance of children's toys. She explains that although Barbie as icon seems harmless, her own examination reveals that "toys and games play crucial roles in helping children determine what is valuable in and around them." The questions she raises not only grow out of her statement of the issue, but also motivate the concerns she addresses in her essay: "More than simple instruments of pleasure and amusement, toys and games play crucial roles in helping children determine what is valuable in and around them." The issue she seizes on is the role toys play in shaping cultural attitudes; but her personal stake in the issue — what may have attracted her to it in the first place — was her own experience playing with dolls that did not reflect her ethnicity.

■ Identify What Is Open to Dispute

We have said that an issue is something that is open to dispute. Sometimes the way to clarify an issue is to think of it as a fundamental tension between two or more conflicting points of view. If you can identify conflicting points of view, an issue may become clear. Consider E. D. Hirsch, who believes that the best approach to educational reform (the subject he writes about) is to change the curriculum in schools. His position: A curriculum based on cultural literacy is the one sure way to reverse the cycle of poverty and illiteracy in urban areas. What is the issue? Hirsch's issue emerges in the presence of an alternative position. Jonathan Kozol, a social activist who has written extensively about educational reform, believes that policymakers need to address reform by providing the necessary resources that all students need to learn. Kozol points out how students in many inner-city schools are reading textbooks that were published twenty years ago, and that the dilapidated conditions in these schools — windows that won't close, for example — make it impossible for students to learn. In tension are two different views of the reform that can reverse illiteracy: Hirsch's view that educational reform should occur through curricular changes, and Kozol's view that educational reform demands socioeconomic resources.

■ Resist Binary Thinking

As you begin to define what is at issue, try to tease out complexities that may not be immediately apparent. That is, try to resist the either/or mindset that signals binary thinking. Looking at what Hirsch and Kozol have to say, it would be easy to characterize the problems facing our schools as either curricular or socioeconomic. But it may be that the real issue combines these arguments with a third or even a fourth, that neither curricular nor socioeconomic changes by themselves can resolve the problems with American schools.

After reading essays by both Hirsch and Kozol, one of our students pointed out that both Hirsch's focus on curriculum and Kozol's socioeconomic focus ignore another concern. She went on to describe her school experience in racial terms. In the excerpt below, notice how this writer uses personal experience (in a new school, she is not treated as she had expected to be treated) to formulate an issue.

> Moving to Tallahassee from Colorado Springs, Colorado, I was immediately struck by the differences apparent in local home life, school life, and community unity, or lack thereof. Ripped from my sheltered world at a small Catholic school characterized by racial harmony, I, both bewildered and unprepared, was thrown into a large public school where outward prejudice from classmates and teachers and "race wars" were common and tolerated. . . .
>
> In a school where students and teachers had the power and free reign to abuse anyone different from them, I was constantly abused. As the only black student in English honors, I was commonly belittled in front of my "peers" by my all-knowing teacher. If I developed courage enough to ask a question, I was always answered with the use of improper grammar and such words as "ain't" as my teacher attempted to simplify the material to "my level" and to give me what he called "a little learning." After discussing several subjects he often turned to me, singling me out of a sea of white faces, and asked, "Do *you* understand, Mila?" When asking my opinion of a subject, he frequently questioned, "What do *your* people think about this?" Although he insisted on including such subjects as Martin Luther King's "I Have a Dream" speech in the curriculum, the speech's themes of tolerance and equity did not accompany his lesson.

Through her reading, this student discovered that few prominent scholars have confronted the issue of racism in schools directly. Although she grants that curricular reform and increased funding may be necessary to improve education, she argues that scholars also need to address race in their studies of teaching and learning.

Our point in using this example is to emphasize that issues may be more complex than you first think they are. For this student, the issue wasn't one of two positions — reform the curriculum or provide more funding. Instead it combined a number of different positions, including race ("prejudice" and "race wars") and the relationship between student and teacher ("Do *you* understand, Mila?") in a classroom. In this passage, the writer uses her experience to challenge binary thinking. Like the student writer, you should examine issues from different perspectives, avoiding either/or propositions that oversimplify the world.

■ Build On and Extend the Ideas of Others

Academic writing builds on and even extends the ideas of others. As an academic writer, you will find that by extending other people's ideas, you will extend your own. You may begin in a familiar place; but as you read more and pursue connections to other readings, you may well end up at an unexpected destination. For example, one of our students was troubled when he read Melissa Stormont-Spurgin's description of homeless children. The student uses details from her work (giving credit, of course) in his own:

> The children . . . went to school after less than three hours of sleep. They wore the same wrinkled clothes that they had worn the day before. What will their teachers think when they fall asleep in class? How will they get food for lunch? What will their peers think? What could these homeless children talk about with their peers? They have had to grow up too fast. Their worries are not the same as other children's worries. They are worried about their next meal and where they will seek shelter. Their needs, however, are the same. They need a home and all of the securities that come with it. They also need an education (Stormont-Spurgin 156).

Initially the student was troubled by his own access to quality schools, and the contrast between his life and the lives of the children Stormont-Spurgin describes. Initially, then, his issue was the fundamental tension between his own privileged status, something he had taken for granted, and the struggle that homeless children face every day. However, as he read further and grew to understand homelessness as a concern in a number of studies, he connected his personal response to a larger conversation about democracy, fairness, and education:

> Melissa Stormont-Spurgin, an author of several articles on educational studies, addresses a very real and important, yet avoided issue in education today. Statistics show that a very high percentage of children who are born into homeless families will remain homeless, or in poverty, for the rest of their lives. How can this be, if everyone actually does have the same educational opportunities? There must be significant educational disadvantages for children without homes. In a democratic society, I feel that we must pay close attention to these disadvantages and do everything in our power to replace them with equality.

Ultimately, the student refined his sense of what was at issue: *Although all people should have access to public education in a democratic society, not everyone has the opportunity to attend quality schools in order to achieve personal success.* In turn, his definition of the issue began to shape his argument:

> Parents, teachers, homeless shelters and the citizens of the United States who fund [homeless] shelters must address the educational needs of homeless children, while steering them away from any more financial or psychological struggles. Without this emphasis on education, the current trend upward in the number of homeless families will inevitably continue in the future of American society.

The student has shifted away from a personal issue — the difference between his status and that of homeless children — to an issue of clashing values: the principle of egalitarian democracy on the one hand and the social reality of citizens in a democracy living in abject poverty on the other. When he started to read about homeless children, he could not have made the claim he ends up making, that policymakers must make education a basic human right. This student offers us an important lesson about the role of inquiry and the value of resisting easy answers. He has built on and extended his own ideas — and the ideas of others — after repeating the process of reading, raising questions, writing, and seeing problems a number of times.

■ Read to Discover a Writer's Frame

A more specialized strategy of building on and extending the ideas of others involves reading to discover a writer's **frame**, the perspective through which a writer presents his or her arguments. Writers want us to see the world a certain way, so they frame their arguments much the same way photographers and artists frame their pictures. For example, if you were to take a picture of friends in front of the football stadium on campus, you would focus on what you would most like to remember — your friends' faces — blurring the images of the people walking behind your friends. Setting up the picture, or framing it, might require using light and shade to make some details stand out more than others. Writers do the same with language.

E. D. Hirsch uses the term *cultural literacy* to frame his argument for curricular reform. For Hirsch, the term is a benchmark, a standard: People who are culturally literate are familiar with the body of information that every educated citizen should know. Hirsch's implication, of course, is that people who are not culturally literate are not well educated. But that is not necessarily true. In fact, a number of educators insist that literacy is simply a means to an end — reading to complete an assignment, for example, or to understand the ramifications of a decision — not an end in itself. By defining and using *cultural literacy* as the goal of education, Hirsch is framing his argument; he is bringing his ideas into focus.

When writers use framing strategies, they also call attention to the specific conversations that set up the situation for their arguments. Framing often entails quoting specific theories and ideas from other authors, and then using those quotations as a perspective, or lens, through which to examine other material. In his memoir *Hunger of Memory: The Education of Richard Rodriguez* (1982), Richard Rodriguez uses this method to examine his situation as a nonnative speaker of English desperate to enter the mainstream culture, even if it means sacrificing his identity as the son of Mexican immigrants. Reflecting on his life as a student, Rodriguez comes across Richard Hoggart's book *The Uses of Literacy* (1957). Hoggart's description of "the scholarship boy" presents a lens through which Rodriguez can see his own experience. Hoggart writes:

> With his family, the boy has the intense pleasure of intimacy, the family's consolation in feeling public alienation. Lavish emotions texture home life.

Then, at school, the instruction bids him to trust lonely reason primarily. Immediate needs set the pace of his parents' lives. From his mother and father the boy learns to trust spontaneity and nonrational ways of knowing. *Then*, at school, there is mental calm. Teachers emphasize the value of a reflectiveness that opens a space between thinking and immediate action.

Years of schooling must pass before the boy will be able to sketch the cultural differences in his day as abstractly as this. But he senses those differences early. Perhaps as early as the night he brings home an assignment from school and finds the house too noisy for study. He has to be more and more alone, if he is going to "get on." He will have, probably unconsciously, to oppose the ethos of the hearth, the intense gregariousness of the working-class family group. . . . The boy has to cut himself off mentally, so as to do his homework, as well as he can.

Here is Rodriguez's response to Hoggart's description of the scholarship boy:

For weeks I read, speed-read, books by modern educational theorists, only to find infrequent and slight mention of students like me. . . . Then one day, leafing through Richard Hoggart's *The Uses of Literacy*, I found, in his description of the scholarship boy, myself. For the first time I realized that there were other students like me, and so I was able to frame the meaning of my academic success, its consequent price — the loss.

Notice how Rodriguez introduces ideas from Hoggart "to frame" his own ideas: "I found, in his description of the scholarship boy, myself. For the first time I realized that there were other students like me, and so I was able to frame the meaning of my academic success, its consequent price — the loss." Hoggart's scholarship boy enables Rodriguez to revisit his own experience with a new perspective. Hoggart's words and idea advance Rodriguez's understanding of the problem he identifies in his life: his inability to find solace at home and within his working-class roots. Hoggart's discription of the scholarship boy's moving between cultural extremes — spontaneity at home and reflection at school — helps Rodriguez bring his own youthful discontent into focus.

Rodriguez's response to Hoggart's text shows how another writer's lens can help frame an issue. If you were using Hoggart's term *scholarship boy* as a lens through which to clarify an issue in education, you might ask how the term illuminates new aspects of another writer's examples or your own. And then you might ask, "To what extent does Hirsch's cultural literacy throw a more positive light on what Rodriguez and Hoggart describe?" or "How do my experiences challenge, extend, or complicate the scholarship-boy concept?"

■ Consider the Constraints of the Situation

In identifying an issue, you have to understand the situation that gives rise to the issue, including the contexts in which it is raised and debated. One of the contexts is the audience. In thinking about your issue, you must consider the extent to which your potential readers are involved in the dialogue you want to enter, and what they know and need to know. In a sense, audience functions as both context and **constraint**, a factor that narrows the choices you can make in responding to an issue. An understanding of your potential readers will help you choose the depth of the discussion; it will also determine the kind of evidence you can present and the language you can use.

Another constraint on your response to an issue is the form that response takes. For example, if you decide to make an issue of government-imposed limits on the music you can download from the Internet, your response in writing might take the form of an editorial or a letter to a legislator. In this situation, length is an obvious constraint: Newspapers limit the word count of editorials, and the best letters to legislators tend to be brief and very selective about the evidence they cite. A few personal examples and a few statistics may be all you can include to support your claim about the issue. By contrast, if you were making your case in an academic journal, a very different set of constraints would apply. You would have more space for illustrations and support, for example.

Finally, the situation itself can function as a major constraint. For instance, suppose your topic is the decline of educational standards. It's difficult to imagine any writer making the case for accelerating that decline or any audience being receptive to any argument that a decline in standards is a good thing.

Steps to Identifying Issues

1. **Draw on your personal experience.** Start with your own sense of what's important, what puzzles you, or what you are curious about. (Then build your argument by moving on to other sources to support your point of view.)

2. **Identify what is open to dispute.** Identify a phenomenon or some idea in a written argument that challenges what you think or believe.

3. **Resist binary thinking.** Think about the issue from multiple perspectives.

4. **Build on and extend the ideas of others.** As you read, be open to new ways of looking at the issue. The issue you finally write about may be very different from what you set out to write about.

5. **Read to discover a writer's frame.** What theories or ideas shape the writer's focus? How can these theories or ideas help you frame your argument?

6. **Consider the constraints of the situation.** Craft your argument to meet the needs of and constraints imposed by your audience and form.

■ **Identify Issues in an Essay**

Consider the situation of writer Anna Quindlen, who in 1992 published an editorial in the *New York Times* addressing the issue of homelessness. At the time, New Yorkers seemed to have accepted homelessness as something that could be studied but not remedied. As you read Quindlen's "No Place Like Home," note the words and phrases Quindlen uses to identify both the situation and her audience. Is her main claim one of fact, value, or policy? Finally, answer the questions that follow the essay to see if you can discern how Quindlen locates, defines, and advances her issue.

ABOUT THE READING

Anna Quindlen is the best-selling author of novels (including *Blessings, Black and Blue, One True Thing,* and *Object Lessons*) and nonfiction books (including *A Short Guide to a Happy Life, Living Out Loud, Thinking Out Loud,* and *How Reading Changed My Life*). She has also written children's books (including *The Tree That Came to Stay* and *Happily Ever After*). She won the Pulitzer Prize in 1992 for her *New York Times* column, "Public & Private." Since 1999 she has been writing a biweekly column for *Newsweek.*

ANNA QUINDLEN

No Place Like Home

Homeless is like the government wanting you locked up
And the people in America do not like you.
They look at you and say Beast!
I wish the people would help the homeless
And stop their talking.

—FRANK S. RICE, *The Rio Times*

The building is beautiful, white and beige and oak, the colors of yuppies. The rehab of the Rio came in $700,000 under budget, two months ahead of schedule. The tenants say they will not mess it up, no, no, no. "When you don't have a place and you get a good place, the last thing you want to do is lose it," said one man who slept in shelters for seven years, seven years during which time you might have gotten married, or lost a loved one, or struck it rich, but all this guy did was live on the streets. *1*

Mayor David Dinkins has announced that he will study parts of the study he commissioned from a commission on the homeless, the newest in a long line of studies. *2*

One study, done in 1981, was called "Private Lives, Public Spaces." It was researched by Ellen Baxter, who now runs the nonprofit company *3* that has brought us the Rio and four other buildings that provide permanent housing for the homeless in Washington Heights.

Another study, done in 1987, was called "A Shelter Is Not a Home" and   *4*
was produced by the Manhattan Borough President David Dinkins, who now runs the City of New York. At the time, the Koch administration said it would study Mr. Dinkins's study, which must have taught Mr. Dinkins something.

Robert Hayes, one of the founding fathers of the movement to help the   *5*
homeless, once told me there were three answers to the problem: housing, housing, housing. It was an overly simplistic answer, and it was essentially correct.

Despite our obsessions with pathology and addiction, Ms. Baxter has   *6*
renovated one apartment building after another and filled them with people. At the Rio, what was once a burnt-out eyesore is now, with its curving facade and bright lobby, the handsomest building on the block; what were once armory transients with dirt etched in the creases of hands and face are now tenants. The building needed people; the people needed a home. The city provided the rehab money; Columbia University provides social service support.

Some of the tenants need to spend time in drug treatment and some go   *7*
to Alcoholics Anonymous and some of them lapse into pretty pronounced fugue states from time to time. So what? How would you behave if you'd lived on the streets for seven years? What is better: to leave them out there while we lament the emptying of the mental hospitals and the demise of jobs? Or to provide a roof over their heads and then get them psychiatric care and job training?

What is better: to spend nearly $20,000 each year to have them   *8*
sleep on cots at night and wander the streets by day? Or to make a one-time investment of $38,000 a unit, as they did in the single rooms with kitchens and baths in the Rio, for permanent homes for people who will pay rent from their future wages or from entitlement benefits?

Years ago I became cynical enough to envision a game plan in which   *9*
politicians, tussling over government stuff like demonstration projects and agency jurisdiction and commission studies, ignored this problem until it went away.

And, in a sense, it has. We have become so accustomed to people sleep-   *10*
ing on sidewalks and in subway stations that recumbent bodies have become small landmarks in our neighborhoods. Mary Brosnahan, executive director of the Coalition for the Homeless, says she was stunned, talking to students, at their assumption that people always had and always would be living on the streets. My children call by pet names — "the man with the cup," "the lady with the falling-down pants" — the homeless people around their school.

And when a problem becomes that rooted in our everyday perceptions,   *11*
it is understood to be without solution. Nonprofit groups like the one that

renovated the Rio prove that this is not so. The cots in the armory are poison; drug programs and job training are icing. A place to shut the door, to sleep without one eye open, to be warm, to be safe — that's the cake. There's no place like home. You didn't need a study to figure that out, did you?

For Analysis and Discussion

1. Can you find evidence of Quindlen's personal responses and experiences?
2. What phenomenon has challenged what Quindlen thinks and believes about homelessness? How has she made it into an issue?
3. Where does she indicate that she has considered the issue from multiple perspectives and is placing her ideas in conversation with those of others?
4. What sort of lens does Quindlen seem to be using to frame her argument?
5. What constraints seem to be in play in the essay?

A Practice Sequence: Identifying Issues

This sequence of activities will give you practice in identifying and clarifying issues based on your own choice of reading and collaboration with your classmates.

1 Draw on your personal experience. Reflect on your own responses to what you have been reading in this or in other classes, or issues that writers have posed in the media. What concerns you most? Choose a story that supports or challenges the claims people are making in what you have read or listened to. What questions do you have? Make some notes in response to these questions, explaining your personal stake in the issues and questions you formulate.

2 Identify what is open to dispute. Take what you have written and formulate your ideas as an issue, using the structure we used in our example of Hirsch's and Kozol's competing arguments:

- Part 1: Your view of a given topic
- Part 2: At least one view that is in tension with your own

If you need to, read further to understand what others have to say about this issue.

3 Resist binary thinking. Share your statement of the issue with one or more peers and ask them if they see other ways to formulate the issue that you may not have thought about. What objections, if any, do they make to your statement in part 1? Write these objections down in part 2 so that you begin to look at the issue from multiple perspectives.

4 Build on and extend the ideas of others. Now that you have formulated an issue from different perspectives, explaining your personal stake in the issue, connect what you think to a broader conversation in what you are reading. Then try making a claim using this structure: "Although some people would argue _____, I think that _____."

5 Read to discover a writer's frame. As an experiment in trying out multiple perspectives, revise the claim you make in exercise 4 by introducing the frame, or lens, through which you want readers to understand your argument. You can employ the same sentence structure. For example, here is a claim framed in terms of race: "Although people should have access to public education, recent policies have exacerbated racial inequalities in public schools." In contrast, here is a claim that focuses on economics: "Although people should have access to public education, the unequal distribution of tax money has created what some would call an 'economy of education.'" The lens may come from reading you have done in other courses or from conversations with your classmates, and you may want to attribute the lens to a particular author or classmate: "Although some people would argue_____, I use E. D. Hirsch's notion of cultural literacy to show_____."

6 Consider the constraints of the situation. Building on these exercises, develop an argument in the form of an editorial for your local newspaper. This means that you will need to limit your argument to about 250 words. You also will need to consider the extent to which your potential readers are involved in the conversation. What do they know? What do they need to know? What kind of evidence do you need to use to persuade readers?

FORMULATING ISSUE-BASED QUESTIONS

When you identify an issue, you need to understand it in the context of its situation. Ideally, the situation and the issue will be both recent and relevant, which will make your task of connecting to your audience that much easier when you write about the issue. For example, the student writer who was concerned about long-standing issues of homelessness and lack of educational opportunity connected to his readers by citing recent statistics and giving the problem of homelessness a face: "The children . . . went to school after less than three hours of sleep. They wore the same wrinkled clothes that they had worn the day before." If your issue does not immediately meet the criteria of timeliness and relevance, you will need to take that into consideration as you continue your reading and research. Ask yourself: What is on people's minds these days? What do they need to know about? Think about why the issue matters to you, and imagine why it might matter to others. By the time you write, you should be prepared to make the issue relevant for your readers.

In addition to understanding the situation and defining the issue that you feel is most timely and relevant, you can formulate an **issue-based question** to help you think through your subject. This question should be specific enough to guide your inquiry into what others have written. An issue-based question should help you

- clarify what you know about the issue and what you still need to learn.
- clearly guide your inquiry.
- organize your inquiry.
- develop an argument — a more complex task than simply collecting information by asking how, why, should, or the extent to which something is true or not.
- consider who your audience is.
- determine what resources you have so that you can ask a question that you have the resources to answer.

A good question develops out of an issue, some fundamental tension that you identify within a conversation. For Anna Quindlen in "No Place Like Home," the tension exists between what she sees as an unacceptable situation in New York and the city's ongoing failure to do something about it. Implicit is a question of how she can change people's attitudes, especially those of city leaders, who seem willing to "spend nearly $20,000 each year to have [homeless people] sleep on cots at night and wander the streets by day" rather than "make a one-time investment of $38,000 a unit" for housing. By identifying what is at issue, you should begin to understand for whom it is an issue — for whom you are answering the question. In turn, the answer to your question will help you craft your thesis.

In the following paragraphs, we trace the steps one of our students took to formulate an issue-based question on the broad topic of language diversity. Although we present the steps in sequence, be aware that they are guidelines only: The steps often overlap, and there is a good deal of room for rethinking and refining along the way.

■ Refine Your Topic

Generally speaking, a **topic** is the subject you want to write about. For example, homelessness, tests, and violence are all topics. So are urban homelessness, standardized tests, and video game violence. And so are homelessness in New York City, aptitude tests versus achievement tests, and mayhem in the video game Grand Theft Auto. As our list suggests, even a specific topic needs refining into an issue before it can be explored effectively in writing.

The topic our student wanted to focus on was language diversity, a subject her linguistics class had been discussing. She was fascinated by the extraordinary range of languages spoken in the United States, not just by immigrant groups but by native speakers whose dialects and varieties of English are considered nonstandard. She herself had relatives for whom English was not a first language. She began refining her topic by putting her thoughts into words:

> I want to describe the experience of being raised in a home where non-Standard English is spoken.

> I'd like to know the benefits and liabilities of growing up bilingual.

> I am curious to know what it's like to live in a community of nonnative speakers of English while trying to make a living in a country where the dominant language is English.

Although she had yet to identify an issue, her attempts to articulate what interested her about the topic were moving her toward the situation of people in the United States who don't speak Standard English or don't have English as their first language.

▪ Explain Your Interest in the Topic

At this point, the student encountered E. D. Hirsch's *Cultural Literacy* in her reading, which had both a provocative and a clarifying effect on her thinking. She began to build on and extend Hirsch's ideas. Reacting to Hirsch's assumption that students should acquire the same base of knowledge and write in Standard Written English, her first, somewhat mischievous thought was, "I wonder what Hirsch would think about cultural literacy being taught in a bilingual classroom?" But then her thinking took another turn, and she began to contemplate the effect of Hirsch's cultural-literacy agenda on speakers whose English is not standard or for whom English is not a first language. She used a demographic fact that she had learned in her linguistics class in her explanation of her interest in the topic: "I'm curious about the consequences of limiting language diversity when the presence of ethnic minorities in our educational system is growing."

▪ Identify an Issue

The more she thought about Hirsch's ideas, and the more she read about language diversity, the more concerned our student grew. It seemed to her that Hirsch's interest in producing students who all share the same base of knowledge and all write in Standard Written English was in tension with her sense that this kind of approach places a burden on people whose first language is not English. That tension clarified the issue for her. In identifying the issue, she wrote:

> Hirsch's book actually sets some priorities, most notably through his list of words and phrases that form the foundations of what it means to be "American." However, this list certainly overlooks several crucial influences in American culture. Most oversights generally come at the expense of the minority populations.

These two concerns — with inclusion and with exclusion — helped focus the student's inquiry.

■ Formulate Your Topic as a Question

To further define her inquiry, the student formulated her topic as a question that pointed toward an argument: "To what extent can E. D. Hirsch's notion of 'cultural literacy' coexist with our country's principles of democracy and inclusion?" Notice that her choice of the phrase *To what extent* implies that both goals do not go hand in hand. If she had asked, "Can common culture coexist with pluralism?" her phrasing would imply that a yes or no answer would suffice, possibly foreclosing avenues of inquiry and certainly ignoring the complexity of the issue.

Instead, despite her misgivings about the implications of Hirsch's agenda, the student suspended judgment, opening the way to genuine inquiry. She acknowledged the usefulness and value of sharing a common language and conceded that Hirsch's points were well taken. She wrote:

> Some sort of unification is necessary. Language, . . . on the most fundamental level of human interaction, demands some compromise and chosen guidelines. . . . How can we learn from one another if we cannot even say hello to each other?

Suspending judgment led her to recognize the complexity of the issue, and her willingness to examine the issue from different perspectives indicated the empathy that is a central component of developing a conversational argument.

■ Acknowledge Your Audience

This student's question ("To what extent can E. D. Hirsch's notion of 'cultural literacy' coexist with our country's principles of democracy and inclusion?") also acknowledged an audience. By invoking cultural literacy, she assumed an audience of readers who are familiar with Hirsch's ideas, probably including policymakers and educational administrators. In gesturing toward democracy, she cast her net very wide: Most Americans probably admire the "principles of democracy." But in specifying inclusion as a democratic principle, she wisely linked all Americans who believe in democratic principles, including the parents of schoolchildren, with all people who have reason to feel excluded by Hirsch's ideas, especially non-native speakers of English, among them immigrants from Mexico and speakers of African American Vernacular English. Thus this student was acknowledging an audience of policymakers, administrators, parents (both mainstream and marginalized), and those who knew about and perhaps supported cultural literacy.

Steps to Formulating an Issue-Based Question

1 **Refine your topic.** Examine your topic from different perspectives. For example, what are the causes of homelessness? What are its consequences?

2 **Explain your interest in the topic.** Explore the source of your interest in this topic and what you want to learn.

3 **Identify an issue.** Consider what is open to dispute.

4 **Formulate your topic as a question.** Use your question to focus your inquiry.

5 **Acknowledge your audience.** Reflect on what readers may know about the issue, why they may be interested, and what you would like to teach them.

A Practice Sequence: Formulating an Issue-Based Question

As you start developing your own issue-based question, it might be useful to practice a five-step process that begins with a topic, a word or phrase that describes the focus of your interests. Here, apply the process to the one-word topic homelessness.

1 Expand your topic into a phrase. "I am interested in the *consequences* of homelessness," "I want to *describe* what it means to be homeless," or "I am interested in discussing the *cause* of homelessness."

2 Explain your interest in this topic. "I am interested in the consequences of homelessness because it challenges democratic principles of fairness."

3 Identify an issue. "The persistence of homelessness contradicts my belief in social justice."

4 Formulate your topic as a question. "To what extent can we allow homelessness to persist in a democratic nation that prides itself on providing equal opportunity to all?"

5 Acknowledge your audience. "I am interested in the consequences of homelessness because I want people who believe in democracy to understand that we need to work harder to make sure that everyone has access to food, shelter, and employment."

The answer to the question you formulate in step 4 should lead to an assertion, your main claim, or *thesis*. For example, you could state your main claim this way: "Although homelessness persists as a widespread problem in our nation, we must develop policies that eliminate homelessness, ensuring that everyone has access to food, shelter, and employment. This is especially important in a democracy that embraces social justice and equality."

The thesis introduces a problem and makes an assertion that you will need to support: "We must develop policies that eliminate homelessness, ensuring that everyone has access to food, shelter, and employment." What is at issue? Not everyone would agree that policies must be implemented to solve the problem. In fact, many would argue that homelessness is an individual problem, that individuals must take responsibility for lifting themselves out of poverty, homelessness, and unemployment. Of course, you would need to read quite a bit to reach this final stage of formulating your thesis.

Try using the five-step process we describe above to formulate your own topic as a question, or try formulating the following topics as questions:

- Downloading music
- Violence in video games
- Gender and employment
- The popularity of a cultural phenomenon (a book, a film, a performer, an icon)
- Standardized tests
- Civil rights
- Town-gown relationships
- Media and representation
- Government and religion
- Affirmative action

5

From Formulating to Developing a Thesis

Academic writing explores complex issues that grow out of relevant, timely conversations in which something is at stake. An academic writer reads as a writer to understand the issues, situations, and questions that lead other writers to make claims. Readers expect academic writers to take a clear, specific, logical stand on an issue, and they evaluate how writers support their claims and anticipate counterarguments. The logical stand is the **thesis**, an assertion that academic writers make at the beginning of what they write and then support with evidence throughout their essay. The illustrations and examples that a writer includes must relate to and support the thesis. Thus, a thesis encompasses all of the information writers use to further their arguments; it is not simply a single assertion at the beginning of an essay.

One of our students aptly described the thesis using the metaphor of a shish kebab: The thesis penetrates every paragraph, holding the paragraphs together, just as a skewer penetrates and holds the ingredients of a shish kebab together. Moreover, the thesis serves as a signpost throughout an essay, reminding readers what the argument is and why the writer has included evidence — examples, illustrations, quotations — relevant to that argument.

An academic thesis

- makes an assertion that is clearly defined, focused, and supported.
- reflects an awareness of the conversation from which the writer has taken up the issue.
- is placed at the beginning of the essay.

- penetrates every paragraph like the skewer in a shish kebab.
- acknowledges points of view that differ from the writer's own, reflecting the complexity of the issue.
- demonstrates an awareness of the readers' assumptions and anticipates possible counterarguments.
- conveys a significant fresh perspective.

It is a myth is that writers first come up with a thesis and then write their essays. The reality is that writers use issue-based questions to read, learn, and develop a thesis throughout the process of writing. Through revising and discussing their ideas, writers hone their thesis, making sure that it threads through every paragraph of the final draft. The position writers ultimately take in writing — their thesis — comes at the end of the writing process, after not one draft but many.

WORKING VERSUS DEFINITIVE THESES

Writers are continually challenged by the need to establish their purpose and to make a clear and specific assertion of it. To reach that assertion, you must first engage in a prolonged process of inquiry, aided by a well-formulated question. The question serves as a tool for inquiry that will help you formulate your **working thesis**, your first attempt at an assertion of your position. A working thesis is valuable in the early stages of writing because it helps you read selectively, in the same way that your issue-based question guides your inquiry. Reading raises questions, helping you see what you know and need to know, and challenging you to read on. Never accept your working thesis as your final position. Instead, continue testing your assertion as you read and write, and modify your working thesis as necessary. A more definitive thesis will come once you are satisfied that you have examined the issue from multiple perspectives.

For example, one of our students wanted to study representations of femininity in the media. In particular, she focused on why the Barbie doll has become an icon of femininity despite what many cultural critics consider Barbie's "outrageous and ultimately unattainable physical characteristics." Our student's working thesis suggested she would develop an argument about the need for change:

> The harmful implications of ongoing exposure to these unattainable ideals, such as low self-esteem, eating disorders, unhealthy body image, and acceptance of violence, make urgent the need for change.

The student assumed that her research would lead her to argue that Barbie's unattainable proportions have a damaging effect on women's self-image and that something needs to be done about it. However, as she read scholarly research to support her tentative thesis, she realized that a more compelling project would be less Barbie-centric. Instead, she chose to examine the broader phenomenon of how the idea of femininity is created and reinforced by society. That is, her personal interest in Barbie was supplanted by her discoveries about cultural norms of beauty and the power they have to influence self-perception and behavior. In her final draft, this was her definitive thesis:

> Although evidence may be provided to argue that gender is an innate characteristic, I will show that it is actually the result of one's actions, which are then labeled *masculine* or *feminine* according to society's definitions of ideal gender. Furthermore, I will discuss the communication of such definitions through the media, specifically in music videos, on TV, and in magazines, and the harmful implications of being exposed to these ideals.

Instead of arguing for change, the student chose to show her readers how they were being manipulated, leaving it to them to decide what actions they might want to take.

DEVELOPING A WORKING THESIS: THREE MODELS

What are some ways to develop a working thesis? We suggest three models that may help you organize the information you gather in response to the question guiding your inquiry.

■ The Correcting-Misinterpretations Model

This model is used to correct writers whose arguments you believe have misconstrued one or more important aspects of an issue. The thesis typically takes the form of a factual claim. Consider this example and the words we have underlined:

> <u>Although scholars have addressed curriculum</u> to explain low achievement in schools, <u>they have failed to fully appreciate the impact of limited resources</u> to fund up-to-date textbooks, quality teachers, and computers. Therefore, reform in schools must focus on economic need as well as curriculum.

The clause beginning with "Although" lays out the assumption that many scholars make, that curriculum explains low educational achievement; the clause beginning with "they have failed" identifies the error those scholars have made by ignoring the economic reasons for low achievement in schools. Notice that the structure of the sentence reinforces the author's position. He offers the faulty assumption in a subordinate clause, reserving the main clause for his own position. The two clauses also reinforce that there are conflicting opinions here. One more thing: Although it is a common myth that a thesis must be phrased in a single sentence, this example shows that a thesis can be written in two (or more) sentences.

▪ The Filling-the-Gap Model

The gap model points to what other writers may have overlooked or ignored in discussing a given issue. The gap model typically makes a claim of value. Consider this student's argument that discussions of cultural diversity in the United States are often framed in terms of black and white. Our underlining indicates the gap the writer has identified:

> If America is truly a "melting pot" of cultures, as it is often called, then why is it that stories and events seem only to be in black and white? Why is it that when history courses are taught about the period of the civil rights movement, only the memoirs of African Americans are read, like those of Melba Pattillo Beals and Ida Mae Holland? Where are the works of Maxine Hong Kingston, who tells the story of alienation and segregation in schools through the eyes of a Chinese child? African Americans were denied the right to vote, and many other citizenship rights; but Chinese Americans were denied even the opportunity to become citizens. I am not diminishing the issue of discrimination against African Americans, nor belittling the struggles they went through. I simply want to call attention to discrimination against other minority groups and their often-overlooked struggles to achieve equality.

In the student's thesis, the gap in people's knowledge stems from their limited understanding of history — that many minority groups were denied their rights.

A variation on the gap model also occurs when a writer suggests that although something might appear to be the case, a closer look reveals something different. For example: "Although it would *appear* that women and people of color have achieved equality in the workplace, their paychecks suggest that this is not true." One of our students examined two poems by the same author that appeared to contradict each other. She noticed a gap others had not seen:

> In both "The Albatross" and "Beauty," Charles Baudelaire chooses to explore the plight of the poet. Interestingly, despite their common author, the two poems' portrayals of the poet's struggles appear contradictory. "The Albatross" seems to give a somewhat sympathetic glimpse into the exile of the

poet — the "winged voyager" so awkward in the ordinary world. "Beauty" takes what appears to be a less forgiving stance: The poet here is docile, simply a mirror. Although both pieces depict the poet's struggles, a closer examination demonstrates how the portrayals differ.

In stating her thesis, the student indicates that although readers might expect Baudelaire's images of poets to be similar, a closer examination of his words would prove them wrong.

■ The Modifying-What-Others-Have-Said Model

The modification model of thesis writing is premised on the possibility of mutual understanding. For example, in proposing a change in policy, one student asserts:

> Although scholars have claimed that the only sure way to reverse the cycle of homelessness in America is to provide an adequate education, we need to build on this work, providing school-to-work programs that ensure graduates have access to employment.

Here the writer seeks to modify other writers' claims, suggesting that education alone does not solve the problem of homelessness; the challenge he sets for himself is to understand the complexity of the problem by building on and extending the ideas of others. In effect, he is in a constructive conversation with those whose work he wants to build on, helping readers see that he shares common ground with the other writers and hopes to find a mutually acceptable solution to the agreed-on problem.

Steps to Formulating a Working Thesis: Three Models

1 **Misinterpretations model:** "Although many scholars have argued about X and Y, a careful examination suggests Z."

2 **Gap model:** "Although scholars have noted X and Y, they have missed the importance of Z."

3 **Modification model:** "Although I agree with the X and Y ideas of other writers, it is important to extend/refine/limit their ideas with Z."

A Practice Sequence: Identifying Types of Theses

Below is a series of working theses. Read each one and then identify the model — misinterpretations, gap, or modification — it represents.

1 A number of studies indicate that violence on television has a detrimental effect on adolescent behavior. However, few researchers have examined key environmental factors like peer pressure, music, and home life. In fact, I would argue that many researchers have oversimplified the problem.

2 Although research indicates that an increasing number of African American and Hispanic students are dropping out of high school, researchers have failed to fully grasp the reasons why this has occurred.

3 I want to argue that studies supporting single-sex education are relatively sound. However, we don't really know the long-term effects of single-sex education, particularly on young women's career paths.

4 Although recent studies of voting patterns in the United States indicate that young people between the ages of 18 and 24 are apathetic, I want to suggest that not all of the reasons these studies provide are valid.

5 Indeed, it's not surprising that students are majoring in fields that will enable them to get a job after graduation. But students may not be as pragmatic as we think. Many students choose majors because they feel that learning is an important end in itself.

6 Although good teachers are essential to learning, we cannot ignore the roles that race and class play in students' access to a quality education.

7 It is clear that cities need to clean up the dilapidated housing projects that were built over half a century ago; but few, if any, studies have examined the effects of doing so on the life chances of those people who are being displaced.

8 In addition to its efforts to advance the cause of social justice in the new global economy, the university must make a commitment to ending poverty on the edge of campus.

9 Although the writer offers evidence to explain the sources of illiteracy in America, he overstates his case when he ignores other factors, among them history, culture, and economic well-being. Therefore, I will argue that we place the discussion in a broader context.

10 More and more policymakers argue that English should be the national language in the United States. Although I agree that English is important, we should not limit people's right to maintain their own linguistic and cultural identity.

ESTABLISHING A CONTEXT FOR A THESIS

In addition to defining the purpose and focus of an essay, a thesis must set up a **context** for the writer's claim. The process of establishing a background for understanding an issue typically involves four steps:

1. Establish that the topic of conversation, the issue, is current and relevant — that it is on people's minds or should be.

2. Briefly summarize what others have said to show that you are familiar with the topic or issue.

3. Explain what you see as the problem — a misinterpretation, gap, or a modification that needs to be made in how others have addressed the topic or issue — perhaps by raising the questions you believe need to be answered.

4. State your thesis, suggesting that your view on the issue may present readers with something new to think about as it builds on and extends what others have argued.

You need not follow these steps in this order as long as your readers come away from the first part of your essay knowing why you are discussing a given issue and what your argument is.

We trace these four steps below in our analysis of the opening paragraphs of one of our student's essays. She was writing in response to what many call the English-only movement. Specifically, she responds to the effects of Proposition 227 in California, a piece of legislation that prevents non-English-speaking students from using their first language in school. Our discussion of how she provides a context for her thesis follows the excerpt.

Nuestra Clase   1

Jenny Eck
Professor Walters
English 200
March 18, 20--

         Nuestra Clase: Making the Classroom a Welcoming Place
               for English Language Learners

         With the Latino population growing exponentially and Spanish quickly becoming one of the most widely spoken languages in the United States, the question arises of how the American educational system is meeting the needs of a growing Hispanic population. What does our educational system do to address the needs of students whose primary language is not English?

1

Nuestra Clase   2

In 1998, the state of California passed Proposition 227, which   2
prohibited bilingual instruction in public schools. Ron Unz, a former
Republican gubernatorial candidate and software developer, launched
the initiative under the name "English for the Children." Unz argued
that the initiative would help Latinos and other recent immigrants
free themselves from bilingual education, which he avowed would
hinder the ability of immigrants to assimilate into American culture
(Stritikus, 2002). Supporters of Proposition 227 assert that bilingual
education has failed English language learners (ELLs) because it does
not adequately equip them with the English language skills essential
to success in school. Eradicating bilingual education, they believe,
will help students learn English more effectively and consequently
achieve more in their educational careers.

Since its passage, Proposition 227 has been hotly debated.   3
Many researchers claim that its strictures have stunted the education
of Spanish-speaking students (Halcón, 2001; Stritikus, 2002). Many
studies have indicated the harmful effects of what Gutiérrez and
her colleagues describe as "backlash pedagogy" (Gutiérrez, Asato,
Santos & Gotanda, 2002), which prohibits the use of students' complete linguistic, sociocultural, and academic repertoire. In essence,
they claim that Proposition 227's backlash pedagogy, in attempting
to emphasize "colorblindness" in education, has instead eradicated
differences that are crucial to students' efforts to become educated.
They argue that by devaluing these differences, the educational
system devalues the very students it is attempting to help.

A sociocultural theory of learning, with its emphasis on the   4
significant impact that factors such as language, culture, family,
and community have on a student's potential for educational success
(Halcón, 2001), calls attention to growing concerns that schools may
not be meeting the needs of ELLs. Russian psychologist Lev Vygotsky
(1978) introduced this viewpoint to educators when he proposed that
development and learning are firmly embedded in and influenced by
society and culture. With Vygotsky's theory in mind, other researchers
have embraced the idea that the failure of minority students is more
often than not a systematic failure, rather than an individual failure
(Trueba, 1989). Sociocultural theory posits that learning needs to be
understood not only in the broader context of the sociocultural lives

Nuestra Clase 3

of students, teachers, and schools, but also in their sociopolitical lives. A sociocultural context takes a student's culture, race, religion, language, family, community, and other similar factors into consideration, while a sociopolitical context takes into account the inherent ideologies and prejudices that exist in society today. In order for teaching to be effective, both sociocultural and sociopolitical factors must be identified and addressed.

Many educators seem to dismiss sociocultural and sociopolitical factors, perhaps not realizing that by ignoring these factors, they are inadvertently privileging the students in their classrooms for whom English is a first language (Larson, 2003). Such a dismissive attitude does not reckon with other studies that have shown how important it is for English language learners to explore and express their bilingual/bicultural identities (McCarthey, García, López-Velásquez, Lin & Guo, 2004). Some of these other studies have even proposed that schooling acts as a "subtractive process" for minority students, not only denying them opportunities to express their identities, but also divesting them of important social and cultural resources, which ultimately leaves them vulnerable to academic failure (Valenzuela, 1999). These other studies convincingly show that sociocultural factors are essential to the educational success of English language learners. Therefore, although many educators believe they know the best way to teach these students, I will argue that the educational system, by not taking into account factors that sociocultural theory emphasizes, has mostly failed to create classrooms that embrace cultural differences, and by so doing has failed to create optimal conditions for teaching and learning.

5

Nuestra Clase 9

References

Gutiérrez, K., Asato, J., Santos, M. & Gotanda, N. (2002). Backlash pedagogy: Language and culture and the politics of reform. *The review of education, pedagogy, and cultural studies, 24*, 335–351.

Nuestra Clase   10

Halcón, J. J. (2001). Mainstream ideology and literacy instructions for Spanish-speaking children. In M. Reyes & J. J. Halcón (Eds.), *The best for our children: Critical perspectives on literacy for Latino students* (pp. 65–77). New York, NY: Teacher's College Press.

Larson, J. (2003). Negotiating Race in Classroom Research: Tensions and Possibilities. In S. Greene & D. Abt-Perkins (Eds.), *Making race visible: Literacy research for cultural understanding* (pp. 89–106). New York, NY: Teacher's College Press.

McCarthey, S. J., López-Velásquez, A. M., García, G. E., Lin, S., & Guo, Y. (2004). Understanding writing contexts for English language learners. *Research in the teaching of English, 38,* 351–394.

Stritikus, T. (2002). *Immigrant children and the politics of English-only: Views from the classroom.* New York, NY: LFB Scholarly Publishing LLC.

Trueba, H. T. (1989). *Raising silent voices: Educating the linguistic minorities for the 21st century.* Cambridge, MA: Newbury House.

Valenzuela, A. (1999). *Subtractive schooling: U.S. Mexican youth and the politics of caring.* Albany, NY: State University of New York Press.

Vygotsky, L. S. (1978). *Thought and language.* Cambridge, MA: MIT Press.

■ Establish That the Issue Is Current and Relevant

Ideally, you should convey to readers that the issue you are discussing is both current (what's on people's minds) and relevant (of sufficient importance to have generated some discussion and written conversation). In the first sentence, Eck tells readers of a trend she feels they need to be aware of, the dramatic growth of the Hispanic population in the United States. Her issue is what the schools are doing to meet the needs of a growing population of students "whose primary language is not English." At the beginning of the third paragraph, she signals the relevance of the issue when she observes that the passage of Proposition 227 has been "hotly debated."

■ Briefly Present What Others Have Said

It is important to introduce who has said what in the conversation you are entering. After all, you are interrupting that conversation to make your contribution, and those who are already in that conversation expect you to have done your homework and acknowledge those who have already made important contributions. (For more on presenting the ideas of others, see Chapter 7.)

In the second paragraph, Eck sets the stage for her review with a brief history of Proposition 227. Here she describes what was at issue for supporters of the law and what they hoped the law would accomplish. Starting with paragraph 3, Eck acknowledges the researchers who have participated in the debate surrounding Proposition 227 and reviews a number of studies that challenge the premises on which Proposition 227 rested. Notice that she introduces the frame of sociocultural theory to help her readers see that denying students the use of their native language in the classroom is a problem.

By pointing out the ways that researchers on language learning challenge the assumptions underlying the English-only movement, Eck is doing more than listing sources. She is establishing that a problem, or issue, exists. Moreover, her review gives readers intellectual touchstones, the scholars who need to be cited in any academic conversation about bilingual education. A review is not a catchall for anyone writing on a topic; instead, it should reflect a writer's selection of the most relevant participants in the conversation. Eck's choice of sources, and how she presents them, conveys that she is knowledgeable about her subject. (Of course, it is her readers' responsibility to read further to determine whether she has reviewed the most relevant work and has presented the ideas of others accurately. If she has, readers will trust her whether or not they end up agreeing with her on the issue.)

■ Explain What You See as the Problem

If a review indicates a problem, as Eck's review does, the problem can often be couched in terms of the models we discussed earlier: misinterpretations, gap, or modification. In paragraph 5, Eck identifies what she concludes is a misunderstanding of how students learn a new language. She suggests that the misunderstanding stems from a gap in knowledge (notice our underlining):

> Many educators seem to dismiss sociocultural and sociopolitical factors, perhaps not realizing that by ignoring these factors, they are inadvertently privileging the students in their classrooms for whom English is a first language (Larson, 2003). Such a dismissive attitude does not reckon with other studies that have shown how important it is for English language learners to explore and express their bilingual/bicultural identities (McCarthey, García, López-Velásquez, Lin & Guo, 2004). Some of these other studies have even proposed that schooling acts as a "subtractive process" for minority students, not only denying them opportunities to express their identities, but also divesting them of important social and

cultural resources, which ultimately leaves them vulnerable to academic failure (Valenzuela, 1999).

While Eck concedes that efforts to understand the problems of language learning have been extensive and multifaceted, her review of the research culminates with her assertion that ignoring students' language practices could have devastating results — that educators, by denying students "important social and cultural resources," may be leaving those students "vulnerable to academic failure."

■ State Your Thesis

An effective thesis statement helps readers see the reasoning behind the author's claim; it also signals what readers should look for in the remainder of the essay. Eck closes paragraph 5 with a statement that speaks to both the purpose and the substance of her writing:

> Therefore, although many educators believe they know the best way to teach ELL students, I will argue that the educational system, by not taking into account factors that sociocultural theory emphasizes, has mostly failed to create classrooms that embrace cultural differences, and by so doing has failed to create optimal conditions for teaching and learning.

In your own writing, you can make use of the strategies that Eck uses in her essay. Words like *although* and *though* can set up problem statements: "Although [though] some people think that nonnative speakers of English can best learn English by not using their first language, the issue is more complex than most people realize." Words like *but, however,* and *yet* can serve the same purpose: "One might argue that nonnative speakers of English can best learn English by not using their first language; but [however, yet] the issue is more complex than most people realize."

Steps to Establishing a Context for a Thesis

1. **Establish that the issue is current and relevant.** Point out the extent to which others have recognized the problem, issue, or question that you are writing about.

2. **Briefly review what others have said.** Explain how others have addressed the problem, issue, or question you are focusing on.

3. **Explain what you see as the problem.** Identify what is open to dispute.

4. **State your thesis.** Help readers see your purpose and how you intend to achieve it — by correcting a misconception, filling a gap, or modifying a claim others have accepted.

■ Analyze the Context of a Thesis

In "Protean Shapes in Literacy Events," cultural anthropologist and linguist Shirley Brice Heath argues that communities of practice shape the ways in which people use reading and writing. Heath points out the problem of holding up a standard of literacy from one community to measure the extent to which another community is or is not literate. Her essay, originally published in 1982, is addressed to a community of scholars who study literacy. As you read the excerpt that follows, you will likely find yourself puzzled by Heath's vocabulary and possibly even excluded from the conversation at times. Our point in reprinting this excerpt is not to initiate you into Heath's academic community but to show, through our annotations, how Heath has applied the strategies we have been discussing in this chapter. As you read, feel free to make your own annotations, and then try to answer the questions — which may involve some careful rereading — that we pose after the excerpt. In particular, watch for signpost words (*but, few, little, however*) that signal the ideas the writer is challenging.

SHIRLEY BRICE HEATH

From Protean Shapes in Literacy Events: Ever-Shifting Oral and Literate Traditions

The first sentence establishes that the issue that interests Heath has been discussed for more than a few years, helping us see the continuing relevance of the area of study.

From the sentence that begins "Much of this research" to the end of the paragraph, Heath reviews some of the relevant literature and points to a problem: that previous work has seen literate and oral cultures as somehow opposed to one another. The author gives us more than a list of sources.

Since the mid-1970s, anthropologists, linguists, historians, and psychologists have turned with new tools of analysis to the study of oral and literate societies. They have used discourse analysis, econometrics, theories of schemata and frames, and proposals of developmental performance to consider the possible links between oral and written language, and between literacy and its individual and societal consequences. Much of this research is predicated on a dichotomous view of oral and literate traditions, usually attributed to researchers active in the 1960s. Repeatedly, Goody and Watt (1963), Ong (1967), Goody (1968), and Havelock (1963) are cited as having suggested a dichotomous view of oral and literate societies and as having asserted certain cognitive, social, and linguistic effects of literacy on both the society and the individual. Survey research tracing the invention and diffusion of writing systems across numerous societies (Kroeber, 1948) and positing the effects of the spread of literacy on social and individual

1

memory (Goody and Watt, 1963; Havelock, 1963, 1976) is cited as supporting a contrastive view of oral and literate social groups. Research which examined oral performance in particular groups is said to support the notion that as members of a society increasingly participate in literacy, they lose habits associated with the oral tradition (Lord, 1965).

In short, existing scholarship makes it easy to interpret a picture which depicts societies existing along a continuum of development from an oral tradition to a literate one, with some societies having a restricted literacy, and others having reached a full development of literacy (Goody, 1968:11). One also finds in this research specific characterizations of oral and written language associated with these traditions.

In the first sentence in this paragraph, Heath suggests that a close reading would raise some important unanswered questions about the relationship between orality and literacy.

But a close reading of these scholars, especially Goody (1968) and Goody and Watt (1963), leaves some room for questioning such a picture of consistent and universal processes or products—individual or societal—of literacy. Goody pointed out that in any traditional society, factors such as secrecy, religious ideology, limited social mobility, lack of access to writing materials and alphabetic scripts could lead to restricted literacy. Furthermore, Goody warned that the advent of a writing system did not amount to technological determinism or to sufficient cause of certain changes in either the individual or the society. Goody went on to propose exploring the concrete context of written communication (1968:4) to determine how the potentialities of literacy developed in traditional societies. He brought together a collection of essays based on the ethnography of literacy in traditional societies to illustrate the wide variety of ways in which *traditional,* i.e., pre-industrial but not necessarily pre-literate, societies played out their uses of oral and literate traditions.

The previous paragraph sets up the problem and the gap that Heath believes her research — indicated in the first two sentences of this paragraph — should address.

Few researchers in the 1970s have, however, heeded Goody's warning about the possible wide-ranging effects of societal and cultural factors on literacy and its uses. In particular, little attention has been given in *modern* complex industrial societies to the social and cultural correlates of literacy or to the work experiences adults have which may affect the

The underlined sentence indicates the gap: The media focus on one set of concerns when they should be attending to a very different set of issues.

maintenance and retention of literacy skills acquired in formal schooling. The public media today give much attention to the decline of literacy skills as measured in school settings and the failure of students to acquire certain levels of literacy. However, the media pay little attention to occasions for literacy retention—to the actual uses of literacy in work settings, daily interactions in religious, economic, and legal institutions, and family habits of socializing the young into uses of literacy. In the clamor over the need to increase the teaching of basic skills, there is much emphasis on the positive effects extensive and critical reading can have on improving oral language.

Heath elaborates on what she sees as a troubling gap between what educators know and what they need to know.

Yet there are scarcely any data comparing the forms and functions of oral language with those of written language produced and used by members of social groups within a complex society. One of the most appropriate sources of data for informing discussions of these issues is that which Goody proposed for traditional societies: the concrete context of written communication. Where, when, how, for whom, and with what results are individuals in different social groups of today's highly industrialized society using reading and writing skills? How have the potentialities of the literacy skills learned in school developed in the lives of today's adults? Does modern society

In the last four sentences of the excerpt, Heath raises the questions that she wants readers to consider and that guide her own research.

contain certain conditions which restrict literacy just as some traditional societies do? If so, what are these factors, and are groups with restricted literacy denied benefits widely attributed to full literacy, such as upward socioeconomic mobility, the development of logical reasoning, and access to the information necessary to make well-informed political judgments?

For Analysis and Discussion

1. What specific places can you point to in the selection that illustrate what is at issue for Heath?
2. How does Heath use her review to set up her argument?
3. What specific words and phrases does Heath use to establish what she sees as the problem? Is she correcting misinterpretations, filling a gap, or modifying what others have said?

4. What would you say is Heath's thesis? What specifics can you point to in the text to support your answer?

5. What would you say are the arguments Heath wants you to avoid? Again, what specific details can you point to in the text to support your answer?

■ Analyze a Student Argument

Now, drawing on the lessons of this chapter, try your own analysis of the following student essay. Read through it with pen or pencil in hand, looking for (1) the author's thesis, (2) the gap it addresses, (3) the problem or issue she sees, (4) evidence of her audience, and (5) her use of sources. Then answer the questions that follow the essay.

Potish 1

Jessie Potish
Professor Riley
English 1020
April 5, 20--

AIDS in Women: A Growing Educational Concern

Due to the fervent efforts of health educators, young people   1
today have a very intimate knowledge of HIV and AIDS. These students were born in the early eighties at the beginning of the AIDS epidemic. Teachers guided students through years of health classes in their junior high and high school years and informed students about the destructive nature of the AIDS virus and ways in which it can and cannot be contracted. Health educators made sure that students were well informed about HIV and presented the topic as being gender-neutral. Although pop culture and the media claimed that homosexual males were responsible for the epidemic, this idea was never presented in the classroom. Though I am grateful for this aspect of AIDS education, it seems that there was an important aspect missing from the curriculum: the more numerous negative effects that the disease has on women. Health education needs to present the effects of AIDS on women and encourage them to be more concerned about contracting and living with the disease.

In spite of this need for reform, health educators may feel   2
uneasy about changing their curriculum and argue that there are a number of reasons to keep the HIV and AIDS curriculum the same.

One reason that they might have for maintaining the current curriculum is that they fear that presenting HIV as more of a woman's issue could decrease awareness of the disease in men. However, this probably will not happen. Many people, though not necessarily health educators, already view HIV as more of a man's disease. In fact, according to Allen E. Carrier of AIDS Project Los Angeles, gay men ages 17 to 24 are at very high risk for HIV infection and realize the dangers of unsafe sex, but continue to engage in high-risk behavior (quoted in DeNoon and Key, "National"). In other words, most men are aware and informed, but some are choosing to ignore some of the education that they have received. In reality, men need to make as many changes as women in order to stop the AIDS epidemic. Peter Piot, the executive director of the Joint United Nations Program on HIV/AIDS, says that "men have a crucial role to play in bringing about this radical change" (Henderson). Therefore, the new AIDS curriculum would be encouraging both men and women to change their attitudes and actions in order to bring about changes.

Health educators might also claim that by focusing more on   3
HIV education, they will have to ignore other important health topics. However, few other health topics today are as important or as relevant to young people as HIV; it is a worldwide epidemic that is constantly affecting them. In addition, it is one of the few diseases that can be controlled with sufficient knowledge and responsible behavior. Teachers should not feel as though they are ignoring more important topics; they are merely focusing on an issue of growing prevalence. Health educators might also argue that they should not be the only ones responsible for making young women more aware of this issue. They could say that parent education and community programs could be used in lieu of education in the classroom. I would argue, though, that while education in the home and through the community could certainly be useful as well, many students do not have a strong support system at home or access to a wealth of materials about health subjects. Therefore, health education in the schools is surely the most effective way to reach young people, and this is where HIV and AIDS education should have the strongest presence.

One of the most important points missing from current AIDS   4
education is the fact that women are, for the most part, more susceptible to the disease. Heterosexual contact is the chief mode of

transmission for women infected with the disease, followed by intra-venous drug use. Women should be especially concerned about con-tracting this disease through sexual contact because, according to Saglio, Kurtzman, and Radner's article in American Family Physician, the sexual transmissibility of the virus from men to women is much greater, up to 19 times more likely than the transmission from women to men. This figure is quite astounding, and I felt concerned that I had never before heard it when learning about HIV. Though abstinence and safe sex were repeatedly taught and encouraged in the classroom, teachers never fully explained how important it is for women to protect themselves. To make this clear to students, health educators should empower young women and encourage them to have more control over their sexuality. C. W. Henderson, editor-in-chief of AIDS Weekly, states that social expectations limit a woman's access to materials about sexual matters. He also claims that high-risk sexual behaviors are more common and socially acceptable in males, who can in turn transmit the infection to their partners. These social norms should not be acceptable. Women should not feel uneasy about getting information or asking about their partner's sex-ual history. Young women need to be taught this in the classroom.

Young women should also be told about the numerous physi-cal conditions that can afflict them if they contract HIV or AIDS. These effects include some that are unique to women in addition to the tragic course that AIDS normally takes on the body. Disease pro-gression in both men and women is similar, and treatment methods are the same; but, according to a study published in the December 28, 1994, issue of the Journal of the American Medical Association, women have lower survival rates than men (cited in DeNoon and Key, "At Last"). In addition, women have complications, mainly gynecol-ogical disorders due to HIV or AIDS, that can have very adverse effects. Pelvic inflammatory disease and vaginal candidiasis are par-ticularly common and difficult to treat in infected women. Also, infected women with herpes require long-term treatment to keep outbreaks under control. There is even an increased frequency of abnormal cervical cells and cervical cancer in HIV-infected women (Saglio et al.). These are definitely very serious health conditions for a woman to consider, as they can do a lot of damage to her

5

Potish   4

reproductive system and even lead to death. In health classes,
I learned very clearly the risks of gynecological diseases and the
adverse permanent effects that they can have. However, I never once
heard that HIV could worsen the effects of these pelvic disorders or
that they were in any way connected. This is a very important topic
that should be stressed among young women. Perhaps health educators should consider discussing this important health connection
that until now has been ignored in the classroom.

In addition, a woman must consider the ramifications of
being infected with HIV and carrying a child. Many young women
probably do not see how much of an effect this disease can have on
their decision to have children. An estimated 84 percent of infected
women are between the ages of 15 and 44, the prime childbearing
years. Nearly 2,000 babies are born each year in the United States
infected with HIV, and 90 percent of children under the age of 15
acquire the disease through vertical transmission (Saglio et al.). That
is, they acquire it from their infected mother while in the womb, during the birth process, or through breast-feeding. There are drugs,
namely zidovudine, that can help decrease the chance of vertical
transmission, but nothing is completely effective. Also, the side
effects of the use of the drug are not fully understood in the mother
or the child (Blanco). There needs to be increased awareness about
HIV among pregnant women and more encouragement for women to
be tested for the disease prior to conception or during the first
trimester of pregnancy. Many young women are not planning on having children for several years, and they may not be prepared to think
that far ahead. This is when the educator should step in and explain
the adverse effects that AIDS can have on a pregnancy. Health educators need to help young women understand the effects that HIV
can have on their unborn children and encourage them to think more
about their futures.

The changes in AIDS education that I am suggesting are necessary and relatively simple to make. Although the current curriculum
in high school health classes is helpful and informative, it simply
does not pertain to young women as much as it should. AIDS is
killing women at an alarming rate, and many people do not realize
this. According to Daniel DeNoon and Keith Key, AIDS is one of the

6

7

Potish 5

six leading causes of death among women ages 18 to 45, and women "bear the brunt of the worldwide AIDS epidemic." For this reason, DeNoon and Key argue, women are one of the most important new populations that are contracting HIV at a high rate. Young women need to be better informed about AIDS and their link to the disease, or many new cases may develop. As the epidemic continues to spread, women need to realize that they can stop the spread of the disease and protect themselves from infection and a number of related complications. It is the responsibility of health educators to present this to young women and inform them of the powerful choices that they can make.

Potish 6

Works Cited

Bianco, Mabel. "Women, Vulnerability and HIV/AIDS — A Human Rights Perspective (Part 22 of 37)." Women, Vulnerability and HIV/AIDS — A Human Rights Perspective. 1998. Contemporary Women's Issues. WebSPIRS. 5 October 2000. <http://webspirs4 .silverplatter.com>

DeNoon, Daniel J., and Keith K. Key. "At Last, a Sex-Based Study of HIV Disease." Infectious Disease Weekly 16 January 1995: 5–7. Academic Search Elite. Ebsco Publishing. 22 October 2000. <http://www.ehostvgw.12.epnet.com>

———. "National Model Launched in HIV/AIDS Prevention." AIDS Weekly Plus 8 July 1996: 16. Academic Search Elite. Ebsco Publishing. 22 October 2000. <http://www.ehostvgw.12 .epnet.com>

Henderson, C. W. "Gender Is Crucial Issue in Slowing the Spread of HIV." AIDS Weekly 10 July 2000: 12–14. Academic Search Elite. Ebsco Publishing. 22 October 2000. <http://www.ehostvgw.12 .epnet.com>

Saglio, Stephen Dower, James Todd Kurtzman, and Allen Bruce Radner. "HIV Infection in Women: An Escalating Health Concern." American Family Physician, 54.5, October 1996: 1541–1549. Academic Search Elite. Ebsco Publishing. 5 October 2000. <http://www.ehostvgw.12.epnet.com>

For Analysis and Discussion

1. What is Potish's thesis? Which sentences spell out her argument most clearly?
2. In what way does Potish's thesis address a misinterpretation, a gap, or the need for a modification?
3. Who do you think Potish's audience is? What passages suggest this?
4. How does Potish use what she has read to define a problem or issue?
5. How does Potish use what she has read to establish the conversation she wants to enter?

A Practice Sequence: Building a Thesis

We would like you to practice some of the strategies we have covered in this chapter. If you have already started working on an essay, exercises 1 through 4 present an opportunity to take stock of your progress, a chance to sort through what you've discovered, identify what you still need to discover, and move toward refining your thesis. Jot down your answer to each of the questions below and make lists of what you know and what you need to learn.

1 Have you established that your issue is current and relevant, that it is or should be on people's minds? What information would you need to do so?

2 Can you summarize briefly what others have said in the past to show that you are familiar with how others have addressed the issue? List some of the key texts you have read and the key points they make.

3 Have you identified any misunderstandings or gaps in how others have addressed the issue? Describe them. Do you have any ideas or information that would address these misunderstandings or help fill these gaps? Where might you find the information you need? Can you think of any sources you should reread to learn more? (For example, have you looked at the works cited or bibliographies in the texts you've already read?)

4 At this point, what is your take on the issue? Try drafting a working thesis statement that will present readers with something new to think about, building on and extending what others have argued. In drafting your thesis statement, try out the three models discussed in this chapter and see if one is an especially good fit:

- *Misinterpretations model*: "Although many scholars have argued about X and Y, a careful examination suggests Z."
- *Gap model*: "Although scholars have noted X and Y, they have missed the importance of Z."

- *Modification model*: "Although I agree with X and Y ideas of other writers, it is important to extend/refine/limit their ideas with Z."

5 If you haven't chosen a topic yet, try a group exercise. Sit down with a few of your classmates and choose one of the following topics to brainstorm about as a group. Choose a topic that everyone in the group finds interesting, and work through exercises 1 through 4 in this practice sequence. Here are some suggestions:

- The moral obligation to vote
- The causes or consequences of poverty
- The limits of academic freedom
- Equity in education
- The popularity of _____
- The causes or consequences of teen violence
- Gender stereotypes in the media
- Linguistic diversity
- On the uses of a liberal education
- Journalism and truth

We cannot overstate the role your working thesis statement plays in helping you organize your evidence, illustrations, and quotations from other texts. Remember that the writing you do should begin with reading, identifying issues, formulating questions, and reading again before you try to state your thesis. Accept that you may have to write a few drafts of your essay before you actually decide on your thesis. An academic thesis statement is complex: It must help readers understand what is at issue, what the writer thinks is true, and what will follow in the essay itself. In this way, the thesis statement is as important for you as a writer as it is for your readers. Readers need signposts to grasp the meaning of what you write, to follow your ideas through every paragraph, and to understand how every paragraph contributes to your argument. The ability to write a good thesis statement is essential to persuading your readers to see your issue through fresh eyes — through your eyes as a writer.

6

From Finding
to Evaluating Sources

In this chapter, we look at strategies for expanding the base of sources
you work with to support your argument. The habits and skills of close
reading and analysis that we have discussed and that you have practiced
are essential for evaluating the sources you find. Once you find sources,
you will need to assess the claims the writers make, the extent to which
they provide evidence in support of those claims, and the recency, relevance, accuracy, and reliability of the evidence. The specific strategies we
discuss here are those you will use to find and evaluate the sources you
find in your library's electronic catalog or on the Internet. These strategies
are core skills for developing a researched academic argument. They are
also essential to avoid being overwhelmed by the torrent of information
unleashed at the click of a computer mouse.

Finding sources is not difficult; finding and identifying good sources is
challenging. You know how simple it is to look up a subject in an encyclopedia or to use a search engine like Google or Yahoo! to discover basic
information on a subject or topic. Unfortunately, this kind of research will
only take you so far. What if the information you find doesn't really address
your question? True, we have emphasized the importance of thinking
about an issue from multiple perspectives — and finding multiple perspectives is easy when you search the Internet. But how do you know whether a
perspective is authoritative or trustworthy or even legitimate? Without
knowing how to find and identify good sources, you can waste a lot of time
reading material that will not contribute to your essay. Our goal is to help
you use your time wisely to collect the sources you need to support your
argument.

IDENTIFYING SOURCES

We assume that by the time you visit the library or log on to the Internet to find sources, you are not flying blind. At the very least, you will have chosen a topic to explore (something in general you want to write about), possibly identified an issue (a question or problem about the topic that is arguable), and perhaps even have a working thesis (a main claim that you want to test against other sources) in mind. Let's say you are already interested in the topic of mad cow disease. Perhaps you have identified an issue: Is mad cow disease a significant threat in the United States given the massive scale of factory farming? And maybe you have drafted a working thesis: "Although factory farming is rightly criticized for its often unsanitary practices and lapses in quality control, the danger of an epidemic of mad cow disease in the United States is minimal." The closer you are to having a working thesis, the more purposeful your research will be. With the working thesis above, instead of trying to sift through hundreds of articles about mad cow disease, you can probably home in on materials that examine mad cow disease in relation to epidemiology and agribusiness.

Once you start expanding your research, however, even a working thesis is just a place to begin. As you digest all the perspectives your research yields, you may discover that your thesis, issue, and perhaps even interest in the topic will shift significantly. Maybe you'll end up writing about factory farming rather than mad cow disease. This kind of shift happens more often than you may think. What is important is to follow what interests you and to keep in mind what is going to matter to your readers.

■ Consult Experts Who Can Guide Your Research

Before you embark on a systematic hunt for sources, you may want to consult with experts who can help guide your research. The following experts are nearer to hand and more approachable than you may think.

Your Writing Instructor.   Your first and best expert is likely to be your writing instructor, who can help you define the limits of your research and the kinds of sources that would prove most helpful. Your writing instructor can probably advise you on whether your topic is too broad or too narrow, help you identify your issue, and perhaps even point you to specific reference works or readings you should consult. He or she can also help you figure out whether you should concentrate mainly on popular or scholarly sources (for more about popular and scholarly sources, see pp. 111–12).

Librarians at Your Campus or Local Library.   In all likelihood, there is no better repository of research material than your campus or local library, and no better guide to those resources than the librarians who work there. Their job is to help you find what you need (although it's up to you to make the most of what you find). Librarians can give you a map or tour of the library, and provide you with booklets or other handouts that instruct you in the specific resources available and their uses. They can explain the catalog system and reference system. And, time allowing, most librarians are willing to give you personal help in finding and using specific sources, from books and journals to indexes and databases.

Experts in Other Fields.   Perhaps the idea for your paper originated outside your writing course, in response to a reading assigned in, say, your psychology or economics course. If so, you may want to discuss your topic or issue with the instructor in that course, who can probably point you to other readings or journals you should consult. If your topic originated outside the classroom, you can still seek out an expert in the appropriate field. If so, you may want to read the advice on interviewing we present in Chapter 11.

Manuals, Handbooks, and Dedicated Web Sites.   These exist in abundance, for general research as well as for discipline-specific research. They are especially helpful in identifying a wide range of authoritative search tools and resources, although they also offer practical advice on how to use and cite them. Indeed, your writing instructor may assign one of these manuals or handbooks, or recommend a Web site, at the beginning of the course. If not, he or she can probably point you to the one that is best suited to your research.

■ Develop a Working Knowledge of Standard Sources

As you start your hunt for sources, it helps to know broadly what kinds of sources are available and what they can help you accomplish. Table 6.1 lists a number of the resources you are likely to rely on when you are looking for material, the purpose and limitations of each type of resource, and some well-known examples. Although it may not help you pinpoint specific resources that are most appropriate for your research, the table does provide a basis for finding sources in any discipline. And familiarizing yourself with the types of resources here should make your conversations with the experts more productive.

■ Distinguish Between Primary and Secondary Sources

As you define the research task before you, you will need to understand the difference between primary and secondary sources, and figure out which you will need to answer your question. Your instructor may specify which he or she prefers, but chances are you will have to make the decision

TABLE 6.1   Standard Types of Sources for Doing Research

Source	Type of Information	Purpose	Limitations	Examples
Abstract	Brief summary of a text and the bibliographic information needed to locate the complete text	To help researchers decide whether or not they want to read the entire source		*Biological Abstracts* *Historical Abstracts* *New Testament Abstracts* *Reference Sources in History: An Introductory Guide*
Bibliography	List of works, usually by subject and author, with full publication information	For an overview of what has been published in a field and who the principal researchers in the field are	Difficult to distinguish the best sources and the most prominent researchers	*Bibliography of the History of Art* *MLA International Bibliography*
Biography	Story of an individual's life and the historical, cultural, or social context in which he or she lived	For background on a person of importance	Lengthy and reflects the author's bias	Biography and Genealogy Master Index Biography Resource Center Biography .com Literature Resource Center *Oxford Dictionary of National Biography*
Book review	Description and usually an evaluation of a recently published book	To help readers stay current with research and thought in their field and to evaluate scholarship	Reflects the reviewer's bias	ALA *Booklist* *Book Review Digest* Book Review Index *Books in Print* with Book Reviews on Disc

Source	Type of Information	Purpose	Limitations	Examples
Database, index	Large collection of citations and abstracts from books, journals, and digests, often updated daily	To give researchers access to a wide range of current sources	Lacks evaluative information	Education Resources Information Center (ERIC) Humanities International Index Index to Scientific & Technical Proceedings United Nations Bibliographic Information System
Data, statistics	Measurements derived from studies or surveys	To help researchers identify important trends (e.g., in voting, housing, residential segregation)	Requires a great deal of scrutiny and interpretation	American FactFinder American National Election Studies Current Index to Statistics Current Population Survey *Statistical Abstract of the United States*
Dictionary	Alphabetical list of words and their definitions	To explain key terms and how they are used		*Merriam-Webster's Collegiate Dictionary* *Oxford English Dictionary*
Encyclopedia	Concise articles about people, places, concepts, and things	A starting point for very basic information	Lack of in-depth information	*The CQ Researcher* Encyclopedia Brittanica Online *Information Please Almanac*

(*continued on next page*)

TABLE 6.1   (*continued*)

Source	Type of Information	Purpose	Limitations	Examples
				McGraw-Hill Encyclopedia of Science & Technology
Internet search engine	Web site that locates online information by keyword or search term	For quickly locating a broad array of current resources	Reliability of information open to question	Google Yahoo!
Newspaper, other news sources	Up-to-date information	To locate timely information	May reflect reporter's or medium's bias	America's Historical Newspapers LexisNexis Academic Newspaper Source ProQuest Historical Newspapers World News Connection
Thesaurus	Alphabetical list of words and their synonyms	For alternative search terms		*Roget's II: The New Thesaurus*

yourself. A **primary source** is a firsthand, or eyewitness, account, the kind of account you find in letters or newspapers or research reports in which the researcher explains his or her impressions of a particular phenomenon. For example, "Hidden Lessons," the Sadkers' study of gender bias in schools, is a primary source. The authors report their own experiences of the phenomenon in the classroom. A **secondary source** is an analysis of information reported in a primary source. For example, even though it may cite the Sadkers' primary research, an essay that analyzes the Sadker's findings along with other studies of gender dynamics in the classroom would be considered a secondary source.

If you were exploring issues of language diversity and the English-only movement, you would draw on both primary and secondary sources. You would be interested in researchers' firsthand (primary) accounts of language learning and use by diverse learners for examples of the challenges nonnative speakers face in learning a standard language. And you would also want to know from secondary sources what others think about whether national unity and individuality can and should coexist in communities and homes as well as in schools. You will find that you are often expected to use both primary and secondary sources in your research.

■ Distinguish Between Popular and Scholarly Sources

To determine the type of information to use, you also need to decide whether you should look for popular or scholarly books and articles. **Popular sources** of information — newspapers like *USA Today* and *The Chronicle of Higher Education,* and large-circulation magazines like *Newsweek* and *Field & Stream* — are written for a general audience. This is not to say that popular sources cannot be specialized: *The Chronicle of Higher Education* is read mostly by academics; *Field & Stream,* by people who love the outdoors. But they are written so that any educated reader can understand them. **Scholarly sources**, by contrast, are written for experts in a particular field. *The New England Journal of Medicine* may be read by people who are not physicians, but they are not the journal's primary audience. In a manner of speaking, these readers are eavesdropping on the journal's conversation of ideas; they are not expected to contribute to it (and in fact would be hard pressed to do so). The articles in scholarly journals undergo **peer review**. That is, they do not get published until they have been carefully evaluated by the author's peers, other experts in the academic conversation being conducted in the journal. Reviewers may comment at length about an article's level of research and writing, and an author may have to revise an article several times before it sees print. And if the reviewers cannot reach a consensus that the research makes an important contribution to the academic conversation, the article will not be published.

When you begin your research, you may find that popular sources provide helpful information about a topic or issue — the results of a national poll, for example. Later, however, you will want to use scholarly sources to advance your argument. You can see from Table 6.2 that popular magazines and scholarly journals can be distinguished by a number of characteristics. Does the source contain advertisements? If so, what kinds of advertisements? For commercial products? Or for academic events and resources? How do the advertisements appear? If you find ads and glossy pictures and illustrations, you are probably looking at a popular magazine. This is in contrast to the tables, charts, and diagrams you are likely to find in an education, psychology, or microbiology journal. Given your experience with rhetorical analyses, you should also be able to determine the makeup of your audience — specialists or nonspecialists — and the level of language you need to use in your writing.

TABLE 6.2   Popular Magazines Versus Scholarly Journals

Criteria	Popular Magazines	Scholarly Journals
Advertisements	Numerous full-page color ads	Few if any ads
Appearance	Eye-catching; glossy; pictures and illustrations	Plain; black-and-white graphics, tables, charts, and diagrams
Audience	General	Professors, researchers, and college students
Author	Journalists	Professionals in an academic field or discipline
Bibliography	Occasional and brief	Extensive bibliography at the end of each article; footnotes and other documentation
Content	General articles to inform, update, or introduce a contemporary issue	Research projects, methodology, and theory
Examples	*Newsweek, National Review, PC World, Psychology Today*	*International Journal of Applied Engineering Research, New England Journal of Medicine*
Language	Nontechnical, simple vocabulary	Specialized vocabulary
Publisher	Commercial publisher	Professional organization, university, research institute, or scholarly press

SOURCE: Adapted from materials at the Hessburg Library, University of Notre Dame.

Again, as you define your task for yourself, it is important to consider why you would use one source or another. Do you want facts? Opinions? News reports? Research studies? Analyses? Personal reflections? The extent to which the information can help you make your argument will serve as your basis for determining whether or not a source of information is of value.

Steps to Identifying Sources

1 **Consult experts who can guide your research.** Talk to people who can help you formulate issues and questions.

2 **Develop a working knowledge of standard sources.** Identify the different kinds of information that different types of sources provide.

3 **Distinguish between primary and secondary sources.** Decide what type of information can best help you answer your research question.

4 **Distinguish between popular and scholarly sources.** Determine what kind of information will persuade your readers.

A Practice Sequence: Identifying Sources

We would now like you to practice using some of the strategies we have discussed so far: talking with experts, deciding what sources of information you should use, and determining what types of information can best help you develop your paper and persuade your readers. We assume you have chosen a topic for your paper, identified an issue, and perhaps formulated a working thesis. If not, think back to some of the topics mentioned in earlier chapters. Have any of them piqued your interest? If not, here are five very broad topics you might work with:

- The civil rights movement
- The media and gender
- Global health
- Science and religion
- Immigration

Once you've decided on a topic, talk to experts and decide which types of sources you should use: primary or secondary, popular or scholarly. Consult with your classmates to evaluate the strengths and weaknesses of different sources of information and the appropriateness of using different types of information. Here are the steps to follow:

1 Talk to a librarian about the sources you might use to get information about your topic (for example, databases, abstracts, or bibliographies). Be sure to take notes.

2 Talk to an expert who can provide you with some ideas about current issues in the field of interest. Be sure to take detailed notes.

> **3** Decide whether you should use primary or secondary sources. What type of information would help you develop your argument?
>
> **4** Decide whether you should use popular or scholarly sources. What type of information would your readers find compelling?

SEARCHING FOR SOURCES

Once you've decided on the types of sources you want to use — primary or secondary, popular or scholarly — you can take steps to locate the information you need. You might begin with a tour of your university or local library, so that you know where the library keeps newspapers, government documents, books, journals, and other sources of information. Notice where the reference desk is: This is where you should head to ask a librarian for help if you get stuck. You also want to find a computer where you can log on to your library's catalog to start your search. Once you have located your sources in the library, you can begin to look through them for the information you need.

You may be tempted to rely on the Internet and a search engine like Google or Yahoo! But keep in mind that the information you retrieve from the Internet may not be trustworthy: Anyone can post his or her thoughts on a Web site. Of course, you can also find excellent scholarly sources on the Internet. (For example, Johns Hopkins University Press manages Project MUSE, a collection of 300-plus academic journals that can be accessed online through institutional subscription.) School libraries also offer efficient access to government records and other sources essential to scholarly writing.

Let's say you are about to start researching a paper on language diversity and the English-only movement. When you log on to the library's site, you find a menu of choices: Catalog, Electronic Resources, Virtual Reference Desk, and Services & Collections. (The wording may vary slightly from library to library, but the means of locating information will be the same.) When you click on Catalog, another menu of search choices appears: Keyword, Title, Author, and Subject (Figure 6.1). The hunt is on.

Search type:

Keyword Anywhere
Title begins with...
Title Keyword
Author (last name first)
Author Keyword
Subject begins with...
Subject Keyword
Call Number begins with...

More Search Options

FIGURE 6.1   Menu of Basic Search Strategies

■ Perform a Keyword Search

A **keyword** is essentially your topic: It defines the topic of your search. To run a keyword search, you can look up information by author, title, or subject. You would search by author to locate all the works a particular author has written on a subject. So, for example, if you know that Paul Lang is an expert on the consequences of the English-only movement, you might begin with an author search. You can use the title search to locate all works with a key word or phrase in the title. The search results are likely to include a number of irrelevant titles, but you should end up with a list of authors, titles, and subject headings to guide another search.

A search by subject is particularly helpful as you begin your research, while you are still formulating your thesis. You want to start by thinking of as many words as possible that relate to your topic. (A thesaurus can help you come up with different words you can use in a keyword search.) Suppose you type in the phrase "English only." A number of different sources appear on the screen, but the most promising is Paul Lang's book *The English Language Debate: One Nation, One Language*? You click on this record, and another screen appears with some valuable pieces of information, including the call number (which tells you where in the library you can find the book) and an indication that the book has a bibliography, something you can make use of once you find the book (Figure 6.2). Notice that the subject listings — *Language policy, English language – Political aspects, English-only movement, Bilingual education* — also give

Full View of Record

Record 12 out of 18

Source	Author :	Lang, Paul (Paul C.)
	Title :	The English language debate : one nation, one language? / Paul Lang.
	Published :	Springfield, N.J. : Enslow Publishers, c1995.
		112 p. : ill. ; 24 cm.

ND Has :   All items

Hesburgh Library General Collection
P 119.32 .U6 E55 1995   [Call number

Notes :   Includes bibliographical references (p. 107-109) and index.   ] Indicates book has a bibliography

Series :   Multicultural issues
Subjects :   Language policy – United States – Juvenile literature.
English language – Political aspects – United States – Juvenile literature.
English-only movement – United States – Juvenile literature.
Education, Bilingual – United States – Juvenile literature.
English-only movement.
English language – Political aspects.
Education, Bilingual.

Additional list of related subjects

Done

FIGURE 6.2   Full-View Bibliographic Entry

you additional keywords to use in finding relevant information. The lesson here is that it is important to generate keywords to get initial information and then to look at that information carefully for more keywords and to determine if the source has a bibliography. Even if this particular source isn't relevant, it may lead you to other sources that are.

■ Try Browsing

Browse is a headings search; it appears in the menu of choices in Figure 6.1 as "Subject begins with . . ." This type of search allows you to scroll through an alphabetical index. Some of the indexes available are the Author Index, the Title Index, and the Library of Congress Subject Headings, a subject index. Browse

- displays an alphabetical list of entries;
- shows the number of records for each entry;
- indicates whether or not there are cross-references for each entry.

What appears in the window is "Browse List: Choose a field, enter a phrase and click the 'go' button." Figure 6.3 shows the results of a preliminary browse when the words "English-only" are entered. Notice that a list of headings or titles appears on the screen. This is not a list of books, and not all of the entries are relevant. But you can use the list to determine which headings are relevant to your topic, issue, or question.

For your paper on the English-only movement, the first two headings seem relevant: *English-only debate* and *English-only movement.* A further

Browse List: Subjects

No. of Recs	Entry
	English one-act plays - [LC Authority Record]
	See: One-act plays, English
	English-only debate - [LC Authority Record]
	See: English-only movement
4	English-only movement - [LC Authority Record]
1	English-only movement – California – Case studies
1	English-only movement – Colorado
4	English-only movement – United States
1	English-only movement – United States – Juvenile literature
	English-only question - [LC Authority Record]
	See: English-only movement
1	English – Ontario – Correspondence
1	English oration

FIGURE 6.3   Preliminary Browse of "English-only" Subject Heading

click would reveal the title of a relevant book and a new list of subject headings (Figure 6.4) that differs from those of your initial search. This list gives you a new bibliography from which you can gather new leads and a list of subject headings to investigate.

We suggest that you do a keyword search first and then a browse search to home in on a subject. Especially when you don't know the exact subject, you can do a quick keyword search, retrieve many sets of results, and then begin looking at the subjects that correspond to each title. Once you find a subject that fits your needs, you can click on the direct subject (found in each bibliographic record) and execute a new search that will yield more-relevant results.

▪ Perform a Journal or Newspaper Title Search

Finally, you can search by journal or newspaper title. For this kind of search, you will need exact information. You can take the name of a journal, magazine, or newspaper cited in your keyword or browse search. The journal or newspaper title search will tell you if your library subscribes to the publication and in what format — print, microform or -film, or electronic.

Suppose you want to continue your search in the *New York Times* for information on the English-only movement by searching for articles in the *New York Times*. You would run a basic search under the category "Periodicals": "Periodical Title begins with . . ." That would give you access to a limited number of articles that focused on the debate surrounding the English-only movement. To find more recent articles, you could go to the *New York Times* Web site (nytimes.com) where you could find many potentially useful listings. Recent newspaper articles will lack the depth and complexity of more scholarly studies, but they are undeniably useful in helping you establish the timeliness and relevance of your research. To see the full text of the articles, you must subscribe or pay a nominal fee,

#	Year	Author	Title
1	☐ 2006	United States.	**English as the official language : hearing before the Subcommittee on Education Reform of the Co** <Book> Click for ONLINE ACCESS (Text version:) Documents Center Owned: 1 Checked Out: 0 Display full record
2	☐ 1996	United States.	**S. 356—Language of Government Act of 1995 : hearings before the Committee on Governmental Affai** <Book> Documents Center Display full record
3	☐ 1996	United States.	**Hearing on English as the common language : hearing before the Subcommittee on Early Childhood,** <Book> Documents Center Display full record
4	☐ 1995	United States.	**Hearing on English as a common language : hearing before the Subcommittee on Early Childhood, Yo** <Book> Documents Center Display full record

Done

FIGURE 6.4   Results of Browsing Deeper: A New List of Sources

although you can usually preview the articles because the Web site will include a few sentences describing the content of each article.

Steps to Searching for Sources

1 **Perform a keyword search.** Choose a word or phrase that best describes your topic.

2 **Try browsing.** Search an alphabetical list by subject.

3 **Perform a journal or newspaper title search.** Find relevant citations by identifying the exact title of a journal or newspaper, or by subject.

A Practice Sequence: Searching for Sources

If you tried the practice sequence on identifying sources (p. 113), explore your topic further by practicing the types of searches discussed in this section: a keyword search; a browse; and a journal or newspaper title search (or a subject search).

EVALUATING LIBRARY SOURCES

The information you collect can and will vary in terms of its relevance and overall quality. You will want to evaluate this information as systematically as possible to be sure that you are using the most appropriate sources to develop your argument. Once you have obtained at least some of the sources you located by searching your library's catalog, you should evaluate the material as you read it. In particular, you want to evaluate the following information for each article or book:

- the author's background and credentials (What is the author's educational background? What has he or she written about in the past? Is this person an expert in the field?)
- the writer's purpose
- the topic of discussion
- the audience the writer invokes and whether you are a member of that audience
- the nature of the conversation (How have others addressed the problem?)
- what the author identifies as a misinterpretation or a gap in knowledge, or an argument that needs modifying

- what the author's own view is
- how the author supports his or her argument (that is, with primary or secondary sources, with facts or opinions)
- the accuracy of the author's evidence (can you find similar information elsewhere?)

If your topic is current and relevant, chances are your searches are going to turn up a large number of possible sources. How do you go about choosing which sources to rely on in your writing? Of course, if time were not an issue, you would read them all from start to finish. But in the real world, assignments come with due dates. To decide whether a library source merits a close reading and evaluation, begin by skimming each book or article. **Skimming** — briefly examining the material to get a sense of the information it offers — involves four steps:

1. Read the introductory sections.
2. Examine the table of contents and index.
3. Check the notes and bibliographic references.
4. Skim deeper.

■ Read the Introductory Sections

Turn to the introductory sections of the text first. Many authors use a preface or introduction to explain the themes they focus on in a book. An **abstract** serves a similar purpose, but article abstracts are usually only 250 words long. In the introductory sections, writers typically describe the issue that motivated them to write, whether or not they believe the work corrects a misconception, fills a gap, or builds on and extends the research of others. For example, in the preface to her book *Learning and Not Learning English: Latino Students in American Schools* (2001), Guadalupe Valdés explains that even after two years of language instruction, many students remain at a low level of language competence. In this passage, Valdés makes clear the purpose of her work:

> This book examines the learning of English in American schools by immigrant children. It focuses on the realities that such youngsters face in trying to acquire English in settings in which they interact exclusively with other non-English-speaking youngsters the entire school day. It is designed to fill a gap in the existing literature on non-English-background youngsters by offering a glimpse of the challenges and difficulties faced by four middle-school students enrolled in the United States for the first time when they were 12 or 13 years old. It is my purpose here to use these youngsters' lives and experiences as a lens through which to examine the policy and instructional dilemmas that now surround the education of immigrant children in this country. (p. 2)

If you were looking for sources for a paper on the English-only movement, in particular the consequences of that movement for young students, you might very well find Valdés's words compelling and decide the book is worth a closer reading.

▪ Examine the Table of Contents and Index

After reading the introductory sections, it is useful to analyze the table of contents to see how much emphasis the writer gives to topics that are relevant to your own research. For example, the table of contents to *Learning and Not Learning English* includes several headings that may relate to your interest: "Educating English-Language Learners," "Challenges and Realities," "Implications for Policy and Practice," and the "Politics of Teaching English." You also should turn to the back of the book to examine the **index**, an alphabetical list of the important and likely to be repeated concepts in a book, and the page numbers on which they appear. An index also would include the names of authors cited in the book. In the index to Valdés's book, you would find references to "English-language abilities and instruction" with specific page numbers where you can read what the author has to say on this subject. You would also find references to "English-only instruction," "equal educational opportunities," and "sheltered instruction."

▪ Check the Notes and Bibliographic References

Especially in the initial stages of writing, you should look closely at writers' notes and bibliographies to discern who they feel are the important voices in the field. Frequent citation of a particular researcher's work may indicate that the individual is considered to be an expert in the field you are studying. Notes usually provide brief references to people, concepts, or context; the bibliography includes a long list of related works. Mining Valdés's bibliography, you would find such titles as "Perspectives on Official English," "Language Policy in Schools," "Not Only English," "Language and Power," and "The Cultural Politics of English."

▪ Skim Deeper

Skimming a book or article entails briefly looking over the elements we have discussed so far: the preface or abstract, the table of contents and the index, and the notes and bibliography. Skimming also can mean reading chapter titles, headings, and the first sentence of each paragraph to determine the relevance of a book or article.

Skimming the first chapter of *Learning and Not Learning English*, several topic sentences reveal the writer's purpose:

> "In this book, then, I examine and describe different expressions that both learning and not-learning English took among four youngsters."
>
> "In the chapters that follow . . ."
>
> "What I hope to suggest . . ."

These are the types of phrases you should look for to get a sense of what the writer is trying to accomplish and whether the writer's work will be of use to you.

If after you've taken these steps, a source still seems promising, you should read it closely, from start to finish, to determine how effectively it can help you answer your research question. Keep in mind all you've learned about critical reading. Those skills are what you'll rely on most as you work through the texts and choose the ones you should use in your paper. Remember the steps of rhetorical analysis: identifying the writer's situation, purpose, claims, and audience. And remember how to identify claims and evaluate the reasons used to support the claims: Is the evidence recent, relevant, accurate, and reliable?

Steps to Evaluating Library Sources

1 **Read the introductory section(s).** Get an overview of the researcher's argument.

2 **Examine the table of contents and index.** Consider the most relevant chapters to your topic and the list of relevant subjects.

3 **Check the notes and bibliographic references.** Identify the authors a researcher refers to (do the names come up in many different books?) and the titles of both books and articles.

4 **Skim deeper.** Read chapter titles and headings and topic sentences to determine the relevance of what you are reading for your own research.

A Practice Sequence: Evaluating Library Sources

For this exercise, we would like you to choose a specific book or article to examine in order to practice these strategies. If you are far along on your own research, use a book or article you have identified as potentially useful.

1 Read the introductory section(s). What issue is the author responding to? What is the writer's purpose? To correct a misconception? To fill a gap? To build on or extend the work of others?

2 Examine the table of contents and index. What key words or phrases are related to your own research? Which topics does the author focus on? Are you intending to give these topics similar emphasis? (Will you give more or less?)

3 Check the notes and bibliographic references. Make a list of the sources you think you want to look up for your own research. Do certain sources seem more important than others?

4 Skim deeper. What is the writer's focus? Is that focus relevant to your own topic, issue, question, or working thesis?

EVALUATING INTERNET SOURCES

Without question, the World Wide Web has revolutionized how research is conducted. It has been a particular boon to experienced researchers who have a clear sense of what they are looking for, giving them access to more information more quickly than ever before. But the Internet is rife with pitfalls for inexperienced researchers. That is, sites that appear accurate and reliable may prove not to be. The sources you find on the Internet outside your school library's catalog pose problems because anyone can post anything he or she wants. Unfortunately, there is no way to monitor the accuracy of what is published on the Internet. Although Internet sources can be useful, particularly because they are current, you must take steps to evaluate them before using information from them.

■ Evaluate the Author of the Site

If an author's name appears on a Web site, ask: Who is this person? What is this person's background? Can I contact this person?

One of our students googled "English only" and clicked on the first result, "Language Policy — English Only Movement," which eventually led her to James Crawford's Language Policy Web Site & Emporium. On the site, Crawford explains that he is "a writer and lecturer — formerly the Washington editor of *Education Week* — who specializes in the politics of language."* He notes that "since 1985, I have been reporting on the English Only movement, English Plus, bilingual education, Native American language revitalization, and language rights in the U.S.A." Between 2004 and 2006, he served as executive director of the National Association for Bilingual Education. Perhaps most important, Crawford has authored four books and a number of articles, and has testified before Congress on "Official English Legislation." From this biographical sketch, the student inferred that Crawford is credentialed to write about the English-only movement.

Less certain, however, are the credentials of the writer who penned an article titled "Should the National Anthem Be Sung in English Only?" which appeared on another Web site our student visited. Why? Because the writer's name never appears on the site. An anonymous posting is the first clue that you want to move on to a more legitimate source of information.

■ Evaluate the Organization That Supports the Site

You have probably noticed that Internet addresses usually end in with a suffix: .edu, .gov, .org, or .com. The .edu suffix means the site is associated

---

Education Week has been published since 1981 by Editorial Projects in Education, a nonprofit organization that was founded with the help of a Carnegie grant. The publication covers issues related to primary and secondary education. If you are not familiar with a publication and are uncertain about its legitimacy, you can always ask your instructor, a librarian, or another expert to vouch for its reliability.

with a university or college, which gives it credibility. The same holds true for .gov, which indicates a government agency. Both types of sites have a regulatory body that oversees their content. The suffix .org indicates a nonprofit organization; .com, a commercial organization. You will need to approach these Web sites with a degree of skepticism because you cannot be sure that they are as carefully monitored by a credentialed regulatory body. (In fact, even .edu sites may turn out to be postings by a student at a college or university.)

Our student was intrigued by James Crawford's site because he appears to be a credible source on the English-only movement. She was less sure about the reference to the Institute for Language and Education Policy. Is the institute a regulatory body that oversees what appears on the site? How long has the institute existed? Who belongs to the institute? Who sits on its board of directors? As a critical thinker, the student had to ask these questions.

■ Evaluate the Purpose of the Site

Information is never objective, so whenever you evaluate a book, an article, or a Web site, you should consider the point of view the writer or sponsor is taking. It's especially important to ask if there is a particular bias among members of the group that sponsors the site. Can you tell what the sponsors of the site advocate? Are they hoping to sell or promote a product, or to influence opinion?

Not all Web sites provide easy answers to these questions. However, James Crawford's Language Policy Web Site & Emporium is quite explicit. In fact, Crawford writes that "the site is designed to encourage discussion of language policy issues, expose misguided school 'reforms,'" and, among other goals, "promote [his] own publications." (Notice "Emporium" in the name of the site.) He is candid about his self-interest, which does raise a question about his degree of objectivity.

What about a site like Wikipedia ("The Free Encyclopedia")? The site appears to exist to convey basic information. Although the popularity of Wikipedia recommends it as a basic resource, you should approach the site with caution because it is not clear whether and how information posted on the site is regulated. It is prudent to confirm information from Wikipedia by checking on sites that are regulated more transparently rather than take Wikipedia as an authoritative source.

■ Evaluate the Information on the Site

In addition to assessing the purpose of a Web site like Wikipedia, you need to evaluate the extent to which the information is recent, accurate, and consistent with information you find in print sources and clearly regulated sites. For example, clicking on "The modern English-only movement" on Wikipedia takes you to a timeline of sorts with a number of links to other sites. But again, what is the source of this information? What is included?

What is left out? You should check further into some of these links, reading the sources cited and keeping in mind the four criteria for evaluating a claim — recency, relevance, accuracy, and reliability. Because you cannot be certain that Internet sources are reviewed or monitored, you need to be scrupulous about examining the claims they make: How much and what kind of evidence supports the writer's (or site's) argument? Can you offer counterarguments?

In the last analysis, it comes down to whether the information you find stands up to the criteria you've learned to apply as a critical reader and writer. If not, move on to other sources. In a Web-based world of information, there is no shortage of material, but you have to train yourself not to settle for the information that is most readily available if it is clearly not credible.

Steps to Evaluating Internet Sources

1 **Evaluate the author of the site.** Determine whether or not the author is an expert.

2 **Evaluate the organization that supports the site.** Find out what the organization stands for and the extent of its credibility.

3 **Evaluate the purpose of the site.** What interests are represented on the site? What is the site trying to do? Provide access to legitimate statistics and information? Advance an argument? Spread propaganda?

4 **Evaluate the information on the site.** Identify the type of information on the site and the extent to which the information is recent, relevant, accurate, and reliable.

A Practice Sequence: Evaluating Internet Sources

For this exercise, we would like you to work in groups on a common topic. The class can choose its own topic or use one of the topics we suggest on page 113. Then google the topic and agree on a Web site to analyze:

    Group 1: Evaluate the author of the site.

    Group 2: Evaluate the organization that supports the site.

    Group 3: Evaluate the purpose of the site.

    Group 4: Evaluate the information on the site.

Next, each group should share its evaluation. The goal is to determine the extent to which you believe you could use the information on this site in writing an academic essay.

7

From Summarizing to Documenting Sources

When you start to use sources to build your argument, there are certain strategies for working with the words and ideas of others that you will need to learn. Often you can quote the words of an author directly; but just as often you will restate and condense the arguments of others (paraphrasing and summarizing) or make comparisons to the ideas of others in the process of developing your own argument (synthesizing). We walk you through these more challenging strategies in this chapter. We also briefly discuss plagiarism and ways to avoid it. Finally, we provide some guidelines for quoting, citing, and documenting sources in your writing.

SUMMARIES, PARAPHRASES, AND QUOTATIONS

In contrast to quotations, which involve using another writer's exact words, paraphrases and summaries are both restatements of another writer's ideas in your own words. The key difference: A paraphrase is usually about the same length as the original passage; a summary generally condenses a significantly longer text, conveying the argument not only of a few sentences, but also of entire paragraphs, essays, or books. In your own writing, you might paraphrase a few sentences or even a few paragraphs, but you certainly would not paraphrase a whole essay (much less a whole book). In constructing your arguments, however, you will often have to summarize the main points of the lengthy texts with which you are in conversation.

Both paraphrasing and summarizing are means to inquiry. That is, the act of recasting someone else's words or ideas into your own language, to suit your argument and reach your readers, forces you to think critically: What does this passage really mean? What is most important about it for my argument? How can I best present it to my readers? It requires making choices, not least of which is the best way to present the information — through paraphrase, summary, or direct quotation. In general, the following rules apply:

- *Paraphrase* when all the information in the passage is important, but the language may be difficult for your readers to understand.

- *Summarize* when you need to present only the key ideas of a passage (or essay or book) to advance your argument.

- *Quote* when the passage is so effective — so clear, so concise, so authoritative, so memorable — that you would find it difficult to improve on.

WRITING A PARAPHRASE

A **paraphrase** is a restatement of all the information in a passage in your own words, using your own sentence structure and composed with your own audience in mind to advance your argument. When you paraphrase a passage, start by identifying key words and phrases and substituting synonyms for them. A dictionary or thesaurus can help, but you may also have to reread what led up to the passage to remind yourself of the context. For example, did the writer define terms earlier that he or she uses in the passage and now expects you to know? Continue by experimenting with word order and sentence structure, combining and recombining phrases to convey what the writer says without replicating his or her style, in the best sequence for your readers. As you shuffle words and phrases, you should begin arriving at a much better understanding of what the writer is saying. By thinking critically, then, you are clarifying the passage for yourself as much as for your readers.

Let's look at a paraphrase of a passage from science fiction writer and scholar James Gunn's essay "Harry Potter as Schooldays Novel"*:

ORIGINAL PASSAGE

The situation and portrayal of Harry as an ordinary child with an extraordinary talent make him interesting. He elicits our sympathy at every turn. He plays a Cinderella-like role as the abused child of mean-spirited foster parents who favor other, less-worthy children, and also fits another fantasy role, that

---

*Gunn's essay appears in *Mapping the World of Harry Potter: An Unauthorized Exploration of the Bestselling Fantasy Series of All Time,* edited by Mercedes Lackey (Dallas: BenBella, 2006), p. 145.

of changeling. Millions of children have nursed the notion that they cannot be the offspring of such unremarkable parents; in the Harry Potter books, the metaphor is often literal truth.

PARAPHRASE

According to James Gunn, the circumstances and depiction of Harry Potter as a normal boy with special abilities captivate us by playing on our empathy. Gunn observes that, like Cinderella, Harry is scorned by his guardians, who treat him far worse than they treat his less-admirable peers. And like another fairy-tale figure, the changeling, Harry embodies the fantasies of children who refuse to believe that they were born of their undistinguished parents (146).

In this paraphrase, synonyms have replaced main words (*circumstances and depiction* for "situation and portrayal," *guardians* for "foster parents"), and the structure of the original sentences has been rearranged. But the paraphrase is about the same length as the original and says essentially the same things as Gunn's original.

Now, compare the paraphrase with this summary:

SUMMARY

James Gunn observes that Harry Potter's character is compelling because readers empathize with Harry's fairy tale–like plight as an orphan whose gifts are ignored by his foster parents (144–45).

The summary condenses the passage, conveying Gunn's main point without restating the details. Notice how both the paraphrase and the summary indicate that the ideas are James Gunn's, not the writer's — "According to James Gunn," "James Gunn observes" — and signal, with page references, where Gunn's ideas end. *It is essential that you acknowledge your sources*, a subject we come back to in our discussion of plagiarism on page 150. The point we want to make here is that borrowing from the work of others is not always intentional. Many students stumble into plagiarism, especially when they are attempting to paraphrase. Remember that it's not enough to change the words in a paraphrase; you also must change the structure of the sentences. The only sure way to protect yourself is to cite your source.

You may be wondering: If paraphrasing is so tricky, why bother? What does it add? I can see how the summary of Gunn's paragraph presents information more concisely and efficiently than the original, but the paraphrase doesn't seem to be all that different from the source, and doesn't seem to add anything to it. Why not simply quote the original or summarize it? Good questions. The answer is that you paraphrase when the ideas in a passage are important but are conveyed in language your readers may have difficulty understanding. When academics write for their peers, they draw on the specialized vocabulary of their disciplines to make their arguments. By paraphrasing, you may be helping your readers, providing a translation of sorts for those who do not speak the language.

Consider this paragraph by George Lipsitz from his academic book *Time Passages: Collective Memory and American Popular Culture,* 1990), and compare the paraphrase that follows it:

ORIGINAL PASSAGE

The transformations in behavior and collective memory fueled by the contradictions of the nineteenth century have passed through three major stages in the United States. The first involved the establishment and codification of commercialized leisure from the invention of the telegraph to the 1890s. The second involved the transition from Victorian to consumer-hedonist values between 1890 and 1945. The third and most important stage, from World War II to the present, involved extraordinary expansion in both the distribution of consumer purchasing power and in both the reach and scope of electronic mass media. The dislocations of urban renewal, suburbanization, and deindustrialization accelerated the demise of tradition in America, while the worldwide pace of change undermined stability elsewhere. The period from World War II to the present marks the final triumph of commercialized leisure, and with it an augmented crisis over the loss of connection to the past.

PARAPHRASE

Historian George Lipsitz argues that Americans' sense of the past is rooted in cultural changes dating from the 1800s, and has evolved through three stages. In the first stage, technological innovations of the nineteenth century gave rise to widespread commercial entertainment. In the second stage, dating from the 1890s to about 1945, attitudes toward the consumption of goods and services changed. Since 1945, in the third stage, increased consumer spending and the growth of the mass media have led to a crisis in which Americans find themselves cut off from their traditions and the memories that give meaning to them (12).

Notice that the paraphrase is not a word-for-word translation of the original. Instead, the writer has made choices that resulted in a slightly briefer and more accessible restatement of Lipsitz's thinking. (Although this paraphrase is shorter than the original passage, a paraphrase can also be a little longer than the original if extra words are needed to help readers understand the original.) Notice too that several specialized terms and phrases from the original passage — "the codification of commercialized leisure," "the transition from Victorian to consumer-hedonist values," "the dislocations of urban renewal, suburbanization, and deindustrialization" — have disappeared. The writer not only looked up these terms and phrases in the dictionary, but also reread the several pages that preceded the original passage to understand what Lipsitz meant by them. The paraphrase is not an improvement on the original passage — in fact, historians would probably prefer what Lipsitz wrote — but it may help readers who do not share Lipsitz's expertise understand his point without distorting his argument.

Now compare this summary to the paraphrase:

SUMMARY

Historian George Lipsitz argues that technological, social, and economic changes dating from the nineteenth century have culminated in what he calls a "crisis over the loss of connection to the past," in which Americans find themselves cut off from the memories of their traditions (12).

Which is better, the paraphrase or the summary? Neither is better or worse in and of itself. Their correctness and appropriateness depend on how the restatements are used in a given argument. That is, the decision to paraphrase or summarize depends entirely on the information you need to convey. Would the details in the paraphrase strengthen your argument? Or is a summary sufficient? In this case, if you plan to focus your argument on the causes of America's loss of cultural memory (the rise of commercial entertainment, changes in spending habits, globalization), then a paraphrase might be more helpful. But if you plan to define *loss of cultural memory*, then a summary may provide enough context for the next stage of your argument.

Steps to Writing a Paraphrase

1 Decide whether to paraphrase. If your readers don't need all the information in the passage, consider summarizing it or presenting the key points as part of a summary of a longer passage. If a passage is clear, concise, and memorable as originally written, consider quoting instead of paraphrasing. Otherwise, and especially if the original was written for an academic audience, you may want to paraphrase the original to make its substance more accessible to your readers.

2 Understand the passage. Start by identifying key words, phrases, and ideas. If necessary, reread the pages leading up to the passage, to place it in context.

3 Draft your paraphrase. Replace key words and phrases with synonyms and alternative phrases (possibly gleaned from the context provided by the surrounding text). Experiment with word order and sentence structure until the paraphrase captures your understanding of the passage, in your own language, for your readers.

4 Acknowledge your source. That's the only sure way to protect yourself from a charge of plagiarism.

> ## A Practice Sequence: Paraphrasing
>
> **1** In one of the sources you've located in your research, find a sentence of some length and complexity, and paraphrase it. Share the original and your paraphrase of it with a classmate, and discuss the effectiveness of your restatement. Is the meaning clear to your reader? Is the paraphrase written in your own language, using your own sentence structure?
>
> **2** Repeat the activity using a short paragraph from the same source. You and your classmate may want to attempt to paraphrase the same paragraph and then compare results. What differences do you detect?

WRITING A SUMMARY

As you have seen, a **summary** condenses a body of information, presenting the key ideas and acknowledging their source. Summarizing is not an active way to make an argument, but summaries do provide a common ground of information for readers so that you can make your argument more effectively. You can summarize a paragraph, several paragraphs, an essay, a chapter in a book, or even an entire book, depending on the use you plan to make of the information in your argument.

We suggest a method of summarizing that involves (1) describing the author's key claims, (2) selecting examples to illustrate the author's argument, (3) presenting the gist of the author's argument, and (4) contextualizing what you summarize. We demonstrate these steps following the excerpt from "Debating the Civil Rights Movement: The View from the Nation," by Steven F. Lawson. Read Lawson's essay, and then follow along as we write a summary of it.

ABOUT THE READING

A professor of history at Rutgers University, Steven F. Lawson's main area of research is the history of the civil rights movement, especially the expansion of black voting rights and black politics. His major publications include *Black Ballots: Voting Rights in the South, 1944–1969* (1976); *In Pursuit of Power: Southern Blacks and Electoral Politics, 1965–1982* (1985); and *Running for Freedom: Civil Rights and Black Politics in America Since 1941* (1990). The following excerpt is from *Debating the Civil Rights Movement: 1945–1968*, where it appeared with Charles Payne's essay (see p. 139) in 1998.

STEVEN F. LAWSON

From Debating the Civil Rights Movement: The View from the Nation

The federal government played an indispensable role in shaping the   *1*
fortunes of the civil rights revolution. It is impossible to understand
how Blacks achieved first-class citizenship rights in the South without
concentrating on what national leaders in Washington, D.C., did to
influence the course of events leading to the extension of racial equality.
Powerful presidents, congressional lawmakers, and members of the
Supreme Court provided the legal instruments to challenge racial segregation and disfranchisement. Without their crucial support, the struggle
against white supremacy in the South still would have taken place but
would have lacked the power and authority to defeat state governments
intent on keeping Blacks in subservient positions.

Along with national officials, the fate of the civil rights movement   *2*
depended on the presence of national organizations. Groups such as the
National Association for the Advancement of Colored People (NAACP),
founded in 1901, drew on financial resources and legal talent from all
over the country to press the case for equal rights in Congress and the
courts. In similar fashion, Dr. Martin Luther King, Jr., and the Southern
Christian Leadership Conference (SCLC), established in the mid-1950s,
focused their attention on spotlighting white southern racism before a
national audience to mobilize support for their side. Even if white Americans outside the South had wanted to ignore the plight of southern
Blacks, NAACP lawyers and lobbyists, SCLC protesters, and their like-
minded allies made that choice impossible. They could do what Black
residents of local communities could not do alone: turn the civil rights
struggle into a national cause for concern and prod the federal government into throwing its considerable power to overturn the entrenched
system of white domination that had prevailed for centuries in the South.

Historical accounts that center on the national state in Washington   *3*
and the operations of national organizations take on a particular narrative. The story begins with World War II, which stimulated Black protests
against racism, and winds its way through the presidencies of Franklin D.
Roosevelt, Harry S. Truman, Dwight D. Eisenhower, John F. Kennedy,
and Lyndon B. Johnson. This period witnessed significant presidential
executive orders promulgating desegregation in the military and in
housing, five pieces of pioneering civil rights legislation, and landmark
Supreme Court rulings toppling segregationist practices and extending the right to vote. The familiar geographical signposts of civil rights
demonstrations — Montgomery, Birmingham, Selma, Albany, Little Rock
— derive their greatest importance as places that molded the critical
national debate on ending racial discrimination.

Overall, a nuanced account of the Black freedom struggle requires an   4
interconnected approach. A balanced portrayal acknowledges that Black
activists had important internal resources at their disposal, derived from
religious, economic, educational, and civic institutions, with which to
make their demands. But it does not belittle African-American creativity
and determination to conclude that given existing power relationships
heavily favoring whites, southern Blacks could not possibly eliminate
racial inequality without outside federal assistance. Furthermore, Washington officials had to protect African Americans from intimidation
and violence to allow them to carry out their challenges to discrimination. Without this room for maneuvering, civil rights advocates would
encounter insurmountable hurdles in confronting white power.

At the same time, the federal government could shape the direction of   5
the struggle by choosing whether and when to respond to Black protest
and by deciding on whom to bestow its support within Black communities. Although united around the struggle against white supremacy,
African Americans were not monolithic in their outlook and held various
shades of opinion on how best to combat racial bias. By allocating precious resources and conferring recognition on particular elements within
local Black communities, national leaders could accelerate or slow down
the pace of racial change.

■ Describe the Key Claims of the Text

As you read through a text with an eye to summarizing it, you want to recognize how the author develops his or her argument. You can do this by
"chunking," grouping related material together into the argument's key
claims. Here are two strategies to try:

Pay Attention to the Beginnings and Endings of Paragraphs.   Often,
underlining the first and last sentences of paragraphs will alert you to the
shape and direction of an author's argument. For example, consider the
first and last sentences of Lawson's opening paragraphs:

> *Paragraph 1:* The federal government played an indispensable role in shaping
> the fortunes of the civil rights revolution. . . . Without their crucial support,
> the struggle against white supremacy in the South still would have taken
> place but would have lacked the power and authority to defeat state govern-
> ments intent on keeping Blacks in subservient positions.

> *Paragraph 2:* Along with national officials, the fate of the civil rights movement
> depended on the presence of national organizations. . . . They could do what
> Black residents of local communities could not do alone: turn the civil rights
> struggle into a national cause for concern and prod the federal government
> into throwing its considerable power to overturn the entrenched system of
> white domination that had prevailed for centuries in the South.

Right away you can see that Lawson has introduced a topic in each paragraph — the federal government in the first, and national civil rights organizations in the second — and has indicated a connection between them. How will Lawson elaborate on this connection? What major points does he seem to be developing?

Notice the Author's Point of View and Use of Transitions.   Another strategy for identifying major points is to pay attention to descriptive words and transitions. Notice the words Lawson uses to describe how the federal government advanced the cause of civil rights: *indispensable, significant, pioneering, landmark,* and *precious.* His word choices suggest an aspect of Lawson's point of view: that he highly values government action. Once you identify an author's point of view, you will start noticing contrasts and oppositions in the argument — instances where the words are less positive, or neutral, or even negative — which often are signaled by how the writer uses transitions.

For example, Lawson begins his fourth paragraph with two neutral-sounding sentences: "Overall, a nuanced account of the Black freedom struggle requires an interconnected approach. A balanced portrayal acknowledges that Black activists had important internal resources . . . with which to make their demands." However, in the next two sentences (the sentences that begin with the transition words *But* and *Furthermore*) Lawson signals that he is not neutral on what he believes was most important to the "Black freedom struggle": help from federal institutions.

These strategies can help you recognize the main points of an essay and describe them in a few sentences. For example, you could describe the key claims of Lawson's essay this way:

1. The civil rights movement would have failed without the support of the federal government.

2. Certainly the activism of national organizations with a local presence in the South was vital to making the struggle for civil rights a national cause.

3. But the primary importance of local activism was providing the executive, legislative, and judicial branches of the federal government with choices of where best to throw the weight of their support for racial equality in the nation.

■ Select Examples to Illustrate the Author's Argument

A summary should be succinct, which means you should limit the number of examples or illustrations you use. As you distill the major points of the argument, try to choose one or two examples to illustrate each major point. Here are the examples you might use to support Lawson's main points:

1. The civil rights movement would have failed without the support of the federal government. *Examples of federal support: Desegregation in*

the military and in housing; Supreme Court rulings toppling segrega-
tionist practices and extending the right to vote (para. 3).

2. Certainly the activism of national organizations with a local presence
   in the South was vital to making the struggle for civil rights a national
   cause. *Examples of activism: NAACP drew on nationwide resources to
   press the case for equal rights; SCLC spotlighted white southern racism*
   (para. 2).

3. But the primary importance of local activism was providing the executive, legislative, and judicial branches of the federal government with
   choices of where best to throw the weight of their support for racial
   equality in the nation. *Examples of events prompting federal support:
   Local struggles in Montgomery, Birmingham, Selma, Albany, and Little
   Rock* (para. 3).

A single concrete example may be sufficient to clarify the point you want
to make about an author's argument. In his five paragraphs, Lawson cites
numerous examples to support his argument, but the most concrete, specific
instance of federal involvement appears in paragraph 3, where he cites the
series of presidential orders that mandated desegregation. This one example
may be sufficient for the purposes of a summary of Lawson's passage.

■ Present the Gist of the Author's Argument

When you present the **gist of an argument**, you are expressing the
author's central idea in a sentence or two. The gist of an argument is not
the same thing as the author's thesis statement; it is your formulation of
the author's main idea, written with the needs of your own argument in
mind. Certainly you need to understand the author's thesis when you formulate the gist. Lawson's first sentence — "The federal government played
an indispensable role in shaping the fortunes of the civil rights movement" — is his thesis statement: It clearly expresses his central idea. But in
formulating the gist of his argument, you want to do more than paraphrase
Lawson. You want to use his position to support your own. For example,
suppose you want to expand on how the three branches of the federal government each played an important role in the civil rights movement. You
would want to mention each branch when you describe the gist of Lawson's argument:

GIST

In his essay, "Debating the Civil Rights Movement: The View from the Nation,"
Steven Lawson argues that actions taken by the president, Congress, and the Supreme Court were all vital to advancing the struggle for civil rights.

Notice that this gist could not have been written based only on Lawson's
thesis statement. It reflects a knowledge of Lawson's major points and his
examples (of executive orders, legislation, and judicial rulings).

■ Contextualize What You Summarize

Your summary should help readers understand the context of the conversation:

- Who is the author?
- What is the author's expertise?
- What is the title of the work?
- Where did the work appear?
- What was the occasion of the work's publication? What prompted the author to write the work?
- What are the issues?
- Who else is taking part in the conversation, and what are their perspectives on the issues?

Again, because a summary must be concise, you must make decisions about how much of the conversation your readers need to know. If your assignment is to practice summarizing, it may be sufficient to include only information about the author and the source. However, if you are using the summary to build your own argument, you may need to provide more context. Your practice summary of Lawson's essay should mention that he is an historian and should cite the title of and page references to his essay. Depending on what else your argument needs, you may want to mention that this piece appeared as one of two essays, each of which sets the stage for a series of primary documents focusing on the roots of the civil rights movement. You also may want to include information about Lawson's audience (historians, other academics, policymakers, general readers), publication information (publisher, date); and what led to the work's publication. Was it published in response to another essay or book, or to commemorate an important event?

We compiled our notes on Lawson's essay (key claims, examples, gist, context) in a worksheet (Figure 7.1). All of our notes in the worksheet constitute a type of prewriting, our preparation for writing the summary. Creating a worksheet like this can help you track your thoughts as you plan to write a summary. (You can download a template of this worksheet at bedfordstmartins.com/frominquiry.)

FIGURE 7.1   Worksheet for Writing a Summary

Key Claims (by paragraph)	Examples (by key claim)	Gist	Context
1. The civil rights movement would have failed without the support of the federal government.	Desegregation in the military and in housing; Supreme Court rulings toppling segregationist practices and extending the right to vote (para. 3).	In his essay, "Debating the Civil Rights Movement: The View from the Nation," Steven Lawson argues that actions taken by the president, Congress, and the Supreme Court were all vital to advancing the struggle for civil rights.	Lawson is a historian. His essay "Debating the Civil Rights Movement: The View from the Nation" appeared in *Debating the Civil Rights Movement*, 1945–1968 by Lawson and Charles Payne (Lanham, MD: Rowman & Littlefield, 1998). Lawson's essay runs from pages 3 to 42; under consideration are his opening paragraphs on pages 3 to 5.
2. Certainly the activism of national organizations with a local presence in the South was vital to making the struggle for civil rights a national cause.	NAACP drew on nationwide resources to press the case for equal rights; SCLC spotlighted white southern racism (para. 2).

Local struggles in Montgomery, Birmingham, Selma, Albany, and Little Rock (para. 3). | | |
| 3. But the primary importance of local activism was providing the executive, legislative, and judicial branches of the federal government with choices of where best to throw the weight of their support for racial equality in the nation. | | | |

Here is our summary of Lawson's essay:

The gist of Lawson's argument, with supporting examples.

In his essay "Debating the Civil Rights Movement: The View from the Nation," historian Steven Lawson argues that actions taken by the president, Congress, and the Supreme Court were all vital to advancing the struggle for civil rights. Lawson's emphasis on the role the federal government played in the civil rights movement comes at a time when other historians are challenging that thinking.

Sentence places Lawson's argument in context, explaining the larger conversation.

Many of these historians believe that the success of the movement rested on activists' participation in the struggle to create change and achieve equality. Although Lawson

Lawson's main point.

recognizes the value of black activism in the South, he also makes clear that desegregation could only have occurred as a result of the federal government's intervention (3–5).

Steps to Writing a Summary

1 **Describe the key claims of the text.** To understand the shape and direction of the argument, study how paragraphs begin and end, and pay attention to the author's point of view and use of transitions. Then combine what you have learned into a few sentences describing the key claims.

2 **Select examples to illustrate the author's argument.** Find one or two examples to support each key claim. You may need only one example when you write your summary.

3 **Present the gist of the author's argument.** Describe the author's central idea in your own language with an eye to where you expect your argument to go.

4 **Contextualize what you summarize.** Cue your readers into the conversation. Who is the author? Where and when did the text appear? Why was the author writing? Who else is in the conversation?

A Practice Sequence: Summarizing

1 Summarize a text that you have been studying for research or for one of your other classes. You may want to limit yourself to an excerpt of just a few paragraphs or a few pages. Follow the four steps we've described, using a summary worksheet for notes, and write a summary of the text. Then share the excerpt and your summary of it with two of your peers. Be prepared to justify your choices in composing the summary. Do your peers agree that your summary captures what is important in the original?

2 With a classmate, choose a brief text of about three pages. Each of you use the method we describe above to write a summary of the text. Exchange your summaries and worksheets, and discuss the effectiveness of your summaries. Each of you should be prepared to discuss your choice of key claims and examples and your wording of the gist. Did you set forth the context effectively?

SYNTHESIS VERSUS SUMMARY

A **synthesis** is a discussion that forges connections between the arguments of two or more authors. Like a summary, a synthesis requires you to understand the key claims of each author's argument, including his or her use of supporting examples and evidence. Also like a summary, a synthesis requires you to present a central idea, a *gist*, to your readers. But in contrast to a summary, which explains the context of a source, a synthesis creates a context for your own argument. That is, when you write a synthesis comparing two or more sources, you demonstrate that you are aware of the larger conversation about the issue, and begin to claim your own place in that conversation. Most academic arguments begin with a synthesis that sets the stage for the argument that follows. By comparing what others have written on a given issue, writers position themselves in relation to what has come before them, acknowledging the contributions of their predecessors as they advance their own points of view.

Like a summary, a synthesis requires analysis: You have to break down arguments and categorize their parts to see how they work together. In our summary of Lawson's passage (p. 137), the parts we looked at were the key claims, the examples and evidence that supported them, the central idea (conveyed in the gist), and the context. But in a synthesis, your main purpose is not simply to report what another author has said. Rather, you must think critically about how multiple points of view intersect on your issue, and decide what those intersections mean.

Comparing different points of view prompts you to ask why they differ. It also makes you more aware of *counterarguments* — passages where claims conflict ("writer X says this, but writer Y asserts just the opposite") or at least differ ("writer X interprets this information this way, while writer Y sees it differently"). And it starts you formulating your own counterarguments: "Neither X nor Y has taken this into account. What if they had?"

Keep in mind that the purpose of a synthesis is not merely to list the similarities and differences you find in different sources, nor to assert your agreement with one source as opposed to others. Instead, it sets up your argument. Once you discover connections between texts, you have to decide what those connections mean to you and your readers. What bearing do they have on your own thinking? How can you make use of them in your argument?

WRITING A SYNTHESIS

To compose an effective synthesis, you must (1) make connections between ideas in different texts, (2) decide what those connections mean, and (3) formulate the gist of what you've read, much like you did when you wrote a summary. The difference is that in a synthesis, your gist should be a succinct statement that brings into focus not the central idea of one text but the relationship among different ideas in multiple texts.

To help you grasp the strategies of writing a synthesis, read the essays below by historians Charles Payne and Ronald Takaki which, like Steven Lawson's essay, deal with race in America. You will see that we have annotated the Payne and Takaki readings not only to comment on their ideas, but also to connect their ideas with those of Lawson. Annotating your texts in this manner is a useful first step in writing a synthesis.

Following the Payne and Takaki selections, we explain how annotating contributes to writing a synthesis. Then we show how you can use a worksheet to organize your thinking on the way to formulating the gist of your synthesis. Finally, we present our own synthesis based on the texts of Lawson, Payne, and Takaki.

ABOUT THE READING

Charles Payne is a professor of history and African American studies at Duke University, where his current research focuses on urban education, the civil rights movement, social change, and social inequality. He is the principal investigator in an ethnographic study of the most improved low-income schools in Chicago. The following selection on the civil rights movement appears with Steven Lawson's essay in *Debating the Civil Rights Movement, 1945–1968*.

CHARLES PAYNE

From Debating the Civil Rights Movement: The View from the Trenches

Point of paragraph seems to be that the language used to describe the civil rights movement distorts the actual goals and results of the movement. Is this Payne's main claim?

The [civil rights] movement continues to exercise a considerable hold on the American imagination. Our understanding of social change, our conceptions of leadership, our understanding of the possibilities of interracial cooperation are all affected by how we remember the movement. Even much of the language that we use to discuss social issues derives from movement days. We think of the movement as a movement for "civil rights" and against "segregation." Even those seemingly innocuous terms carry their own historical baggage.   *1*

"Segregation" became the accepted way to describe the South's racial system among both Blacks and whites. In its denotative meaning, suggesting separation between Blacks and whites, it is not a very accurate term to describe that system. The system involved plenty of integration; it just had to be on terms acceptable to white people. Indeed, the agricultural economy of the early-twentieth-century South probably afforded a good deal more interracial contact than the modern urban ghetto. "White supremacy" is a more accurate description of what the system was about. "Segregation" is the way apologists for the South liked to think of it. It implies, "We're not doing anything to Black people: we just want to keep them separate from us." It was the most innocent face one could put on that system. When we use the term as a summary term for what was going on in the South, we are unconsciously adopting the preferred euphemism of nineteenth-century white supremacist leadership.

Supports the claim that "movement" language hides or distorts reality.

If "segregation" is a poor way to describe the problem, "integration" may not tell us much about the solution. It is not at all clear what proportion of the Black population was interested in "integration" as a general goal. African Americans have wanted access to the privileges that white people have enjoyed and have been interested in integration as a possible avenue to those privileges, but that view is different from seeing integration as important in and of itself. Even in the 1950s, it was clear that school integration, while it would potentially put more resources into the education of Black children, also potentially meant the loss of thousands of teaching jobs for Black teachers and the destruction of schools to which Black communities often felt deeply attached, however resource-poor they were. There was also something potentially demeaning in the idea that Black children had to be sitting next to white children to learn. The first Black children to integrate the schools in a given community often found themselves in a strange position, especially if they were

Payne talks about African Americans' preferring "privileges" and "resources" to "integration."

Integration might lead to fewer resources — what's gained economically on the one hand would be lost on the other.

2

3

teenagers. While some Black people thought of them as endangering themselves for the greater good of the community, others saw them as turning their backs on that community and what it had to offer. It is probably safest to say that only a segment of the Black community had anything like an ideological commitment to "integration," while most Black people were willing to give it a try to see if it really did lead to a better life.

We might also ask how "civil rights" came to be 4 commonly used as a summary term for the struggle of African Americans. In the late 1960s, after several civil rights bills had been passed, a certain part of white America seemed not to understand why Black Americans were still angry about their collective status. "You have your civil rights. Now what's the problem?" In part, the problem was that "civil rights" was always a narrow way to conceptualize the larger struggle. For African Americans, the struggle has always been about forging a decent place for themselves within this society, which has been understood to involve the thorny issues of economic participation and self-assertion as well as civil rights. Indeed, in the 1940s, Gunnar Myrdal had demonstrated that economic issues were the ones that Black Americans ranked first in priority. At the 1963 March on Washington — which was initially conceived as a march for jobs — [the Student Nonviolent Coordinating Committee's] John Lewis wanted to point out that SNCC was not sure it could support what became the Civil Rights Act of 1964 partly because it did not have an economic component:

> What is in the bill that will protect the homeless and starving people of this nation? What is there in this bill to insure the equality of a maid who earns $5.00 a week in the home of a family whose income is $100,000 a year?

One hypothesis, of course, would be that "civil 5 rights" becomes so popular precisely because it is so narrow, precisely because it does not suggest that distribution of privilege is a part of the problem.

Margin notes:

Is this "segment" the activists Lawson refers to? Are Lawson and Payne on the same page about the black community's not being "monolithic" (Lawson, para. 5) in its approach to civil rights?

Lawson, by contrast, emphasizes that civil rights were vital to the struggle for equality.

Payne's examples suggest that economic equality, not legal rights, is what the civil rights movement was about.

Payne's main point — that the language of civil rights is limited because it ignores economic factors.

ABOUT THE READING

Ronald Takaki is a professor of ethnic studies at the University of California, Berkeley. An adviser to the ethnic studies PhD program, he was instrumental in establishing Berkeley's American cultures graduation requirement. Takaki is a prolific writer with several award-winning books to his credit, including *A Pro-Slavery Crusade* (1971), a study of the South's ideological defense of slavery; *Violence in the Black Imagination* (1972), an examination of nineteenth-century black novelists; the Pulitzer Prize–nominated *Strangers from a Different Shore: A History of Asian Americans* (1989); and *A Different Mirror: A History of Multicultural America* (1993). The essay that follows is from a collection he edited, *Debating Diversity: Clashing Perspectives on Race and Ethnicity in America* (2002), and is his response to the Los Angeles riots of April 29, 1992.

RONALD TAKAKI

Policies: Strategies and Solutions

What dream? Civil rights? Economic equality?

Business Week links the riots to economic inequality.

What happens, asked black poet Langston Hughes, to a "dream deferred?" Does it "dry up like a raisin in the sun," or "does it explode?" An answer was hurled at America during the bloody and destructive 1992 Los Angeles race riot. On April 29, a California jury announced its not-guilty verdict in the trial of four white police officers charged with beating Rodney King, an African American who had been stopped for a traffic violation. Videotaped images of King being brutally clubbed had been repeatedly beamed across the country. The jury's shocking decision ignited an explosion of fury and violence in the inner city of Los Angeles. During the days of rage, scores of people were killed, over 2,000 injured, 12,000 arrested, and almost a billion dollars in property destroyed.

"It took a brutal beating, an unexpected jury verdict, and the sudden rampage of rioting, looting, and indiscriminate violence to bring this crisis [of urban America] back to the forefront," *Business Week* reported. "Racism surely explains some of the carnage in Los Angeles. But the day-to-day living conditions with which many of America's urban poor must contend is an equally compelling story — a tale of economic injustice." This usually conservative

The dream is not only deferred; it seems to be moving further away!

magazine pointed out that "the poverty rate, which fell as low as 11 percent in the 1970s, moved higher in the Reagan years and jumped during the last couple of years. Last year [1991], an estimated 36 million people — or about 14.7 percent of the total population — were living in poverty."

More recent examples of economic inequality than Payne's. Decades after the civil rights movement, economic inequality remains an issue.

The explosion unshrouded the terrible conditions   3
and the anger of poor African Americans trapped in inner cities. "South Central Los Angeles is a Third World country," declared Krashaun Scott, a former member of the Los Angeles Crips gang. "There's a South Central in every city, in every state." Describing the desperate conditions in his community, he continued: "What we got is inadequate housing and inferior education. I wish someone would tell me the difference between Guatemala and South Central." This comparison graphically illustrated the squalor and poverty present within one of America's wealthiest and most modern cities. A gang member known as Bone commented that the recent violence was "not a riot — it was a class struggle. When Rodney King asked, 'Can we get along?' it ain't just about Rodney King. He was the lighter and it blew up."

More examples of increasing economic inequality.

What exploded was anguish born of despair.   4
Plants and factories had been moved out of central Los Angeles into the suburbs, as well as across the border into Mexico and overseas to countries like South Korea. The Firestone factory, which had employed many of the parents of these young blacks, was boarded up, like a tomb. In terms of manufacturing jobs, South Central Los Angeles had become a wasteland. Many young black men and women nervously peered down the corridor of their futures and saw no possibility of full-time employment paying above minimum wage, or any jobs at all. The unemployment rate in this area was 59 percent — higher than the national rate during the Great Depression.

"Once again, young blacks are taking to the   5
streets to express their outrage at perceived injustice," *Newsweek* reported, "and once again, whites are fearful that The Fire Next Time will consume them." But

In a multiethnic America, do Payne's and Lawson's focus on black-and-white civil rights still apply?

this time, the magazine noticed, the situation was different from the 1965 Watts riot: "The nation is rapidly moving toward a multiethnic future in which Asians, Hispanics, Caribbean islanders, and many other immigrant groups compose a diverse and changing social mosaic that cannot be described by the old vocabulary of race relations in America." The terms "black" and "white," *Newsweek* concluded, no longer "depict the American social reality."

At the street level, African American community organizer Ted Watkins observed: "This riot was deeper and more dangerous. More ethnic groups were involved." Watkins had witnessed the Watts fury; since then, he had watched the influx of Hispanics and Koreans into South Central Los Angeles. Shortly after the terrible turmoil, social critic Richard Rodriguez reflected on the significance of these changes: "The Rodney King riots were appropriately multiracial in this multicultural capital of America. We cannot settle for black and white conclusions when one of the most important conflicts the riots revealed was the tension between Koreans and African Americans." He also noted that "the majority of looters who were arrested . . . turned out to be Hispanic."

Another comment on the new multicultural — black versus white — reality.

Out of the ashes emerged a more complex awareness of our society's racial crisis. "I think good will come of [the riot]," stated Janet Harris, a chaplain at Central Juvenile Hall. "People need to take off their rose-colored glasses," she added, "and take a hard look at what they've been doing. They've been living in invisible cages. And they've shut out that world. And maybe the world came crashing in on them and now people will be moved to do something." A black minister called for cross-cultural understanding between African Americans and Korean Americans: "If we could appreciate and affirm each other's histories, there wouldn't be generalizations and stigmatizations, and we could see that we have more in common." The fires of the riot illuminated the harsh reality of class inequality. "At first I didn't notice," a Korean shopkeeper said, "but I slowly realized the

Like Payne, Takaki emphasizes the importance of economic factors — rich versus poor.

6

7

looters were very poor. The riot happened because of
the gap between rich and poor." Executive director of
the Asian Pacific American Legal Center, Steward
Kwoh direly predicted that "the economic polariza-
tion between the 'haves' and 'have nots' would be the
main ingredient for future calamities."

During the 1992 calamity, Rodney King pleaded: 8
"We all can get along. I mean, we're stuck here for a
while. Let's try to work it out." But we find ourselves
wondering, how can we get along and how can we
work it out? Is "the Negro today," as Irving Kristol
contends, "like the immigrant yesterday," or do "race
and class" intersect in the black community? Should
there be limits on immigration from Mexico, or are
these immigrants scapegoats for our nation's problems? What should we do and not do about crime?
What should be the future of affirmative action? Have
American blacks, Nathan Glazer admits, turned out
to be "not like the immigrants of yesterday"?

■ Make Connections Between Different Texts

The texts by Lawson, Payne, and Takaki all deal with race in America, but
race is such a large topic that you cannot assume that connections are
going to leap off the page at you. In fact, each text deals with a main issue
that does not immediately connect with those of the others:

- Lawson emphasizes the importance of federal actions for advancing the
  cause of civil rights.
- Payne contends that the terms we use to talk about the civil rights movement distort its goals and accomplishments.
- Takaki writes about the 1992 Los Angeles riots, arguing that desperate
  economic circumstances led to an outburst of multicultural violence.

But closer reading does suggest connections. Both Lawson and Payne are
writing about the civil rights movement. They seem to agree that civil
rights activists were a crucial minority in the black community, but they
seem to disagree on the importance of legislation versus economic factors.

Notice how our annotations call out these connections: "Payne talks
about African Americans' preferring 'privileges' and 'resources' to 'integration.'" "Are Lawson and Payne on the same page about the black community's not being 'monolithic' . . . in its approach to civil rights?" "Lawson,

by contrast, emphasizes that civil rights were vital to the struggle for equality." "Payne's examples suggest that economic equality, not legal rights, is what the civil rights movement was about."

Turning to Takaki, we notice that he is also writing about economic inequality and race, but in the 1990s, not the 1950s and 1960s: "More recent examples of economic inequality than Payne's. Decades after the civil rights movement, economic inequality remains an issue." But Takaki adds another factor: economic inequality in an increasingly multicultural America. Our comment: "In a multiethnic America, do Payne's and Lawson's focus on black-and-white civil rights still apply?"

With these annotations, we are starting to think critically about the ideas in the essays, speculating about what they mean. Notice, however, that not all of the annotations make connections. Some try to get at the gist of the arguments: "Is this Payne's main claim?" Some note examples: "More examples of increasing economic inequality." Some offer impromptu opinions and reactions: "The dream is not only deferred; it seems to be moving further away!" You should not expect every annotation to contribute to your synthesis. Instead, use them to record your responses and spur your thinking too.

■ Decide What Those Connections Mean

Having annotated the selections, we filled out the worksheet in Figure 7.2, making notes in the grid to help us see the three texts in relation to one another. Our worksheet included columns for

- author and source information,
- the gist of each author's arguments,
- supporting examples and illustrations,
- counterarguments,
- our own thoughts.

A worksheet like this one can help you concentrate on similarities and differences in the texts to determine what the connections between texts mean. (You can download a template for this worksheet at bedfordst martins.com/frominquiry.) Of course, you can design your own worksheet as well, tailoring it to your needs and preferences. If you want to take very detailed notes about your authors and sources, for example, you may want to have separate columns for each.

Once you start noticing connections, including points of agreement and disagreement, you can start identifying counterarguments in the readings — for example, Payne countering Lawson's position that equality can be legislated. Identifying counterarguments gives you a sense of what is at issue for each author. And determining what the authors think in relation to one another can help you realize what may be at issue for you. Suppose

FIGURE 7.2	Worksheet for Writing a Synthesis			
AUTHOR AND SOURCE	GIST OF ARGUMENT	EXAMPLES/ ILLUSTRATIONS	COUNTER- ARGUMENTS	WHAT I THINK
Historian Steven F. Lawson, from "Debating the Civil Rights Movement: The View from the Nation"	Actions taken by the president, Congress, and the Supreme Court were all vital to advancing the struggle for civil rights.	The executive orders, the legislation, and the court decisions that promoted desegregation	Desegregation cannot be legislated. The struggle was not simply about civil rights; it also was about achieving economic equality.	I'm not convinced by Lawson's argument.
Historian Charles Payne, from "Debating the Civil Rights Movement: The View from the Trenches"	By granting African Americans their civil rights, the Supreme Court did not — and could not — guarantee access to economic equality.	Continued inequalities between rich and poor	The executive orders, legislation, and Court rulings that promoted desegregation indicate that there was some attempt to achieve equality.	An interesting argument, but I'm not sure Payne took the best approach by working with definitions.
Ethnic historian Ronald Takaki, "Policies: Strategies and Solutions"	Economic inequality persists in urban areas where ethnic minorities live in poverty and squalor.	Inadequate housing, schools, and employment	Racial equality has been legislated; so poverty is an individual problem, not a systemic one.	The multiethnic connection makes me want to look into his issue more deeply.

you are struck by Payne's argument that the term *civil rights* obscures an equally important issue in African Americans' struggle for equality: economic equality. Suppose you connect Payne's point about economic inequality with Takaki's more-recent examples of racial inequality in the areas of housing, education, and employment. Turning these ideas around in your mind, you may decide that race-based economic inequality in a multicultural society is a topic you want to explore and develop.

■ Formulate the Gist of What You've Read

Remember that your gist should bring into focus the relationship among different ideas in multiple texts. Looking at the information juxtaposed on the worksheet, you can begin to construct the gist of your synthesis:

- The first writer, Lawson, believes that the civil rights movement owes its success to the federal government.

- The second writer, Payne, believes that blacks' struggle for economic equality was not addressed by the actions of the federal government.

- The third writer, Takaki, seems to support Payne when he claims that poverty still exists for African Americans. But he broadens the issue of economic inequality, extending it to people of different racial backgrounds.

How do you formulate this information into a gist? You can use a transition word (we've used *although*) to connect the ideas these authors bring together while conveying their differences (Lawson's emphasis on civil rights versus Payne and Takaki's emphasis on economic inequality). Thus a gist about these essays might read:

GIST OF A SYNTHESIS

Although historian Steven Lawson argues that the federal government played a crucial role in extending civil rights to African Americans, other scholars, among them Charles Payne and Ronald Takaki, point out that the focus on civil rights ignored the devastating economic inequality that persists among people of color today.

Having drafted this gist, we returned to our notes on the worksheet and complete the synthesis, presenting examples and using transitions to signal the relationships among the texts and their ideas. It's a good idea in a synthesis to use at least one illustration from each author's text to support the point you want to make, and to use transition words and phrases to lead your readers through the larger argument you want to make.

Here is our brief synthesis of the three texts:

The gist of our synthesis. "Although" signals that Lawson's argument is qualified or countered later in the sentence.

Although historian Steven Lawson argues that the federal government played a crucial role in extending civil rights to African Americans, other scholars, among them Charles Payne and Ronald Takaki, point out that the focus on civil rights ignored the devastating economic inequality that persists among people of color today. Indeed, Lawson illustrates the extent to which presidents, lawmakers, and judges brought an end to legal segregation, but he largely ignores the economic component of racial discrimination. Unfortunately, integration is still what Langston Hughes would call a "dream deferred" (quoted in Takaki). A historian, Charles Payne also observes that by granting

Transition: Lawson claims one thing, but ignores something else.

Example that backs up the gist: Both Payne and Takaki argue that the negative effects of economic inequality outweigh the positive effects of civil rights protections.

African Americans their civil rights, the federal government did not — and could not — guarantee their access to economic equality. Ronald Takaki, an ethnic historian, supports Payne's argument, demonstrating through a number of examples that economic inequality persists in urban areas where ethnic minorities live in poverty and squalor. Takaki also makes the important point that the problem of economic inequality is no longer a black-white problem, as it was during the civil rights movement. Today's multiracial

Sets up argument to follow

society complicates our understanding of the problem of inequality and of a possible solution.

Writing a synthesis, like writing a summary, is principally a strategy for framing your own argument. In writing a synthesis, you are conveying to your readers how various points of view in a conversation intersect and diverge. The larger point of this exercise is to find your own issue — your own position in the conversation — and make your argument for it.

Steps to Writing a Synthesis

1 **Make connections between different texts**. Annotate the texts you are working with with an eye to comparing them. As you would for a summary, note major points in the texts, choose relevant examples, and formulate the gist of each text.

2 **Decide what those connections mean**. Fill out a worksheet to compare your notes on the different texts, track counterarguments, and record your thoughts. Decide what the similarities and differences mean to you and what they might mean to your readers.

3 **Formulate the gist of what you've read**. Identify an overarching idea that brings together the ideas you've noted, and write a synthesis that forges connections and makes use of the examples you've noted. Use transitions to signal the direction of your synthesis.

A Practice Sequence: Writing a Synthesis

1 Choose at least three texts you expect to work with in your researched argument, read them closely, and fill out a synthesis worksheet to organize your information about them. With the worksheet in hand, write down any similarities and differences you find. Are the ideas weighted in one direction or the other, as they are in our readings? On what points do the authors agree? Formulate the gist of the works, and then write the synthesis, incorporating examples and using transitions to signal the relationships among ideas and authors. Does the synthesis suggest the direction of your argument?

2 As a class, choose three or more texts to synthesize. Then break up into small groups, each group working with the same texts. Within each group, work through the steps in synthesizing. One person in each group should take notes in a format like our worksheet. After you complete the worksheet, identify similarities and differences among the ideas. Are they weighted in one direction or the other? Are there points of agreement among the authors? Your answers to these questions should help you formulate the gist of the synthesis. After you formulate the gist, share what you've written with the other groups. Be sure to explain how you arrived at the gist you formulated. Did each group construct the same gist? What was similar? What was different?

AVOIDING PLAGIARISM

Whether you paraphrase, summarize, or synthesize, it is essential that you acknowledge your sources. Academic writing requires you to use and document sources appropriately, making clear to readers the boundaries between your words and ideas and those of other writers. Setting boundaries can be a challenge because so much of academic writing involves interweaving the ideas of others into your own argument. Still, no matter how difficult, you must acknowledge your sources. It's only fair. Imagine how you would feel if you were reading a text and discovered that the writer had incorporated a passage from one of your papers, something you slaved over, without giving you credit. You would see yourself as a victim of plagiarism, and you would be justified in feeling very angry indeed.

In fact, **plagiarism** — the unacknowledged use of another's work, passed off as one's own — is a most serious breach of academic integrity, and colleges and universities deal with it severely. If you are caught plagiarizing in your work for a class, you can expect to fail that class and may even be expelled from your college or university. Furthermore, although a failing grade on a paper or in a course, honestly come by, is unlikely to deter an employer from hiring you, the stigma of plagiarism can come back to haunt you when you apply for a job. Any violation of the principles set forth in Table 7.1 could have serious consequences for your academic and professional career.

Even if you know what plagiarism is and wouldn't think about doing it, you can still plagiarize unintentionally. Again, paraphrasing can be especially tricky: Attempting to restate a passage without using the original words and sentence structure is, to a certain extent, an invitation to plagiarism. If you remember that your paper is *your* argument, and understand

TABLE 7.1   Principles Governing Plagiarism

1. All written work submitted for any purpose is accepted as your own work. This means it must not have been written even in part by another person.

2. The wording of any written work you submit is assumed to be your own. This means you must not submit work that has been copied, wholly or partially, from a book, article, essay, newspaper, another student's paper or notebook, or any other source. Another writer's phrases, sentences, or paragraphs can be included only if they are presented as quotations and the source acknowledged.

3. The ideas expressed in a paper or report are assumed to originate with you, the writer. Written work that paraphrases a source without acknowledgment must not be submitted for credit. Ideas from the work of others can be incorporated in your work as starting points, governing issues, illustrations, and the like, but in every instance the source must be cited.

4. Remember that any online materials you use to gather information for a paper are also governed by the rules for avoiding plagiarism. You need to learn to cite electronic sources as well as printed and other sources.

5. You may correct and revise your writing with the aid of reference books. You also may discuss your writing with your peers in a writing group or with peer tutors at your campus writing center. However, you may not submit writing that has been revised substantially by another person.

---

that any paraphrasing, summarizing, or synthesizing should reflect *your* voice and style, you will be less likely to have problems with plagiarism. Your paper should sound like you. And, again, the surest way to protect yourself is to cite your sources.

Steps to Avoiding Plagiarism

1 **Always cite the source.** Signal that you are paraphrasing, summarizing, or synthesizing by identifying your source at the outset — "According to James Gunn," "Steven Lawson argues," "Charles Payne and Ronald Takaki . . . point out." And if possible, indicate the end of the paraphrase, summary, or synthesis with relevant page references to the source. If you cite a source several times in your paper, don't assume your first citation has you covered; acknowledge the source as often as you use it.

2 **Provide a full citation in your bibliography.** It's not enough to cite a source in your paper; you must also provide a full citation for every source you use in the list of sources at the end of your paper.

INTEGRATING QUOTATIONS
INTO YOUR WRITING

When you integrate quotations into your writing, bear in mind a piece of advice we've given you about writing the rest of your paper: Take your readers by the hand and lead them step-by-step. When you quote other authors to develop your argument — using their words to support your thinking or to address a counterargument — discuss and analyze the words you quote, showing readers how the specific language of each quotation contributes to the larger point you are making in your essay. When you integrate quotations, then, there are three basic things you want to do: (1) Take an active stance, (2) explain the quotations, and (3) attach short quotations to your own sentences.

■ Take an Active Stance

Critical reading demands that you adopt an active stance toward what you read — that you raise questions in response to a text that is telling you not only what the author thinks but also what you should think. You should be no less active when you are using other authors' texts to develop your own argument. Certainly taking an active stance when you are quoting means knowing when to quote. Don't use a quote when a paraphrase or summary can convey the information from a source more effectively and efficiently. (Don't forget to acknowledge your source!) More important, however, it means you have to make fair and wise decisions about what and how much you should quote to make your researched argument:

- It's not fair (or wise) to quote selectively — choosing only passages that support your argument — when you know you are distorting or misrepresenting the argument of the writer you are quoting. Ideally, you want to demonstrate that you understand the writer's argument and that you want to make evenhanded use of it in your own argument, whether you agree or disagree, in whole or in part, with what the other writer has written.

- It's not wise (or fair to yourself) to flesh out your paper with an overwhelming number of quotations that could make readers think that you either do not know your topic well or do not have your own ideas. Don't allow quotations to take over your paragraphs and shape your own words about the topic. In structuring your paragraphs, remember that your ideas and argument — your thesis — are what is most important to the readers and what justifies a quotation's being included at all.

Above all, taking an active stance when you quote means taking control of your own writing. You want to establish your own argument and guide your readers through it, allowing sources to contribute to but not dictate its direction. You are responsible for plotting and pacing your essay. Always keep in mind that your thesis is the skewer that runs through every paragraph, holding all of the ideas together. When you use quota-tions, then, you must organize them to enrich, substantiate, illustrate, and help support your central claim or thesis.

■ Explain the Quotations

When you quote an author to support or advance your argument, you must be sure that readers know exactly what they should learn from the quotation. Read the excerpt below from one student's early draft of an argument that focuses on the value of service learning in high schools as a means for creating change. The student reviews several relevant studies — but then simply drops in a quotation, expecting readers to know what they should pay attention to in the quotation.

> Other research emphasizes community service as an integral and integrated part of moral identity. In this understanding, community service activities are not iso-lated events but are woven into the context of students' everyday lives (Yates, 1995); the personal, the moral, and the civic become "inseparable" (Colby, Ehrlich, Beaumont, & Stephens, 2003, p. 15). In their study of minority high schoolers at an urban Catholic school who volunteered at a soup kitchen for the homeless as part of a class assignment, Youniss and Yates (1999) found that the students under-went significant identity changes, coming to perceive themselves as lifelong activists. The researchers' findings are worth quoting at length here because they depict the dramatic nature of the students' changed viewpoints. Youniss and Yates write:
>
>> Many students abandoned an initially negative view of homeless people and a disinterest in homelessness by gaining appreciation of the humanity of home-less people and by showing concern for homelessness in relation to poverty, job training, low-cost housing, prison reform, drug and alcohol rehabilitation, care for the mentally ill, quality urban education, and welfare policy.
>> Several students also altered perceptions of themselves from politically impo-tent teenagers to involved citizens who now and in the future could use their talent and power to correct social problems. They projected articulated pictures of themselves as adult citizens who could affect housing policies, education for minorities, and government programs within a clear framework of social justice. (p. 362)

The student's introduction to the quoted passage provided a rationale for quoting Youniss and Yates at length; but it did not help her readers see what was important about the research in relation to the student's own argument. Our student needed to frame the quotation for her readers. Instead of introducing the quotation by saying "Youniss and Yates write," she should have made explicit that the study supports the argument that

community service can create change. A more appropriate frame for the
quotation might have been a summary like this one:

Frames the quotation,   One particular study underscores my argument that service
explaining it in the con-   can motivate change, particularly when that change begins
text of the student's   within the students who are involved in service. Youniss and
argument.   Yates (1999) write that over the course of their research, the
students developed both an "appreciation of the humanity of
homeless people" and a sense that they would someday be
able to "use their talent and power to correct social problems"
(p. 362).

In the following example, notice that the student writer uses Derrick
Bell's text to say something about the ways the effects of desegregation
have been muted by political manipulation.* The writer shapes what he
wants readers to focus on, leaving nothing to chance.

The effectiveness with which the meaning of *Brown v. Board of Education* has
been manipulated, Derrick Bell argues, is also evidenced by the way in which
such thinking has actually been embraced by minority groups. Bell claims that
a black school board member's asking "But of what value is it to teach black
children to read in all-black schools?" indicates this unthinking acceptance that
whiteness is an essential ingredient to effective schooling for blacks. Bell
continues:

The assumption that even the attaining of academic skills is worthless
unless those skills are acquired in the presence of white students illustrates
dramatically how a legal precedent, namely the Supreme Court's decision in
Brown v. Board of Education, has been so constricted even by advocates that
its goal — equal educational opportunity — is rendered inaccessible, even
unwanted, unless it can be obtained through racial balancing of the school
population. (p. 255)

Bell's argument is extremely compelling, particularly when one considers the
extent to which "racial balancing" has come to be defined in terms of large white
majority populations and small nonwhite minority populations.

Notice how the student's last sentence helps readers understand what the
quoted material suggests and why it's important by embedding and
extending Bell's notion of racial balancing into his explanation.

In sum, you should always explain the information that you quote so
that your readers can see how the quotation relates to your own argument.
("Take your readers by the hand . . . ") As you read other people's writing,
keep an eye open to the ways writers introduce and explain the sources
they use to build their arguments.

*This quotation is from Derrick Bell's *Silent Covenants: Brown v. Board of Education
and the Unfulfilled Hopes for Racial Reform* (Oxford UP, 2005).

■ Attach Short Quotations to Your Own Sentences

The quotations we discussed above are **block quotations,** lengthy quotations, generally of more than five lines, that are set off from the text of a paper with indention. Make shorter quotations part of your own sentences so your readers can understand how the quotations connect to your argument and can follow along easily. How do you make a quotation part of your own sentences? There are two main methods:

- Integrate quotations within the grammar of your writing.
- Attach quotations with punctuation.

If possible, use both to make your integration of quotations more interesting and varied.

Integrate Quotations within the Grammar of a Sentence.   When you integrate a quotation into a sentence, the quotation must make grammatical sense and read as if it is part of the sentence:

> Fine, Weiss, and Powell (1998) expanded upon what others call "equal status contact theory" by using a "framework that draws on three traditionally independent literatures — those on community, difference, and democracy" (p. 37).

If you add words to the quotation, use square brackets around them to let readers know that the words are not original to the quotation:

> Smith and Wellner (2002) asserted that they "are not alone [in believing] that the facts have been incorrectly interpreted by Mancini" (p. 24).

If you omit any words in the middle of a quotation, use an **ellipsis,** three periods with spaces between them, to indicate the omission:

> Riquelme argues that "Eliot tries . . . to provide a definition by negations, which he also turns into positive terms that are meant to correct misconceptions" (156).

If you omit a sentence or more, make sure to put a period before the ellipsis points:

> Eagleton writes, "What Eliot was in fact assaulting was the whole ideology of middle-class liberalism. . . . Eliot's own solution is an extreme right-wing authoritarianism: men and women must sacrifice their petty 'personalities' and opinions to an impersonal order" (39).

Whatever you add (using square brackets) or omit (using ellipses), the sentence must read grammatically. And, of course, your additions and omissions must not distort the author's meaning.

Attach Quotations with Punctuation.   You also can attach a quotation to a sentence by using punctuation. For example, this passage attaches the run-in quotation with a colon:

> For these researchers, there needs to be recognition of differences in a way that will include and accept all students. Specifically, they ask: "Within multiracial settings,

when are young people invited to discuss, voice, critique, and re-view the very notions of race that feel so fixed, so hierarchical, so damaging, and so accepted in the broader culture?" (p. 132).

In conclusion, if you don't connect quotations to your argument, your readers may not understand why you've included them. You need to explain some significant point that each quotation reveals as you introduce or end it. This strategy helps readers know what to pay attention to in a quotation, particularly if the quotation is lengthy.

Steps to Integrating Quotations into Your Writing

1 **Take an active stance.** Your sources should contribute to your argument, not dictate its direction.

2 **Explain the quotations.** Explain what you quote so your readers understand how each quotation relates to your argument.

3 **Attach short quotations to your own sentences.** Integrate short quotations within the grammar of your own sentences, or attach them with appropriate punctuation.

A Practice Sequence: Integrating Quotations

1 Using several of the sources you are working with in developing your paper, try integrating quotations into your essay. Be sure you are controlling your sources. Carefully read the paragraphs where you've used quotations. Will your readers clearly understand why the quotations are there — the points the quotations support? Do the sentences with quotations read smoothly? Are they grammatically correct?

2 Working in a small group, agree on a substantial paragraph or passage (from this book or some other source) to write about. Each member should read the passage and take a position on the ideas, and then draft a page that quotes the passage using both strategies for integrating these quotations. Compare what you've written, examining similarities and differences in the use of quotations.

CITING AND DOCUMENTING SOURCES

You must provide a brief citation in the text of your paper for every quotation or idea taken from another writer, and you must list complete information at the end of your paper for the sources you use. This information is essential for readers who want to read the source to understand a quotation or idea in its original context. How you cite sources in the body of your paper and document them at the end of your paper varies from discipline to discipline, so it is important to ask your instructor what documentation style he or she prefers.

Even within academic disciplines, documentation styles can vary. Specific academic journals within disciplines will sometimes have their own set of style guidelines. The important thing is to adhere faithfully to your chosen (or assigned) style throughout your paper, observing all the niceties of form prescribed by the style. You may have noticed small differences in the citation styles in the examples throughout this chapter. That's because the examples are taken from the work of a variety of writers, both professionals and students, who had to conform to the documentation requirements of their publication or of their teachers.

Here we briefly introduce two common documentation styles that may be useful in your college career: the Modern Language Association (MLA) for listing bibliographic information in the humanities, and the American Psychological Association (APA), in the social sciences. The information is basic, for use when you begin drafting your paper. In the final stages of writing, you should consult either the *MLA Handbook for Writers of Research Papers* (6th ed.) or the *Publication Manual of the American Psychological Association* (5th ed.). Although you'll need the manuals for complete style information, both the MLA (http://www.mla.org/style_faq) and the APA (http://www.apastyle.org/faqs.html) maintain Web sites for frequently asked questions. Again, before you start your research, check with your instructor to find out whether you should use either of these styles or if there's another style he or she prefers.

MLA and APA styles have many similarities — for example, both require short citations in the body of an essay linked to a list of sources at the end of the essay. But it is their differences, though subtle, that are crucial. To a great extent, these differences reflect the assumptions writers in the humanities and in the social sciences bring to working with sources. In particular, you should understand each style's treatment of the source's author, publication date, and page numbers in in-text citations, and verb use in referring to sources.

Author.   MLA style requires you give the author's full name on first mention in your paper; APA style uses last names throughout. The humanities emphasize "the human element" — the individual as creative force — so the MLA uses the complete name at first mention to imply the author's importance. Because the social sciences emphasize the primacy of data in studies of human activity, in APA style last names are deemed sufficient.

Publication Date.   In-text citations using MLA style leave out the date of publication. The assumption: that the insights of the past may be as useful as those of the present. By contrast, APA style gives the date of the study after the author's name, reflecting a belief in the progress of research, that recent findings may supersede earlier ones.

Page Numbers.   The MLA requires page numbers be included with paraphrases and summaries as well as quotations (the written text is so important, a reader may want to check the exact language of the original). By contrast, the APA requires attribution but not page numbers for paraphrases and summaries (it is the findings, not how they are described, that are most important).

Verb Use.   The MLA uses the present tense of verbs ("Writer X claims") to introduce cited material, assuming the cited text's timelessness, whether written last week or centuries ago. By contrast, the verbs introducing citations in APA style acknowledge the "pastness" of research ("Writer X claimed" or "Writer Y has claimed") on the assumption that new data may emerge to challenge older research.

Although it is useful to understand that different citation styles reflect different attitudes toward inquiry and research in different disciplines, for the purposes of your writing it is mainly important to know the style you have to follow in your paper, and to stick to it scrupulously. Whenever you consult a source — even if you don't end up using it in your paper — write down complete citation information so you can cite it fully and accurately if you need to. Table 7.2 shows the basic information needed to cite books, chapters in books, journal articles, and online sources. You also should note any other information that could be relevant — a translator's name,

TABLE 7.2   Basic Information Needed for Citing Sources

BOOKS	CHAPTERS IN BOOKS	JOURNAL ARTICLES	ONLINE SOURCES
Author(s) or editor(s)	Author(s)	Author(s)	Author(s)
Title and subtitle	Chapter title and subtitle	Article title and subtitle	Document title and subtitle
Edition information	Book editor(s)	Journal title	Print publication information, if any
Place of publication	Book title	Volume and series number	Site sponsor
Publisher	Edition information	Date of publication	Site title
Year of publication	Place of publication	Page numbers	Year of publication
	Publisher		Date accessed
	Year of publication		URL
	Page numbers		

for example, or a series title and editor. Ideally, you want to be able to cite a source fully without having to go back to it to get more information.

■ The Basics of MLA Style

In-Text Citations. In MLA style, you must provide a brief citation in the body of your essay (1) when you quote directly from a source, (2) when you paraphrase or summarize what someone else has written, and (3) even when you use an idea or concept that originated with someone else. In the excerpt below, the citation tells readers that the student writer's argument about the evolution of Ebonics is rooted in a well-established source of information. Because the writer does not mention the author in the paraphrase of her source in the text, she gives the author's name in the citation:

> The evolution of US Ebonics can be traced from the year 1557 to the present day. In times of great oppression, such as the beginning of the slave codes in 1661, the language of the black community was at its most "ebonified" levels; whereas, in times of racial progress, for example during the abolitionist movement, the language as a source of community identity was forsaken for greater assimilation (Smitherman 119).

The parenthetical citation refers to page 119 of Geneva Smitherman's book *Talkin and Testifyin: The Language of Black America* (1977). Smitherman is a recognized authority on Ebonics. Had the student mentioned Smitherman's name in her introduction to the paraphrase, she would not have had to repeat it in the citation. Notice that there is no punctuation within the parentheses and no *p.* before the page number. Also notice that the citation is considered part of the sentence in which it appears, so the period ending the sentence follows the closing parenthesis.

By contrast, in the example that follows, the student quotes directly from Richard Rodriguez's book *Hunger of Memory: The Education of Richard Rodriguez* (1982):

> Many minority cultures in today's society feel that it is more important to maintain cultural bonds than to extend themselves into the larger community. People who do not speak English may feel a similar sense of community and consequently lose some of the individuality and cultural ties that come with speaking their native or home language. This shared language within a home or community also adds to the unity of the community. Richard Rodriguez attests to this fact in his essay "Aria." He then goes on to say that "it is not healthy to distinguish public words from private sounds so easily" (183).

Because the student mentions Rodriguez in her text right before the quotation ("Richard Rodriguez attests"), she does not need to include his name in the citation; the page number is sufficient.

Works Cited.   At the end of your researched essay, and starting on a new page, you must provide a list of works cited, a list of all the sources you have used (leaving out sources you consulted but did not cite). Entries should be listed alphabetically by author's last name or by title if no author is identified. Figure 7.3 is a sample works cited page in MLA style that illustrates a few (very few) of the basic types of documentation.

Steps to Compiling an MLA List of Works Cited

1 Begin your list of works cited on a new page at the end of your paper.

2 Put your last name and page number in the upper-right corner.

3 Double-space throughout.

4 Center the heading ("Works Cited") on the page.

5 Arrange the list of sources alphabetically by author's last name or by title if no author is identified.

6 Begin the first line of each source flush left; second and subsequent lines should be indented 1/2 inch.

7 Invert the author's name, last name first. In the case of multiple authors, only the first author's name is inverted.

8 Underline the titles of books, journals, magazines, and newspapers. You can put them in italics if your instructor says to do so. Put the titles of book chapters and articles in quotation marks. Capitalize each word in all titles except for articles, short prepositions, and conjunctions.

9 For books, list the place of publication and the name of the publisher, and the year of publication. For chapters, list the editors of the book and the book title, and the publication information. For articles, list the journal title, volume and series numbers, and the date of publication.

10 List the relevant page numbers.

The steps outlined here for compiling a list of works cited apply to printed sources. MLA formats for citing online sources vary, but this is an example of the basic format:

Author. "Document Title." *Name of Site.* Date posted/revised. Site Sponsor.
    Date you accessed the site <URL>.

FIGURE 7.3   Sample List of Works Cited, MLA Format

Eck 10

Works Cited

Gutierrez, Kris. "'English for the Children': The New Literacy of the Old
World Order." Bilingual Research Journal, in press.

Online article,
no author
"History of Bilingual Education." Spring 1998. Rethinking Schools Online.
Retrieved on 8 Apr. 1998 <http://www.rethinkingschools.org/
archive/12_03/langhst.shtml>.

Article in a
scholarly
journal
Lanehart, Sonja L. "African American Vernacular English and Education."
Journal of English Linguistics 26 (1998): 122–37.

Article in a
magazine
Pompa, Delia. "Bilingual Success: Why Two-Language Education Is Critical
for Latinos." Hispanic 13 (1996): 96.

Rawls, John. Political Liberalism. New York: Columbia UP, 1993.

Essay in an
edited collec-
tion; second
source by
same writer
---. "Social Unity and Primary Goods." Utilitarianism and Beyond. Ed.
Amartya Sen and Bernard Williams. Cambridge, Eng.: Cambridge UP,
1982. 159–85.

Rodriguez, Richard. "Aria." Hunger of Memory: The Education of Richard
Rodriguez. New York: Bantam, 1982. 11–40.

Schrag, Peter. "Language Barrier." New Republic 9 Mar. 1998: 14–15.

A book
Smitherman, Geneva. Talkin and Testifyin: The Language of Black
America. Detroit: Wayne State UP, 1977.

Willis, Arlette. "Reading the World of School Literacy: Contextualizing the
Experience of a Young American Male." Harvard Educational Review.
65 (1996): 30–49.

Things to remember:

- Invert the author's name or the first author's name.

- Underline the name of the site. (Again, you can use italics with your
  instructor's okay.)

- MLA accepts both day-month-year and month-day-year formats for
  dates. Just be consistent.

- If the site sponsor — usually an institution or organization — isn't clear,
  check the copyright notice at the bottom of the Web page.

- Notice that there's no punctuation between the date you accessed the
  site and the angle-bracketed URL.

- When a URL runs more than one line, break the URL following a slash.
  And don't insert a hyphen to indicate the break.

In addition to online sources, you will likely use other nonprint sources in researching your papers. Our students, for example, regularly analyze films, recordings, television and radio programs, paintings, and photographs. For details on how to format these sources, consult the *MLA Handbook* or go to Purdue University's Online Writing Lab (OWL) site (http://owl.english.purdue.edu/owl/resource/557/01/).

■ The Basics of APA Style

In-Text Citations.   In APA style, in-text citations identify the author or authors of a source and the publication date. If the author or authors are mentioned in the text, only the publication date is needed:

> Feingold (1992) documented the fact that males perform much better than females do in math and science and other "masculine" areas.

Notice that the in-text citation does not include a page number. Because Feingold is only cited, not quoted, no page reference is necessary. If the source is quoted directly, a page number is added in parentheses following the quote:

> Feingold (1992) argued that "men scored significantly higher than women in situations designed to test aptitude in mathematics and hard sciences" (p. 92).

APA style uses the abbreviation *p.* or *pp.* before page numbers, which MLA style does not. If the author is not identified with a signal phrase, the name, year, and page number would be noted parenthetically after the quotation:

> One study found that "men scored significantly higher than women in situations designed to test aptitude in mathematics and hard sciences" (Feingold, 1992, p. 92).

Many studies in the social sciences have multiple authors. In a work with two authors, cite both authors every time:

> Dlugos and Friedlander (2000) wrote that "sustaining passionate commitment to work as a psychotherapist reflects passionate commitment in other areas of life" (p. 298).

Here, too, if you do not identify the authors in a signal phrase, include their names, the year the source was published, and the relevant page number parenthetically after the quotation — but use an ampersand (&) instead of the word *and* between the authors' names:

> Some believe that "sustaining passionate commitment to work as a psychotherapist reflects passionate commitment in other areas of life" (Dlugos & Friedlander, 2000, p. 298).

Use the same principles the first time you cite a work with three to five authors:

> Booth-Butterfield, Anderson, and Williams (2000) tested . . .
>
> (Booth-Butterfield, Anderson, & Williams, 2000, p. 5)

Thereafter, you can use the name of the first author followed by the abbreviation *et al.* (Latin for "and others") in roman type:

> Booth-Butterfield et al. (2000) tested . . .
>
> (Booth-Butterfield et al., 2000, p. 5)

For a work with six or more authors, use et al. from the first mention.

These are only some of the most basic examples of APA in-text citation. Consult the APA manual for other guidelines.

References. APA style, like MLA style, requires a separate list of sources at the end of a research paper. This list is called "References," not "Works Cited." The list of references starts on a new page at the end of your paper and lists sources alphabetically by author (or title if no author is identified). Figure 7.4 shows a sample list of references with sources cited in APA style.

Steps to Compiling an APA List of References

1 Begin your list of references on a new page at the end of your paper.

2 Put a shortened version of the paper's title (not your last name) and the page number in the upper-right corner.

3 Double-space throughout.

4 Center the heading ("References") on the page.

5 Arrange the list of sources alphabetically by author's last name or by title if no author is identified.

6 Begin the first line of each source flush left; second and subsequent lines should be indented ½ inch.

7 Invert all authors' names. If a source has more than one author, use an ampersand (not *and*) before the last name.

8 Insert the date in parentheses after the last author's name.

9 Italicize the titles of books, capitalizing only the first letter of the title and subtitle and proper nouns.

10 Follow the same capitalization for the titles of book chapters and articles. Do not use quotation marks around chapter and article titles.

11 Italicize the titles of journals, magazines, and newspapers, capitalizing the initial letters of all key words.

> **12** For books, list the place of publication and the name of the publisher. For chapters, list the book editor(s), the book title, the relevant page numbers, and the place of publication and the name of the publisher. For articles, list the journal title, the volume number, and the relevant pages.

FIGURE 7.4   Sample References, APA Format

Gender and Teaching 15

References

Campbell, R. J. (1969). Co-education: Attitudes and self-concepts of girls at three schools. *British Journal of Educational Psychology, 39,* 87.

Journal article, seven authors → Coleman, J., Campbell, E., Hobson, C., McPartland, J., Mood, A., Weinfeld, F., & York, R. (1966). *Equality of educational opportunity (The Coleman report).* Washington, DC: U.S. Government Printing Office.

Feingold, A. (1992, Spring). Sex differences in variability in intellectual abilities: A new look at an old controversy. *Review of Educational Research, 62,* 61–84.

Online source → Haig, P. (2003). K-12 single-sex education: What does the research say? Retrieved September 22, 2004, from http://www.ericdigests.org/2001-2/sex.html

Hallinan, M. T. (1994). Tracking: From theory to practice. *Sociology of Education, 67,* 79–84.

Hanson, S. L. (1994). Lost talent: Unrealized educational aspirations and expectations among U.S. youth. *Sociology of Education, 67,* 159–183.

Jovanovic, J., & King, S. S. (1998, Fall). Boys and girls in the performance-based science classroom: Who's doing the performing? *American Educational Research Journal, 35,* 477–496.

Lee, V. E., & Marks, H. M. (1990). Sustained effects of the single-sex secondary school experience on attitudes, behaviors, and values in college. *Journal of Educational Psychology, 82,* 578–592.

Mickelson, R. A. (1989). Why does Jane read and write so well? The anomaly of women's achievement. *Sociology of Education, 62,* 47–63.

Scholarly book → Rosenberg, M. (1965). *Society and the adolescent self-image.* Princeton, NJ: Princeton University Press.

Schneider, F. W., & Coutts, L. M. (1982). The high school environment: A comparison of coeducational and single-sex schools. *Journal of Educational Psychology, 74,* 898–906.

Essay in edited collection
Spade, J. Z. (2000). Gender education in the United States. In J. H. Ballantine & J. Z. Spade (Eds.). (2001). *Schools and society: A sociological approach to education* (pp. 270–278). Belmont, CA: Wadsworth/Thomson Learning.

Streitmatter, J. L. (1999). *For girls ONLY: Making a case for single-sex schooling.* Albany: State University of New York Press.

Microfilm source
Winslow, M. A. (1995). *Where the boys are: The educational aspirations and future expectations of working-class girls in an all-female high school.* Ann Arbor, MI: University Microfilms, Dissertation Services. Internet.

The *APA Manual* is your best resource for formatting online sources, but here is an example of a basic reference to an online source:

Author/Site Sponsor. (Date posted/revised). Document title. *Name of site.* Retrieved day-month-year, from URL

- If no author is identified, alphabetize the entry under the site sponsor's name.
- Capitalize an online document title like an article title, and don't enclose it in quotes.
- Use the same initial-capital-only style for the site name, but italicize it.
- Notice that there is no end punctuation after the URL.
- APA style asks you to break lengthy URLs after a slash or before a period, again being sure that your program doesn't insert a hyphen at the line break.

The *APA Manual* is also your best resource for formatting references to other nonprint sources. You should know that certain nonprint sources you are likely to rely on in your research in the social sciences — interviews and focus groups, for example — do not have to be included in your list of references. Instead you would cite the person you interviewed or the focus group you conducted in the text of your paper. For example:

(Long, J., interview, April 7, 2007)

■ ■ ■

Throughout this chapter we have emphasized two key points: that academic writing is researched — which means it is connected to a broader conversation — and that you should use sources strategically to develop your own thesis. The decisions you make about how to use the ideas of others matter: Will you paraphrase or summarize? Should you orchestrate a comparison of ideas in a synthesis? Should you use a direct quotation? Have you taken an active stance in using direct quotations? Have you analyzed the information in ways that clarify for readers why you are paraphrasing, summarizing, or quoting? Does the evidence you use support your thesis? Ultimately, sources should enhance and enrich the ideas you have developed through research, giving you the best chance of persuading your readers to listen to you, learn from you, and perhaps change their minds about an issue that is important to you.

8

From Ethos to Logos:
Appealing to Your Readers

W ho you believe your readers are influences how you see a particular
situation, define an issue, explain the ongoing conversation surrounding that issue, and formulate a question. You may need to read
widely to understand how different writers have dealt with the issue you
address. And you will need to anticipate how others might respond to your
argument — whether they will be sympathetic or antagonistic — and to
compose your essay so that readers will "listen" whether or not they agree
with you. To achieve these goals, you will no doubt use reason in the form
of evidence to sway readers. But you can also use other means of persuasion: That is, you can use your own character, by presenting yourself as
someone who is knowledgeable, fair, and just; and you can appeal to your
readers' emotions. Although you may believe that reason alone should provide the means for changing people's minds, people's emotions also color
the way they see the world.

   Your audience is more than your immediate reader, your instructor or
a peer. Your audience encompasses those you cite in writing about a particular issue and those you anticipate responding to your argument. This
is true no matter what you write about, from an interpretation of the novels of a particular author, or an analysis of the cultural work of horror
films, to the ethics of treating boys and girls differently in schools, or the
moral issues surrounding homelessness in America. In this chapter we discuss different ways of engaging your readers, centering on three kinds of
appeals: **ethos**, appeals from character; **pathos**, appeals to emotion; and
logos, appeals to reason. *Ethos, pathos,* and *logos* are terms derived from
ancient Greek writers, but they are still of great value today when considering how to persuade your audience. Readers will judge your argument

on whether or not you present an argument that is fair and just, one that creates a sense of goodwill. All three appeals rely on these qualities. You want your argument to convey that you are reasonable and value fairness, justice, and goodwill, that you trust that your readers are reasonable and value these qualities too; and that your argument makes reasonable use of evidence that appeals to your readers' sense of fairness, justice, and good-will. Your task as a writer is to decide the proper balance of these different appeals in your argument, based on your thesis, the circumstances, and your audience.

CONNECTING WITH READERS: A SAMPLE ARGUMENT

To consider how an author connects with his audience, read the excerpt below from James W. Loewen's book *Lies My Teacher Told Me: Everything Your American History Textbook Got Wrong*. As you read the excerpt, note Loewen's main points, and select key examples that illustrate his argument. As a class, test the claims he makes — To what extent do you believe that what Loewen argues is true? This may entail recalling your own experiences in high school history classes or locating one or more of the books that Loewen mentions.

ABOUT THE READING

In addition to *Lies My Teacher Told Me* (1995), James Loewen, who holds a PhD in sociology, has written several other books, including *Lies Across America: What Our Historic Sites Get Wrong* (1999) and *Sundown Towns: A Hidden Dimension of American Racism* (2005). As the titles of these books suggest, Loewen is a writer who questions the assumptions about history that many people take for granted. This is especially true of the excerpt below, from a chapter in which Loewen challenges a common American belief — that everyone has an equal chance in what he calls the "land of opportunity" — by arguing that we live in a class system that privileges some people and raises barriers for others. History textbook writers, he points out, are guilty of complicity in this class system because they leave a great deal of history out of their textbooks.

JAMES W. LOEWEN

The Land of Opportunity

High school students have eyes, ears, and television sets (all too   *1*
many have their own TV sets), so they know a lot about relative privilege in America. They measure their family's social position against

that of other families, and their community's position against other communities. Middle-class students, especially, know little about how the American class structure works, however, and nothing at all about how it has changed over time. These students do not leave high school merely ignorant of the workings of the class structure; they come out as terrible sociologists. "Why are people poor?" I have asked first-year college students. Or, if their own class position is one of relative privilege, "Why is your family well off?" The answers I've received, to characterize them charitably, are half-formed and naïve. The students blame the poor for not being successful. They have no understanding of the ways that opportunity is not equal in America and no notion that social structure pushes people around, influencing the ideas they hold and the lives they fashion.

High school history textbooks can take some of the credit for this 2
state of affairs. Some textbooks cover certain high points of labor history, such as the 1894 Pullman strike near Chicago that President Cleveland broke with federal troops, or the 1911 Triangle Shirtwaist fire that killed 146 women in New York City, but the most recent event mentioned in most books is the Taft-Hartley Act of fifty years ago. No book mentions the Hormel meat-packers' strike in the mid-1980s or the air traffic controllers' strike broken by President Reagan. Nor do textbooks describe any continuing issues facing labor, such as the growth of multinational corporations and their exporting of jobs overseas. With such omissions, textbook authors can construe labor history as something that happened long ago, like slavery, and that, like slavery, was corrected long ago. It logically follows that unions appear anachronistic. The idea that they might be necessary in order for workers to have a voice in the workplace goes unstated.

Textbooks' treatments of events in labor history are never anchored in 3
any analysis of social class. This amounts to delivering the footnotes instead of the lecture! Six of the dozen high school American history textbooks I examined contain no index listing at all for "social class," "social stratification," "class structure," "income distribution," "inequality," or any conceivably related topic. Not one book lists "upper class," "working class," or "lower class." Two of the textbooks list "middle class," but only to assure students that America is a middle-class country. "Except for slaves, most of the colonists were members of the 'middling ranks,'" says *Land of Promise*, and nails home the point that we are a middle-class country by asking students to "Describe three 'middle-class' values that united free Americans of all classes." Several of the textbooks note the explosion of middle-class suburbs after World War II. Talking about the middle class is hardly equivalent to discussing social stratification, however; in fact, as Gregory Mantsios has pointed out, "such references appear to be acceptable precisely because they mute class differences."

Stressing how middle-class we all are is particularly problematic 4
today, because the proportion of households earning between 75 percent and 125 percent of the median income has fallen steadily

since 1967. The Reagan-Bush administrations accelerated this shrinkage of the middle class, and most families who left its ranks fell rather than rose. This is the kind of historical trend one would think history books would take as appropriate subject matter, but only four of the twelve books in my sample provide any analysis of social stratification in the United States. Even these fragmentary analyses are set mostly in colonial America. *Land of Promise* lives up to its reassuring title by heading its discussion of social class "Social Mobility." "One great difference between colonial and European society was that the colonists had more social mobility," echoes *The American Tradition*. "In contrast with contemporary Europe, eighteenth-century America was a shining land of equality and opportunity — with the notorious exception of slavery," chimes in *The American Pageant*. Although *The Challenge of Freedom* identifies three social classes — upper, middle, and lower — among whites in colonial society, compared to Europe "there was greater *social mobility*."

Never mind that the most violent class conflicts in American   5
history — Bacon's Rebellion and Shays's Rebellion — took place in and just after colonial times. Textbooks still say that colonial society was relatively classless and marked by upward mobility. And things have gotten rosier since. "By 1815," *The Challenge of Freedom* assures us, two classes had withered away and "America was a country of middle class people and of middle class goals." This book returns repeatedly, at intervals of every fifty years or so, to the theme of how open opportunity is in America. "In the years after 1945, *social mobility* — movement from one social class to another — became more widespread in America," *Challenge* concludes. "This meant that people had a better chance to move upward in society." The stress on upward mobility is striking. There is almost nothing in any of these textbooks about class inequalities or barriers of any kind to social mobility. "What conditions made it possible for poor white immigrants to become richer in the colonies?" *Land of Promise* asks. "What conditions made/make it difficult?" goes unasked. Textbook authors thus present an America in which, as preachers were fond of saying in the nineteenth century, men start from "humble origins" and attain "the most elevated positions."

Social class is probably the single most important variable in society.   6
From womb to tomb, it correlates with almost all other social characteristics of people that we can measure. Affluent expectant mothers are more likely to get prenatal care, receive current medical advice, and enjoy general health, fitness, and nutrition. Many poor and working-class mothers-to-be first contact the medical profession in the last month, sometimes the last hours, of their pregnancies. Rich babies come out healthier and weighing more than poor babies. The infants go home to very different situations. Poor babies are more likely to have high levels of poisonous lead in their environments and their bodies. Rich babies get more time and verbal interaction with their parents and

higher quality day care when not with their parents. When they enter kindergarten, and through the twelve years that follow, rich children benefit from suburban schools that spend two to three times as much money per student as schools in inner cities or impoverished rural areas. Poor children are taught in classes that are often 50 percent larger than the classes of affluent children. Differences such as these help account for the higher school-dropout rate among poor children.

Even when poor children are fortunate enough to attend the same school as rich children, they encounter teachers who expect only children of affluent families to know the right answers. Social science research shows that teachers are often surprised and even distressed when poor children excel. Teachers and counselors believe they can predict who is "college material." Since many working-class children give off the wrong signals, even in first grade, they end up in the "general education" track in high school. "If you are the child of low-income parents, the chances are good that you will receive limited and often careless attention from adults in your high school," in the words of Theodore Sizer's best-selling study of American high schools, *Horace's Compromise*. "If you are the child of upper-middle-income parents, the chances are good that you will receive substantial and careful attention." Researcher Reba Page has provided vivid accounts of how high school American history courses use rote learning to turn off lower-class students. Thus schools have put into practice Woodrow Wilson's recommendation: "We want one class of persons to have a liberal education, and we want another class of persons, a very much larger class of necessity in every society, to forgo the privilege of a liberal education and fit themselves to perform specific difficult manual tasks." 7

As if this unequal home and school life were not enough, rich teenagers then enroll in the Princeton Review or other coaching sessions for the Scholastic Aptitude Test. Even without coaching, affluent children are advantaged because their background is similar to that of the test-makers, so they are comfortable with the vocabulary and subtle subcultural assumptions of the test. To no one's surprise, social class correlates strongly with SAT scores. 8

All these are among the reasons why social class predicts the rate of college attendance and the type of college chosen more effectively than does any other factor, including intellectual ability, however measured. After college, most affluent children get white-collar jobs, most working-class children get blue-collar jobs, and the class differences continue. As adults, rich people are more likely to have hired an attorney and to be a member of formal organizations that increase their civic power. Poor people are more likely to watch TV. Because affluent families can save some money while poor families must spend what they make, wealth differences are ten times larger than income differences. Therefore most poor and working-class families cannot 9 accumulate the down payment required to buy a house, which in turn shuts them out from our most important tax shelter, the write-off of home mortgage interest. Working-class parents cannot afford to live in elite subdivisions or hire high-quality day care, so the process of educational inequality replicates itself in the next generation. Finally, affluent Americans also have longer life expectancies than lower- and working-class people, the largest single cause of which is better access to health care. Echoing the results of Helen Keller's study of blindness, research has determined that poor health is not distributed randomly about the social structure but is concentrated in the lower class. Social Security then becomes a huge transfer system, using monies contributed by all Americans to pay benefits disproportionately to longer-lived affluent Americans.

Ultimately, social class determines how people think about social   *10*
class. When asked if poverty in America is the fault of the poor or the fault of the system, 57 percent of business leaders blamed the poor; just 9 percent blamed the system. Labor leaders showed sharply reversed choices: only 15 percent said the poor were at fault while 56 percent blamed the system. (Some replied "don't know" or chose a middle position.) The largest single difference between our two main political parties lies in how their members think about social class: 55 percent of Republicans blamed the poor for their poverty, while only 13 percent blamed the system for it; 68 percent of Democrats, on the other hand, blamed the system, while only 5 percent blamed the poor.

Few of these statements are news, I know, which is why I have not   *11*
documented most of them, but the majority of high school students do not know or understand these ideas. Moreover, the processes have changed over time, for the class structure in America today is not the same as it was in 1890, let alone in colonial America. Yet in *Land of Promise,* for example, social class goes unmentioned after 1670.

For Analysis and Discussion

1. List what you think are Loewen's main points. What appeals does he seem to draw on most when he makes those points: appeals based on his own character (ethos), on the emotions of his reader (pathos), or on the reasonableness of his evidence (logos)? Are the appeals obvious or difficult to tease out? Does he combine them? Discuss your answers with your classmates.

2. Identify what you think is the main claim of Loewen's argument, and choose key examples to support your answer. Compare your chosen claim and examples to those chosen by your classmates. Do they differ significantly? Can you agree on Loewen's gist and his key examples?

3. As a class, test the claims Loewen makes by thinking about your own experiences in high school history classes. Do you remember finding out that

something you were taught from an American history textbook was not true? Did you discover on your own what you considered to be misrepresentations in or important omissions from your textbook? If so, did these misrepresentations or omissions tend to support or contradict the claims about history textbooks that Loewen makes?

APPEALING TO ETHOS

Although we like to believe that our decisions and beliefs are based on reason and logic, in fact often they are based on what amounts to character judgments. That is, if a person you trust makes a reasonable argument for one choice, and a person you distrust makes a reasonable argument for the opposite choice, you are more likely to be swayed by the argument of the person you trust. Similarly, the audience for your argument will be more disposed to agree with you if its members believe you are a fair, just person who is knowledgeable and has good judgment. Even the most well developed argument will fall short if you do not leave this kind of impression on your readers. Thus it is not surprising that ethos may be the most important component of your argument.

There are three strategies for evoking a sense of ethos: (1) Establish that you have good judgment; (2) convey to readers that you are knowledgeable; and (3) show that you understand the complexity of the issue. These strategies are interrelated: A writer who demonstrates good judgment is more often than not someone who is both knowledgeable about an issue and who acknowledges the complexity of it by weighing the strengths *and* weaknesses of different arguments. However, keep in mind that these characteristics do not exist apart from what readers think and believe.

■ Establish That You Have Good Judgment

Most readers of academic writing expect writers to demonstrate good judgment by identifying a problem that readers agree is worth addressing. In turn, good judgment gives writers credibility. Loewen crafts his introduction to capture the attention of educators as well as concerned citizens when he claims that students leave high school unaware of class structure and as a consequence "have no understanding of the ways that opportunity is not equal in America and no notion that social structure pushes people around, influencing the ideas they hold and the lives they may fashion" (para. 1). Loewen does not blame students, or even instructors, for this lack of awareness. Instead, he writes, "textbooks can take some of the credit for this state of affairs" (para. 2) because, among other shortcomings, they leave out important events in "labor history" and relegate issues facing labor to the past. Whether or not an educator — or a general reader for that matter — will ultimately agree with Loewen's case is, at this point, up for grabs, but certainly the possibility that high schools in general, and history textbooks in particular, are failing students by leaving them vulnerable to class-based manipulation would be recognized as a problem by readers who believe America should be a society that offers equal opportunity for all. At this point, Loewen's readers are likely to agree that the problem of omission he identifies may be significant if its consequences are as serious as he believes them to be.

One could also argue that writers establish good judgment by conveying to readers that that they are fair-minded, just, and have the best interests of readers in mind. Loewen is particularly concerned that students understand the persistence of poverty and inequality in the United States and the historical circumstances of the poor, which they cannot do unless textbook writers take a more inclusive approach to addressing labor history, especially "the growth of multinational corporations and their exporting of jobs overseas" (para. 2). It's not fair to deny this important information to students, and it's not fair to the poor to leave them out of official histories of the United States. Loewen further demonstrates that he is fair and just when he calls attention in paragraph 6 to the inequality between rich and poor children in schools, a problem that persists despite our forebears' belief that class would not determine the fate of citizens of the United States.

■ Convey to Readers That You Are Knowledgeable

Being thoughtful about a subject goes hand in hand with being knowledgeable about the subject. Loewen demonstrates his knowledge of class issues and their absence from textbooks in a number of ways (not the least of which is his awareness that a problem exists — many people, including educators, may not be aware of this problem). In paragraph 3, Loewen makes a bold claim: "Textbooks' treatments of events in labor history are never anchored in any analysis of social class." As readers, we cannot help wondering: How does the author know this? How will he support this claim? Loewen anticipates these questions by demonstrating that he has studied the subject through a systematic examination of American history textbooks. He observes that six of the twelve textbooks he examined "contain no index listing at all for 'social class,' 'social stratification,' 'class structure,' 'income distribution,' 'inequality,' or any conceivably related topic; and that "not one book lists 'upper class,' 'working class,' or 'lower class.'" Loewen also demonstrates his grasp of class issues in American history, from — the "violent class conflicts" that "took place in and just after colonial times" (para. 5), which contradict textbook writers' assertions that class conflicts did not exist during this period, to the more recent conflicts in the 1980s and early 1990s (paras. 2 and 4). Moreover, Loewen backs up his own study of textbooks with references to a number of studies from the social sciences to illustrate that "social class is probably the single most important variable in society" (para. 6). Witness the statistics and findings he cites in paragraphs 6 through 10. The breadth of Loewen's historical knowledge and the range of his reading should convince readers that he is knowledgeable, and his trenchant analysis contributes to the authority he brings to the issue and to his credibility.

■ Show That You Understand the Complexity of a Given Issue

Recognizing the complexity of an issue helps readers see the extent to which authors know that any issue can be understood in a number of different ways. Academic readers value writing that displays inquisitiveness and curiosity. Loewen acknowledges that most of the history he recounts is "not news" (para. 11) to his educated readers, who by implication "know" and "understand" his references to historical events and trends. What may be news to his readers, he explains, is the extent to which class structure in the United States has changed over time. With the steady erosion of middle-class households since 1967, "class inequalities" and "barriers . . . to social mobility" (para. 5) are limiting more and more Americans' access to even the most fundamental of opportunities in a democratic society — health care and education.

Still, even though Loewen has introduced new thinking about the nature of class in the United States and has demonstrated a provocative play of mind by examining an overlooked body of data (high school history textbooks) that may influence the way class is perceived in America, there are still levels of complexity he hasn't addressed explicitly. Most important, perhaps, is the question of why history textbooks continue to ignore issues of class when there is so much research that indicates its importance in shaping the events history textbooks purport to explain.

***

Steps to Appealing to Ethos

1 **Establish that you have good judgment.** Identify an issue your readers will agree is worth addressing, and demonstrate that you are fair-minded and have the best interests of your readers in mind when you address it.

2 **Convey to readers that you are knowledgeable.** Support your claims with credible evidence that shows you have read widely, thought about, and understand the issue.

3 **Show that you understand the complexity of the issue.** Demonstrate that you understand the variety of viewpoints your readers may bring — or may not be able to bring — to the issue.

***

APPEALING TO PATHOS

An appeal to pathos recognizes that people are moved to action by their emotions as well as by reasonable arguments. In fact, pathos is a vital part of argument that can predispose readers one way or another. Do you want to arouse readers' sympathy? Anger? Passion? You can do that by knowing what readers value. Appeals to pathos are typically indirect. You can appeal to pathos by using examples or illustrations that you believe will arouse the appropriate emotions, and by presenting them using an appropriate tone.

To acknowledge that writers play on readers' emotions is not to endorse manipulative writing. Rather, it is to acknowledge that effective writers use all available means of persuasion to move readers to agree with them. After all, if your thoughtful reading and careful research have led you to believe that you must weigh in with a useful insight on an important issue, it stands to reason that you would want your argument to convince your readers to believe as strongly in what you assert as you do. For example, if you genuinely believe that the conditions some families are living in are abysmal and unfair, you want your readers to believe it too. And an effective way to persuade them to believe as you do, in addition to convincing them of the reasonableness of your argument and of your own good character and judgment, is to establish a kind of emotional common ground in your writing — the common ground of pathos.

■ Show That You Know What Your Readers Value

Let's consider some of the ways James Loewen signals that he knows what his readers value. In the first place, Loewen assumes that readers feel the same way he does: Educated people should know that the United States has a class structure despite the democratic principles that the nation was founded on. He also expects readers to identify with his unwillingness to accept the injustice that results from that class structure. He believes that women living in poverty should have access to appropriate health care, that children living in poverty should have a chance to attend college, and that certain classes of people should not be written off to "perform specific difficult manual tasks" (para. 7). Time and again, Loewen cites examples that reveal that the poor are discriminated against by the class structure in the United States not for lack of ability, lack of desire, lack of ambition, or lack of morality, but for no better reason than lack of money — and that such discrimination has been going on for a long time. He expects his readers also will find such discrimination an unacceptable affront to their values of fair play and democracy, and that they will experience the same sense of outrage that he does.

■ Use Illustrations and Examples
That Appeal to Readers' Emotions

You can appeal to readers' emotions indirectly through the illustrations and examples you use to support your argument. In paragraph 2, Loewen contends that textbook writers share responsibility for high school students' not knowing about the continued relevance of class issues in American life.

Loewen's readers — parents, educators, historians — may very well be angered by the omissions he points out. Certainly he would expect them to be angry when they read about the effects of economic class on the health care expectant mothers and then their children receive (para. 6) and on their children's access to quality education (paras. 6–8). In citing the fact that social class "correlates strongly with SAT scores" (para. 8) and so "predicts the rate of collage attendance and the type of college chosen" (para. 9), Loewen forces his readers to acknowledge that the educational playing field is far from level. Finally, he calls attention to the fact that accumulated wealth accounts for deep class divisions in our society — that their inability to save prevents the poor from hiring legal counsel, purchasing a home, or taking advantage of tax shelters. The result, Loewen observes, is that "educational inequality replicates itself in the next generation" (para. 9). Together, these examples strengthen both Loewen's argument and what he hopes will be readers' outrage that history textbooks do not address class issues. Without that information, Americans cannot fully understand or act to change the existing class structure.

■ Consider How Your Tone May Affect Your Audience

The **tone** of your writing is your use of language that communicates your attitude toward yourself, your material, and your readers. Of course, your tone is important in everything you write, but it is particularly crucial when you are appealing to pathos. When you are appealing to your readers' emotions, it is tempting to use loaded, exaggerated, and even intemperate language to convey how you feel (and hope your readers will feel) about an issue. Consider these sentences. "The Republican Party has devised the most ignominious means of filling the pockets of corporations." "These wretched children suffer heartrending agonies that can barely be imagined, much less described." "The ethereal beauty of the Brandenburg concertos thrill one to the deepest core of one's being." All of these sentences express strong and probably sincere beliefs and emotions, but some readers might find them overwrought and coercive, and question the writer's reasonableness.

Some writers rely on irony or sarcasm to set the tone of their work. **Irony** is the use of language to say one thing while meaning quite another. **Sarcasm** is the use of heavy-handed irony to ridicule or attack someone or something. Although irony and sarcasm can make for vivid and entertaining writing, they also can backfire and end up alienating readers. The sentence "Liberals will be pleased to hear that the new budget will be making liberal use of their hard-earned dollars" may entertain some readers with its irony and wordplay, but others may assume that the writer's attitude toward liberals is likely to result in an unfairly slanted argument. And the sentence "In my opinion, there's no reason why Christians and Muslims shouldn't rejoice together over the common ground of their both being deluded about the existence of a God" may please some readers, but it risks alienating those who are uncomfortable with breezy comments about religious beliefs. Again, think of your readers and what they value, and weigh the benefits of a clever sentence against its potential to detract from your argument or offend your audience.

You often find colorful wording and irony in op-ed and opinion pieces, where a writer may not have the space to build a compelling argument using evidence and has to resort to shortcuts to readers' emotions. However, in academic writing, where the careful accumulation and presentation of evidence and telling examples are highly valued, the frequent use of loaded language, exaggeration, and sarcasm is looked on with distrust.

Consider Loewen's excerpt. Although his outrage comes through clearly, he never resorts to hectoring. For example, in paragraph 1, he writes that students are "ignorant of the workings of the class structure" and that their opinions are "half-formed and naïve." But he does not imply that students are ignoramuses or that their opinions are foolish. What they lack, he contends, is understanding. They need to be taught something about class structure that they are not now being taught. And paragraph 1 is about as close to name-calling as Loewen comes. Even textbook writers, who are the target of his anger, are not vilified. True, Loewen occasionally makes use of irony, for example in paragraph 5, where he points out inconsistencies and omissions in textbooks: "Never mind that the most violent class conflicts in American history — Bacon's Rebellion and Shays's Rebellion — took place in and just after colonial times. Textbooks still say that colonial society was relatively classless and marked by upward mobility. And things have gotten rosier since." But he doesn't resort to ridicule. Instead, he relies on examples and illustrations to connect with his readers' sense of values and appeal to their emotions.

Steps to Appealing to Pathos

1. **Show that you know what your readers value.** Start from your own values and imagine what assumptions and principles would appeal to your readers. What common ground can you imagine between your values and theirs? How will it need to be adjusted for different kinds of readers?

2. **Use illustrations and examples that appeal to readers' emotions.** Again, start from your own emotional position. What examples and illustrations resonate most with you? How can you present them to have the most emotional impact on your readers? How would you adjust them for different kinds of readers?

3. **Consider how your tone may affect your audience.** Be wary of using loaded, exaggerated, and intemperate language that may put off your readers; and be careful in your use of irony and sarcasm.

A Practice Sequence: Appealing to Ethos and Pathos

Discuss the language and strategies the writers use in the passages below to connect with their audience, in particular their appeals to both ethos and pathos. As you consider each excerpt, discuss who you think the implied audience is and whether you think the strategies the writers use to connect with their readers are effective or not.

1 Almost a half century after the U.S. Supreme Court concluded that Southern school segregation was unconstitutional and "inherently unequal," new statistics from the 1998–99 school year show that segregation continued to intensify throughout the 1990s, a period in which there were three major Supreme Court decisions authorizing a return to segregated neighborhood schools and limiting the reach and duration of desegregation orders. For African American students, this trend is particularly apparent in the South, where most blacks live and where the 2000 Census shows a continuing return from the North. From 1988 to 1998, most of the progress of the previous two decades in increasing integration in the region was lost. The South is still much more integrated than it was before the civil rights revolution, but it is moving backward at an accelerating rate.

> —GARY ORFIELD, "Schools More Separate:
> Consequences of a Decade of Resegregation"
> (http://www.civilrightsproject.ucla.edu/research/deseg/
> Schools_More_Separate.pdf)

2 No issue has been more saturated with dishonesty than the issue of racial quotas and preferences, which is now being examined by the Supreme Court of the United States. Many defenders of affirmative action are not even honest enough to admit that they are talking about quotas and preferences, even though everyone knows that that is what affirmative action amounts to in practice.

Despite all the gushing about the mystical benefits of "diversity" in higher education, a recent study by respected academic scholars found that "college diversity programs fail to raise standards" and that "a majority of faculty members and administrators recognize this when speaking anonymously."

This study by Stanley Rothman, Seymour Martin Lipset, and Neil Nevitte found that "of those who think that preferences have some impact on academic standards those believing it negative exceed those believing it positive by 15 to 1."

Poll after poll over the years has shown that most faculty members and most students are opposed to double standards in college admissions. Yet professors who will come out publicly and say what they say privately in these polls are as rare as hens' teeth.

Such two-faced talk is pervasive in academia and elsewhere. A few years ago, in Berkeley, there was a big fight over whether a faculty vote on affirmative action would be by secret ballot or open vote. Both sides knew that the result of a secret ballot would be the direct opposite of the result in a public vote at a faculty meeting.

—Thomas Sowell, "The Grand Fraud:
Affirmative Action for Blacks"
(http://www.capmag.com/article.asp?ID=2637)

3 When the judgment day comes for every high school student — that day when a final transcript is issued and sent to the finest institutions, with every sin of class selection written as with a burning chisel on stone — on that day a great cry will go up throughout the land, and there will be weeping, wailing, gnashing of teeth, and considerable grumbling against guidance counselors, and the cry of a certain senior might be, "WHY did no one tell me that Introduction to Social Poker wasn't a solid academic class?" At another, perhaps less wealthy school, a frustrated and under-nurtured sculptress will wonder, "Why can't I read, and why don't I care?" The reason for both of these oversights, as they may eventually discover, is that the idea of the elective course has been seriously mauled, mistreated, and abused under the current middle-class high school system. A significant amount of the blame for producing students who are stunted, both cognitively and morally, can be traced back to this pervasive fact. Elective courses, as shoddily planned and poorly funded as they may be, constitute the only formation that many students get in their own special types of intelligences. Following the model of Howard Gardner, these may be spatial, musical, or something else. A lack of stimulation to a student's own intelligence directly causes a lack of identification with the intelligence of others. Instead of becoming moderately interested in a subject by noticing the pleasure other people receive from it, the student will be bitter, jealous, and without empathy. These are the common ingredients in many types of tragedy, violent or benign. Schools must take responsibility for speaking in some way to each of the general types of intelligences. Failure to do so will result in students who lack skills, and also the inspiration to comfort, admire, emulate, and aid their fellow humans.

"All tasks that really call upon the power of attention are interesting for the same reason and to an almost equal degree," wrote Simone Weil in her *Reflections on Love and Faith,* her editor having defined attention as "a suspension of one's own self as a center of the world and making oneself available to the reality of another being." In Parker Palmer's *The Courage to Teach,* modern scientific theorist David Bohm describes "a holistic underlying implicate order whose information unfolds into the explicate order of particular fields." Rilke's euphemism for this "holistic . . . implicate order," which Palmer borrows, is "the grace of great things." Weil's term would be "God." However, both agree that eventual perception of this singular grace, or God, is accessible through education of a specific sort, and for both it is doubtless the most necessary experience of a lifetime. Realizing that this contention is raining down from different theorists, and keeping in mind that the most necessary experience of a lifetime should not be wholly irrelevant to the school system, educators should therefore reach the conclusion that this is a matter worth looking into. I assert that the most fruitful and practical results of their attention will be a wider range of electives coupled with a new acknowledgment and handling of them, one that treats each one seriously.

—ERIN MEYERS,
"The Educational Smorgasbord as Saving Grace"

APPEALING TO LOGOS: USING REASON AND EVIDENCE TO FIT THE SITUATION

To make an argument persuasive, you need to be in dialogue with your readers, using your own character (ethos) to demonstrate that you are a reasonable, credible, fair person and appealing to your readers' emotions (pathos), particularly their sense of right and wrong. Each type of appeal goes hand in hand with an appeal to logos, using converging pieces of evidence — statistics, facts, observations — to advance your claim. Remember that the type of evidence you use is determined by the issue, problem, situation, and readers' expectations. As an author, you should try to anticipate and address readers' beliefs and values. Ethos and pathos are concerned with the content of your argument; logos addresses both form and content.

An argument begins with one or more premises and ends with a conclusion. A **premise** is an assumption that you expect your readers to agree with, a statement that is either true or false — for example, "Alaska is cold in the winter" — that is offered in support of a claim. That claim is the **conclusion** you want your readers to draw from your premises. The conclusion is also a sentence that is either true or false. For instance, Loewen's major premise is that class is a key factor in Americans' access to health care, education, and wealth. Loewen also offers a second, more specific premise: that textbook writers provide little discussion of the ways class matters. Loewen crafts his argument to help readers draw the following conclusion: "We live in a class system that runs counter to the democratic principles that underlie the founding of the United States, and history textbooks must tell this story. Without this knowledge, citizens will be uninformed." Whether or not readers accept this as true depends on how Loewen moves from his initial premises to reach his conclusion — that is, whether or not we draw the same kinds of inferences, or reasoned judgments, that he does. He must do so in a way that meets readers' expectations of what constitutes relevant and persuasive evidence and guides them one step at a time toward his conclusion.

There are two main forms of argument: deductive and inductive. A **deductive argument** is an argument in which the premises support (or appear to support) the conclusion. If you join two premises to produce a conclusion that is taken to be true, you are stating a **syllogism.** This is the classic example of deductive reasoning through a syllogism:

1. All men are mortal. (First premise)
2. Socrates is a man. (Second premise)
3. Therefore, Socrates is mortal. (Conclusion)

In a deductive argument, it is impossible for both premises to be true and the conclusion to be false. That is, the truth of the premises means that the conclusion must also be true.

By contrast, an **inductive argument** relies on evidence and observation to reach a conclusion. Although readers may accept a writer's premises as true, it is possible for them to reject the writer's conclusion. Let's consider this for a moment in the context of Loewen's argument. Loewen introduces the premise that class matters, then offers the more specific premise that textbook writers leave class issues out of their narratives of American history, and finally draws the conclusion that citizens need to be informed of this body of knowledge in order to create change:

1. Although class is a key factor in Americans' access to health care, education, and wealth, students know very little about the social structure in the United States.
2. Textbook writers do not address the issue of class in their textbooks, an issue that people need to know about.
3. Therefore, if people had this knowledge, they would understand that poverty cannot be blamed on the poor.

Notice that Loewen's premises are not necessarily true. For example, readers could challenge the premise that "textbook writers do not address issues of class in their textbooks." After all, Loewen examined just twelve textbooks. What if he had examined a different set of textbooks? Would he have drawn the same conclusion? And even if Loewen's evidence convinces us that the two premises are true, we do not have to accept that the conclusion is true.

The conclusion in an inductive argument is never definitive. That is the nature of any argument that deals with human emotions and actions. Moreover, we have seen throughout history that people tend to disagree much more on the terms of an argument than on its form. Do we agree that Israel's leaders practice apartheid? (What do we mean by *apartheid* in this case?) Do we agree with the need to grant women reproductive rights? (When does life begin?) Do we agree that all people should be treated equally? (Would equality mean equal access to resources or to outcomes?)

Deductive arguments are conclusive. In a deductive argument, the premises are universal truths — laws of nature, if you will — and the conclusion must follow from those premises. That is, a^2 plus b^2 always equals c^2, and humans are always mortal. By contrast, an inductive argument is never conclusive. The premises may or may not be true; and even if they are true, the conclusion may be false. We might accept that class matters and that high school history textbooks don't address the issue of class structure in the United States; but we still would not know that students who have studied social stratification in America will necessarily understand the nature of poverty. It may be that social class is only one reason for poverty; or it may be that textbooks are only one source of information about social stratification in the United States, that textbook omissions are simply not as serious as Loewen claims. That the premises of an argument are true only establishes that the conclusion is probably true and, perhaps, only for some readers.

Inductive argument is the basis of academic writing; it is also the basis of any appeal to logos. The process of constructing an inductive argument involves three steps:

1. State the premises of your argument.

2. Use credible evidence to show readers that your argument has merit.

3. Demonstrate that the conclusion follows from the premises.

In following these three steps, you will want to determine the truth of your premises, help readers understand whether or not the inferences you draw are justified, and use word signals to help readers fully grasp the connections between your premises and conclusion.

▪ State the Premises of Your Argument

Stating a premise establishes what you have found to be true and what you want to persuade readers to accept as truth as well. Let's return to Loewen, who asserts his premise at the very outset of the excerpt: "Middle-class students . . . know little about how the American class structure works . . . and nothing at all about how it has changed over time." Loewen elaborates on this initial premise a few sentences later, arguing that students "have no understanding of the ways that opportunity is not equal in America and no notion that the social structure pushes people around, influencing the ideas they hold and the lives they fashion." Implicit here is the point that class matters. Loewen makes this point explicit several paragraphs on, where he states that "social class is probably the single most important variable in society" (para. 6). He states his second, more specific premise in paragraph 2: "High school history textbooks can take some of the credit for this state of affairs." The burden of demonstrating that these premises are true is on Loewen. If readers find that either of the premises is not true, it will be difficult, if not impossible, for them to accept his conclusion that with more knowledge, people will understand that poverty is not the fault of the poor (para. 10).

▪ Use Credible Evidence

The validity of your argument depends on whether or not the inferences you draw are justified, and whether or not you can expect a reasonable person to draw the same conclusion from those premises. Loewen has to demonstrate throughout (1) that students do not have much, if any, knowledge about the class structure that exists in the United States and (2) that textbook writers are in large part to blame for this lack of knowledge. He also must help readers understand how this lack of knowledge contributes to (3) his conclusion that greater knowledge would lead Americans to understand that poor people are not responsible for poverty. He can help readers with the order in which he states his premises and by choosing the type and amount of evidence that will enable readers to draw the inferences that he does.

Interestingly, Loewen seems to assume that one group of readers — educators — will accept his first premise as true. He does not elaborate on what students know or do not know. Instead, he moves right to his second premise, which involves first acknowledging what high school history textbooks typically cover, then identifying what he believes are the important events that textbook writers exclude, and ultimately asserting that "treatments of events in labor history are never anchored in any analysis of social class" (para. 3). He supports this point with his own study of twelve textbooks (paras. 3–5) before returning to his premise that "social class is probably the single most important variable in society" (para. 6). What follows is a series of observations about the rich and references to researchers' findings on inequality (paras. 7–9). Finally, he asserts that "social class determines how people think about social class" (para. 10), implying that fuller knowledge would lead business leaders and conservative voters to think differently about the source of poverty. The question to explore is whether or not Loewen supports this conclusion.

▪ Demonstrate That the Conclusion Follows from the Premises

Authors signal their conclusion with words like *consequently, finally, in sum, in the end, subsequently, therefore, thus, ultimately,* and *as a result.* Here is how this looks in the structure of Loewen's argument:

1. Although class is a key factor in Americans' access to health care, education, and wealth, students know very little about the social structure in the United States.

2. Textbook writers do not address the issue of class in their textbooks, an issue that people need to know about.

3. Ultimately, if people had this knowledge, they would understand poverty cannot be blamed on the poor.

We've reprinted much of paragraph 9 of Loewen's excerpt below. Notice how Loewen pulls together what he has been discussing. He again underscores the importance of class and achievement ("All these are among the reasons."). And he points out that access to certain types of colleges puts people in a position to accumulate and sustain wealth. Of course, this is not true of the poor "because affluent families can save some money while poor families must spend what they make." This causal relationship ("Because") heightens readers' awareness of the class structure that exists in the United States.

> All these are among the reasons why social class predicts the rate of college attendance and the type of college chosen more effectively than does any other factor, including intellectual ability, however measured. After college, most affluent children get white-collar jobs, most working-class children get blue-collar jobs, and the class differences continue. As adults, rich people are more likely to have hired an attorney and to be a member of formal organizations that increase their civic power. Poor people are more likely to watch TV. Because affluent families can save some money while poor families must spend what they make, wealth differences are ten times larger than income differences. Therefore most poor and working-class families cannot accumulate the down payment required to buy a house, which in turn shuts them out from our most important tax shelter, the write-off of home mortgage interest. Working-class parents cannot afford to live in elite subdivisions or hire high-quality day care, so the process of educational inequality replicates itself in the next generation. Finally, affluent Americans also have longer life expectancies than lower- and working-class people, the largest single cause of which is better access to health care.

Once Loewen establishes this causal relationship, he concludes ("Therefore," "Finally") with the argument that poverty persists from one generation to the next.

In paragraph 10, Loewen uses the transition word *ultimately* to make the point that social class matters, so much so that it limits the ways in which people see the world, that it even "determines how people think about social class." (We discuss how to write conclusions in Chapter 9.)

Steps to Appealing to Logos

1 **State the premises of your argument.** Establish what you have found to be true and what you want readers to accept as well.

2 **Use credible evidence.** Lead your readers from one premise to the next, making sure your evidence is sufficient and convincing and your inferences are logical and correct.

3 **Demonstrate that the conclusion follows from the premises.** In particular, use the right words to signal to your readers how the evidence and inferences lead to your conclusion.

RECOGNIZING LOGICAL FALLACIES

We turn now to **logical fallacies**, flaws in the chain of reasoning that lead to a conclusion that does not necessarily follow from the premises, or evidence. Logical fallacies are common in inductive arguments for two reasons: Inductive arguments rely on reasoning about probability, not certainty; and they derive from human beliefs and values, not facts or laws of nature.

Here we list fifteen logical fallacies. In examining them, think about how to guard against the sometimes-faulty logic behind statements you might hear from politicians, advertisers, and the like. That should help you examine the premises on which you base your own assumptions and the logic you use to help readers reach the same conclusions you do.

1. *Erroneous Appeal to Authority.* An authority is someone with expertise in a given subject. An *erroneous authority* is an author who claims to be an authority but is not, or someone an author cites as an authority who is not. In this type of fallacy, the claim might be true, but the fact that an unqualified person is making the claim means there is no reason for readers to accept the claim as true. Because the issue here is the legitimacy of authority, your concern should be to prove to yourself and your readers that you or the people you are citing have expertise in the subject. An awareness of this type of fallacy has become increasingly important as celebrities offer support for candidates running for office or act as spokespeople for curbing global warming or some other cause. The candidate may be the best person for the office, and there may be very good reasons to attack global warming; but we need to question the legitimacy of a nonexpert endorsement.

2. *Ad Hominem.* An ad hominem argument focuses on the person making a claim instead of on the claim itself. (*Ad hominem* is Latin for "to the person.") In most cases, an ad hominem argument does not have a bearing on the truth or the quality of a claim. Keep in mind that it is always important to address the claim or the reasoning behind it, rather than the person making the claim. "Of course Senator Wiley supports oil drilling in Alaska — he's in the pocket of the oil companies!" is an example of an ad hominem argument. Senator Wiley may have good reasons for supporting oil drilling in Alaska that have nothing to do with his alleged attachment to the oil industry. However, if an individual's character is relevant to the argument, then an ad hominem argument can be valid. If Senator Wiley has been found guilty of accepting bribes from an oil company, it makes sense to question both his credibility and his claims.

3. *Shifting the Issue.* This type of fallacy occurs when an author draws attention away from the issue instead of offering evidence that will enable people to draw their own conclusions about the soundness of an argument. For example:

> Affirmative action proponents accuse me of opposing equal opportunity in the workforce. I think my positions on military expenditures, education, and public health speak for themselves.

The author of this statement does not provide a chain of reasoning that would enable readers to judge his or her stance on the issue of affirmative action.

4. *Either/Or Fallacy.* At times, an author will take two extreme positions to force readers to make a choice between two seemingly contradictory positions. For example:

> Either you support the war in Iraq, or you are against it.

Although the author has set up an either/or condition, in reality one position does not exclude the other. Many people support the troops in Iraq even though they do not support the reasons for starting the war.

5. *Sweeping Generalizations.* When an author attempts to draw a conclusion without providing sufficient evidence to support the conclusion or examining possible counterarguments, he or she may be making sweeping generalizations. For example:

> Despite the women's movement in the 1960s and 1970s, women still do not receive equal pay for equal work. Obviously, any attempt to change the status quo for women is doomed to failure.

As is the case with many fallacies, the author's position may be reasonable, but we cannot accept the argument at face value. Reading critically entails testing assumptions like this one — that any attempt to create change is doomed to failure because women do not receive equal pay for equal work. We could ask, for example, whether inequities persist in the public sector. And we could point to other areas where the women's movement has had measurable success. Title IX, for example, has reduced the dropout rate among teenage girls; it has also increased the rate at which women earn college and graduate degrees.

6. *Bandwagon.* This is a fairly common mode of argument in advertising when, for example, a commercial attempts to persuade us to buy a certain product because it's popular.

> Because Harvard, Stanford, and Berkeley have all added a multicultural component to their graduation requirements, other institutions should do so as well.

The growing popularity of an idea is not sufficient reason to accept that it is true.

7. *Begging the Question.* This fallacy entails advancing a circular argument that asks readers to accept a premise that is also the conclusion readers are expected to draw:

> We could improve the undergraduate experience with coed dorms because both men and women benefit from living with members of the opposite gender.

Here readers are being asked to accept that the conclusion is true despite the fact that the premises — men benefit from living with women, and women benefit from living with men — are essentially the same as the conclusion.

Without evidence that a shift in dorm policy could improve on the undergraduate experience, we cannot accept the conclusion as true. Indeed, the conclusion does not necessarily follow from the premise.

8. *False Analogy.* Authors (and others) often try to persuade us that something is true by using a comparison. This approach is not in and of itself a problem, as long as the comparison is reasonable. For example:

> It is ridiculous to have a Gay and Lesbian Program and a Department of African American Culture. We don't have a Straight Studies Program or a Department of Caucasian Culture.

Here the author is urging readers to rethink the need for two academic departments by saying that the school doesn't have two other departments. That, of course, is not a reason for or against the new departments. What's needed is an analysis that compares the costs (economic and otherwise) of starting up and operating the new departments versus the contributions (economic and otherwise) of the new departments.

9. *Technical Jargon.* If you've ever had a salesperson try to persuade you to purchase a television or stereo with capabilities you absolutely *must* have — even if you don't understand a word the salesperson was saying about alternating currents and circuit splicers — then you're familiar with this type of fallacy. We found this passage in one of our student's papers:

> You should use this drug because it has been clinically proven that it inhibits the reuptake of serotonin and enhances the dopamine levels of the body's neurotransmitters.

The student's argument may very well be true, but he hasn't presented any substantive evidence to demonstrate that the premises are true and that the conclusion follows from the premises.

10. *Confusing Cause and Effect.* It is challenging to establish that one factor causes another. For example, how can we know for certain that economic class predicts, or is a factor in, academic achievement? How do we know that a new president's policies are the cause of a country's economic well-being? Authors often assume cause and effect when two factors are simply associated with each other:

> The current recession came right after President Bush was elected.

This fallacy states a fact; but it does not prove that the president's election caused the recession.

11. *Appeal to Fear.* One type of logical fallacy makes an appeal to readers' irrational fears and prejudices, preventing them from dealing squarely with a given issue and often confusing cause and effect:

> We should use whatever means possible to avoid further attack.

The reasoning here is something like this: "If we are soft on defense, we will never end the threat of terrorism." But we need to consider whether there is indeed a threat, and, if so, whether the presence of a threat should lead to action, and, if so, whether that action should include "whatever means possible." (Think of companies that sell alarm systems by pointing to people's vulnerability to harm and property damage.)

12. *Fallacy of Division.* A fallacy of division suggests that what is true of the whole must also be true of its parts:

> Conservatives have always voted against raising the minimum wage, against stem cell research, and for defense spending. Therefore, we can assume that conservative Senator Harrison will vote this way.

The author is urging readers to accept the premise without providing evidence of how the senator has actually voted on the three issues.

13. *Hasty Generalization.* This fallacy is committed when a person draws a conclusion about a group based on a sample that is too small to be representative. Consider this statement:

> Seventy five percent of the seniors surveyed at the university study just 10 hours a week. We can conclude, then, that students at the university are not studying enough.

What you need to know is how many students were actually surveyed. Seventy-five percent may seem high, but not if the researcher surveyed just 400 of the 2,400 graduating seniors. This sample of students from a total population of 9,600 students at the university is too small to draw the conclusion that students in general are not studying enough.

14. *The Straw Man Argument.* A straw man fallacy makes a generalization about what a group believes without actually citing a specific writer or work:

> Democrats are more interested in running than in trying to win the war on terrorism.

Here the fallacy is that the author simply ignores a person's actual position and substitutes a distorted, exaggerated, or misrepresented version of that position. This kind of fallacy often goes hand in hand with assuming that what is true of the group is true of the individual, what we call the fallacy of division.

15. *Fallacy of the Middle Ground.* The fallacy of the middle ground assumes that the middle position between two extreme positions must be correct. Although the middle ground may be true, the author must justify this position with evidence.

> E. D. Hirsch argues that cultural literacy is the only sure way to increase test scores, and Jonathan Kozol believes schools will improve only if state legislators increase funding; but I would argue that school reform will occur if we change the curriculum *and* provide more funding.

This fallacy draws its power from the fact that a moderate or middle position is often the correct one. Again, however, the claim that the moderate or middle position is correct must be supported by legitimate reasoning.

ANALYZING THE APPEALS IN A TEXT

Now that you have studied the variety of appeals you can make to connect with your audience, we would like you to read a chapter from a study of education by Jean Anyon and analyze her strategies for appealing to her readers. The chapter is quite long and carefully argued, so we suggest you take detailed notes about her use of appeals to ethos, pathos, and logos as you read. You may want to refer to the Practice Sequence questions on p. 199 to help focus your reading. Ideally, you should work through the text with your classmates, in groups of three or four, appointing one student to record and share each group's analysis of Anyon's argument.

ABOUT THE READING

Jean Anyon teaches educational policy in the doctoral program in urban education at the City University of New York. Her articles on cities, race, social class, and schools have been reprinted in more than forty edited collections and translated into several languages. This chapter appears in her book *Radical Possibilities: Public Policy, Urban Education, and a New Social Movement* (2005).

JEAN ANYON

The Economic Is Political

It is widely acknowledged that one of the most important causes of poorly funded, staffed, and resourced schools is the poverty of the families and neighborhoods in which the schools are located. What is rarely acknowledged, however, is the proactive role of the federal government in maintaining this poverty and therefore poverty education.   *1*

All economies depend on government regulations in order to function. Capitalism would not be capitalism without constitutional and other federal provisions that make legal the private ownership of property, the right of business to charge more for products than the cost of producing them, or the right of corporations to keep those profits rather than sharing them with workers or employees. The 14th Amendment to the Constitution, passed in 1867, turns corporations into "persons" so they will be free from government "interference." Because economies are maintained by rules made by governments, economic institutions are inescapably political; they function according to determinative macro-economic policies.   *2*

This chapter demonstrates that the poverty of U.S. families is considerably more widespread than commonly believed — and is catastrophic in low-income urban neighborhoods of color. I demonstrate that the   *3* basic reason people are poor is that there are not enough jobs paying decent wages. In cities, the harsh economic realities of poverty shape the lives of parents of school children, and therefore the lives of their children as well. Neighborhood poverty also impacts the education students receive by contributing to low school funding levels, poorly paid teachers, and a lack of resources.

First, I provide an overview of national poverty as a backdrop to the   4
situation in urban America. I then focus specifically on urban families of color. . . .

Income

Almost three-fourths (70%) of all American employees saw their wages   5
fall between 1973 and 1995 (in constant dollars — that is, adjusted for inflation); even with the boom of the late 1990s, a majority of workers made less in 2000 than they had in 1973. New college graduates earned $1.10 less per hour in 1995 than their counterparts did in 1973. The earnings of the average American family did improve slightly over this period, but only through a dramatic increase in the number of hours worked and the share of families in which both parents worked (Lafer, 2002, p. 45; Mishel, Bernstein, and Boushey, 2003, p. 162).

Some of the largest long-term wage declines have been among entry-   6
level workers (those with up to five years' work experience) with a high school education. Average wages for male entry-level high school graduates were 28% lower in 1997 than two decades earlier. The decline for comparable women was 18% (Economic Policy Institute, Feb. 17, 1999, p. 1).

Low wages are an important cause of poverty. Low-wage workers are   7
those whose hourly wage is less than the earnings necessary to lift a family above the official poverty line — in 2004, $15,670 or less for a family of three, and $18,850 for a family of four.

The percentage of people who work full-time, year-round yet are poor   8
is staggering. In 2000, at the height of a booming economy, almost a fifth of all men (19.5%), and almost a third of all women (33.1%) earned poverty-level wages working full-time, year-round. In the same year, over one in four Black men (26.3%), over one in three Black women (36.5%) and Hispanic men (37.6%), and almost half of Hispanic women (49.3%) earned poverty wages working full-time, year-round (Mishel, Bernstein, and Schmitt, 2001, pp. 137–139).

I analyzed figures provided by the Economic Policy Institute to calcu-   9
late the overall percentage of people who work full-time, year-round, yet make *poverty-zone* wages. Poverty zone is defined here as wages up to 125% of the official poverty threshold needed to support a family of four at the poverty level (ibid., p. 133). The analysis demonstrates that in 1999, during the strong economy, almost half of people at work in the

U.S. (41.3%) earned poverty-zone wages — in 1999, $10.24/hour ($21,299/year) or less, working full-time, year-round (ibid., Table 2.10, p. 130). Two years later, in 2001, 38.4 earned poverty-zone wages working full-time, year-round (in 2001, 125% of the poverty line was a $10.88 hourly wage) (ibid., p. 134). These figures indicate that even in "good times" the U.S. pyramid of wages sits squarely on the shoulders of almost half of U.S. employees, who are the working poor.

In 2000, more than half (59.5%) of the working poor were women. Over 10 60% were White (60.4%). Thirty-five percent were Black or Latino (ibid., p. 353). Over 61.8% had a high school degree or less, while a quarter (24.2%) had some college, and 8% had a bachelor's degree (ibid., p. 353). This last figure indicates that *almost one in ten of the working poor is a college graduate.*

Seventy percent of the working poor had jobs in services or retail trade 11 and 10% worked in manufacturing (ibid., p. 353). The vast majority (93.3%) were not in unions. More than half (57.7%) were under the age of 35 (ibid., p. 353). It is important to note that these workers are poor by official standards. As we will see below, a more realistic measure of poverty would literally double the amount of income under which people are defined as poor.

Moving up the income scale in the U.S. is more difficult than in other 12 countries. As *Business Week* pointed out several years ago, economic mobility in the U.S. declined after the 1960s. Because most young people earn less than their parents, mobility here is second worst among similar countries recently studied — only Canada is worse (Dreier, Swanstrom, and Mollenkopf, 2001, pp. 18, 47). Low-wage workers in the U.S. are more likely to remain in the low-wage labor market longer than workers in Germany, France, Italy, the UK, Denmark, Finland, Sweden, and Canada (Mishel, Bernstein, and Schmitt, 2001, p. 12).

Relatively few U.S. individuals or families make high incomes. In 13 2000, only 7.8% of women and 16% of men earned at least three times the official poverty level (Mishel, Bernstein, and Boushey, 2003, p. 133). In 2001, only 19% of *families* earned more than $94,000, and only 4% made more than $164,000 (in 2001 dollars) (ibid., p. 56).

In the last two decades, income has skyrocketed at the tip of the distri- 14 butional pyramid. The top one percent of tax filers, the 2.1 million people earning $700,000 a year or more, had after-tax income that jumped 31% in the last few years, while the after-tax income of the bottom 90% of tax filers rose only 3.4% (Mishel, Bernstein, and Schmitt, 2001, p. 83).

While employee pay has lagged, CEO pay has skyrocketed. And the 15 ratio of CEO to worker pay has increased dramatically: In the 1960s and '70s, the ratio was between 26% and 37%. In the 1990s, it was between 102% and 310%. By 2001, the ratio had grown to 245% (Mishel, Bernstein, and Boushey, 2003, p. 215). In other words, in 2001, a CEO earned more in one workday (there are 260 in a year) than an average worker earned in 52 weeks (Economic Policy Institute, July 24, 2002, p. 1). In recent years, the average ratio of CEO pay to worker pay in all other advanced countries was considerably lower — 18.1 to 1 (Mishel, Bernstein, and Boushey, 2003, p. 216).

Jobs

What job opportunities are available for Americans? For two decades, *16* numerous politicians, educators, and corporate spokespeople have been arguing that the U.S. must improve education because people need advanced skills in order to get a job. This is a myth, however. Most job openings in the next 10 years will not require either sophisticated skills or a college degree. Seventy-seven percent of new and projected jobs will be low-paying. Only a quarter of the new and projected jobs are expected to pay over $26,000 a year (Department of Labor, 2002, Chart 9; see also Economic Policy Institute, July 21, 2004).

Most will require on-the-job training only, and will not require a col- *17* lege education; most will be in service and retail, where poverty-zone wages are the norm. Only 12.6% of new jobs will require a bachelor's degree. Of the 20 occupations expected to grow the fastest, only six require college — these six are in computer systems and information technology (Department of Labor, 2002, Chart 8), and there are relatively few of these jobs.

The typical job of the future is not in information technology. Most *18* job openings will be in food preparation and service and in fast-food restaurants, as telephone customer service representatives, and as cashiers (Department of Labor, 2002, Chart 9). In the next decade, about 5 million new jobs will be created for food workers, including waiters and waitresses. Another 4 million will be for cashiers and retail salespersons, and 3 million for clerks. Over 2 million will be for packagers, laborers, and truck drivers. Managerial and professional occupations will also need more workers, but their numbers pale compared with openings requiring less education.

Indeed, a typical job of the future is retail sales at Wal-Mart. The aver- *19* age pay at Wal-Mart, which employs over a million people and is the largest private employer in the world, was $20,030 in 2000. According to *Business Week,* half of Wal-Mart's full-time employees are eligible for food stamps (households earning up to 130% of the official poverty line are eligible) (March 13, 2000, p. 78).

A main determinant of whether one is poor or not is whether or not *20* one has a decently paying job. The assertion that jobs are plentiful — if only workers were qualified to fill them — has been a central tenet of federal policy for 20 years. In 1982, the Reagan administration eliminated the Comprehensive Employment and Training Administration

(CETA), which by 1978 had created almost 2 million full-time jobs, and substituted a major federal job training program (Job Partnership Training Act) (Lafer, 2002, pp. 1–2). Since then, and continuing today, job training has been the centerpiece of federal and state efforts to solve both the unemployment problem and the poverty problem. For almost all of this time, however, the federal government has not collected data on job availability (vacancies). If they had, and if they had consulted studies that had been carried out, they would have found that all the evidence demonstrates that at any given time there are far more unemployed people than there are job openings (ibid., p. 23; see also Pigeon and Wray, 1999, among others). The federal government has spent $85 billion on job training since the Reagan years, claiming all the while that there are jobs for those who want them (Lafer, 2002, p. 19).

In an exhaustive analysis, labor economist Gordon Lafer demonstrates that "over the period 1984 to 1996 — at the height of an alleged labor shortage — the number of people in need of work exceeded the total number of job openings by an average of five to one. In 1996, for example, the country would have needed 14.4 million jobs in order for all low-income people to work their way out of poverty. However, there were at most 2.4 million job openings available to meet this need; of these, only one million were in full-time, non-managerial positions" (ibid., 3, pp. 29–44). Thus, "there simply are not enough decently paying jobs for the number of people who need them — no matter how well trained they are" — and therefore job training programs cannot hope to address more than a small fraction of either the unemployment or poverty problems (ibid., 3, pp. 88–123; see also Jargowsky, 1998; and Eisenhower Foundation, 1998). 21

Lafer also demonstrates that throughout the 1984 to 1996 period, the total number of vacancies in jobs that paid above poverty wage was never more than one-seventh the number of people who needed those jobs, and "the gap between jobs needed and decently paying jobs available was never less than 16 million" (2002, pp. 34–35). 22

In the last 15 years or so, corporate pronouncements and federal economic policies (regarding expansion of visas for foreign workers, for example) have often been premised on the assumption that there has been a U.S. shortage of highly skilled computer technicians. And employers report that scientific and technical positions are often hard to fill (ibid., p. 54). Large corporations have argued that there are no skilled workers at home as a rationale for transferring computer-based operations to other countries. Although there are some shortages (nursing, for example), the evidence suggests that there is no actual shortage of programmers or systems analysts. "Rather, technology companies have hired lower-wage foreign programmers while thousands of more experienced (and more expensive) American programmers remained unemployed" (ibid., p. 54; see also Lardner, 1998). 23

Even in occupations such as nursing where there have been shortages, *24* most technical professions are quite small as a share of the overall workforce, and therefore the total number of such jobs going begging has never been a significant source of job openings. For example, "the combined total of jobs for mathematicians, computer scientists, computer programmers, numerical control tool programmers, science technicians, electrical and electronic technicians, health technicians, and health assessment and treating occupations amounted to only 4.1% of the total workforce in 1984. After twenty years of unprecedented growth, this share is projected to grow to only 6.4 by the year 2006" (Lafer, 2002, p. 54; see also Galbraith, 1998; and Mishel, Bernstein, and Boushey, 2003).

Furthermore, as the technology has been adapted by business, "com- *25* puter work" has been highly differentiated, with technical knowledge used by a relatively small group of well-paid specialists, and the vast majority of daily computer operators carrying out tasks in relatively low-wage occupations with few educational requirements (social workers, secretaries, credit card and computer call center operators, etc.) (Lafer, 2002, p. 56; see also Frenkel, Korczynski, Shire, and Tam, 1999; Galbraith, 1998; and Osterman, 2001).

To make the case for terminating the job-creation programs of CETA *26* in 1982, Ronald Reagan argued that "if you look at the want ads, you see lots of available jobs" (Lafer, 2002, p. 44). As Lafer points out, however, "A look at the want ads in the newspapers shows that there are, indeed jobs, but only for the number of people the ads specify; and this illusion masks a deeper truth, which is that for large numbers of the poor there are NO decently paying jobs, no matter how hard they work or what training programs they enroll in" (ibid., p. 44).

A report in the *New York Times* in 1999 offered on-the-ground confir- *27* mation of the lack of jobs for workers who need them; Journalist Amy Waldman reported that at the height of the "full economy" in 1999, about 5,000 lined up for a job fair in the Bronx, New York. More than 40 employers were inside the Bronx County Building, trying to fill positions from sales clerk to registered nurse. Many of the people in line, who had been waiting for over three hours, said they had been looking for work, most often entry-level clerical positions, for months. Many of the people in line were on public assistance and were trying to get off it. "There is a huge pool of people with entry-level skills and not enough jobs for them," said Lucy Mayo, an employment specialist. "Most of the jobs that were available," she said, "offered low pay and no benefits. For example, Barnes and Noble, which was scheduled to open a new bookstore at Bay Plaza in the Bronx, had 50–75 jobs to fill. The jobs pay $7.25 an hour, are part-time with no benefits. Some of the large corporations there, however (Montefiore Medical Centers and the Correctional Services Corporation), offered benefits after six months. One man, aged 25, said he had left his last manufacturing job in Chatham,

NJ [a suburb of New York City], because the transportation was eating up half of his $7 hourly pay. With two children to support, he had been looking for work for six months. . . . There were 2,600 jobs created in the Bronx last year [1998], mostly in retail and construction. Still, 250,000 Bronx residents work outside the borough" (Waldman, Oct. 20, 1999).

Compounding the problem for entry-level workers, college-educated persons may be crowding them out. Research by Richard Murnane and Frank Levy shows that controlling for a person's mathematics or reading skill while a high school senior eliminates a substantial portion of the growth in the college-to-high school wage premium in a later period (for women essentially all, and for men about one-third). This suggests that it is basic high school–level skills that are increasingly in demand by employers, who are relying more and more on college completion as a screen to get the people who are more likely to have them (Murnane and Levy, 1996, p. 29; see also Pigeon and Wray, 1999). *28*

That employers hire college-educated workers for jobs that require high school skills helps to explain why a more highly educated workforce does not necessarily earn higher wages. As entry-level employees obtain more education, employers merely ratchet up the requirements (see Galbraith, 1998; and Moss and Tilly, 2001). *29*

Poverty

One consequence of a predominance of low-wage work and too few jobs in the U.S. is the numbers of poor people that approach the figures of 1959 before massive urban poverty became a national issue. Although the percentages are lower now, the numbers are still staggering: There were about as many people officially poor in 1993 (39.2 million) as in 1959 (39.4 million) — three years before Michael Harrington galvanized the nation's conscience, and ultimately a "war on poverty," by demonstrating that upwards of 40 million people were poor (Harrington, 1963, p. 9). (In 2003, almost 36 million — 35.8 million — were officially poor.) *30*

Most poverty today is urban poverty. Demographic researcher Myron Orfield analyzed the distribution of poverty populations in the 25 largest metropolitan areas in the U.S. and found (confirmed by the 2000 Census) that about two-thirds of the U.S. poor today live in central cities and "urbanized," financially distressed suburbs. *31*

As has been the case since the mid-1960s, most of the urban poor are Black or Latino. . . . The concentration of Black and Latino poor in low-income urban areas is due not only to a lack of jobs with decent pay (and insufficient income to support a move out if desired) but to the lack of federal and state implementation of antiracial discrimination laws, the lack of affordable housing outside of urban areas, and state-enabled local zoning exclusions based on social class (income). *32*

The figures on poverty presented so far in this chapter are based on fed-   *33*
eral guidelines, and they underestimate the number of people who are
actually poor. The federal poverty formula in 1998 — during the height of
the '90s boom — determined that 13% of U.S. households (families and
unattached individuals) were poor. A single mother with two children was
officially poor if she earned $13,133 or less in that year. In 2003, a single
mother of two children was officially poor if she earned $15,260 or less.

Many social scientists have come to believe that these amounts are   *34*
too low, and that individuals and families with incomes up to 200% of
government thresholds are poor. The official formula for figuring
poverty — designed by federal employee Molly Orshansky in 1963 and
used in the war on poverty — utilized data collected in the 1950s. The
formula Orshansky devised was based on the price of a minimal food
budget (as determined by the Department of Agriculture). She multi-
plied the cost of food by three, to cover housing and health-care costs.
This figure, adjusted for family size, was the level below which families
and individuals were designated as poor.

Research in the 1950s showed that families spent about a third of   *35*
their budget on food. Since that time, however, the costs of housing and
health care have skyrocketed. Thus, most families today spend only
about a fifth of their income on food, and considerably more on housing
and health care (Bernstein, Brocht, and Spade-Aguilar, 2000, pp. 12–13;
see also Short, Iceland, and Garner, 1999; and recommendations by the
National Research Council, reported in Citro and Michael, 1995).

A recent national assessment of working families concluded that twice   *36*
the official poverty line is a more realistic measure of those who face critical and serious hardships in the U.S. This research documents that
working families with income up to 200% of the poverty line "experience
as many hardships" as families who are officially poor (Boushey,
Brocht, Gundersen, and Bernstein, 2001, p. 2).

A calculation of the individuals who earned less than 200% of the   *37*
poverty level in 2001 demonstrates a much larger percentage of poor
employees than is commonly acknowledged: 84.3% of Hispanic workers,
80% of Black workers, and 64.3% of White workers made wages at or
under 200% of the official poverty line (Mishel, Bernstein, and Schmitt,
2001, pp. 130–139). A calculation of *families* living with earnings up to
200% of the poverty line reveals that Black and Latino families face the
greatest financial hurdles. Over 50% of Black and Latino families earn
less than 200% of the poverty level, compared to only 20.3% of White
families, even though White families make up the majority (50.5%) of
families that fall below 200% of the poverty level (ibid., p. 12).

Families headed by a worker with less than a high school education   *38*
are the most likely to fall below 200% (68.6%), but over three-fourths of
families who fall below are headed by a worker with a high school education or more. An indication of the failure of higher education to
secure good wages is the fact that over a third (33.6%) are headed by a

worker with some college or a college degree (ibid., p. 13). And an indictment of the failure of full-time work to provide a decent living is the fact that a full half (50.0%) of families falling below 200% of the poverty line have a *full-time, year-round worker* (ibid., p. 15).

The statistics in this chapter relate in a fairly staid manner what is *39* actually a potentially inflammatory political situation. A humane reckoning of poverty reveals that the vast majority of African Americans and Latinos who have jobs, and more than two-thirds of employed Whites, do not earn enough to live on. This outrages me, as the experience must anger those who live it. But the situation is not immutable. Economies are indeed political, regulated by officials elected and appointed who formulate legislation, legal decisions, and other policy. These officials, and their mandates, can be changed — but only if all of us who are incensed by the policies' indecency stand together.

In order for injustice to create an outrage that can ultimately be *40* channeled into public demands, knowledge of the facts is necessary, and an appreciation of the consequences must be clear. I hope this chapter clarifies the situation regarding poverty. It is also extremely important . . . that people who are poor come to see their situation not as a result of their own failure but as a result of systemic causes. That is, if governments created enough jobs, and if businesses paid higher wages, workers would not be poor.

And knowledge is crucial to an accurate understanding of what *41* plagues urban education. We must know where the problem lies in order to identify workable solutions. We can win the war against poverty and poor schools only if we know where the poverty originates. The next chapter describes one important source, federal policies that maintain low-wage work and unemployment in urban areas, and ways these can set up failure for the families and schools there.

BIBLIOGRAPHY

Bernstein, Jared, Brocht, Chauna, and Spade-Aguilar, Maggie. (2000). *How much is enough? Basic family budgets for working families.* Washington, DC: Economic Policy Institute.

Boushey, Heather, Brocht, Chauna, Gundersen, Betheny, and Bernstein, Jared. (2001). *Hardships in America: The real story of working families.* Washington, DC: Economic Policy Institute.

Citro, Constance, and Michael, Robert (Eds.). (1995). *Measuring poverty: A new approach.* Washington, DC: National Academy Press.

Department of Labor. (2002). *Occupation projections to 2010.* Washington, DC.

Economic Policy Institute. (1999, Feb. 17). *Entry-level workers face lower wages.* Washington, DC.

Economic Policy Institute. (2002, July 24). *Economic snapshots.* Washington, DC.

Economic Policy Institute. (2004, July 21). *Jobs in the future: No boom in the need for college graduates.* Washington, DC.

Eisenhower Foundation. (1998). *Background report.* Washington DC.

Frenkel, Stephen, Korczynski, Maretk, Shire, Karen, and Tam, May. (1999). *On the front line: Organization of work in the information economy*. Ithaca, NY: Cornell University Press.

Galbraith, James K. (1998). *Created unequal: The crisis in American pay*. Twentieth Century Fund Book. New York: Free Press, Simon and Schuster.

Harrington, Michael. (1963). *The other America: Poverty in the United States*. Baltimore, MD: Penguin.

Jargowsky, Paul. (1998). *Poverty and place: Ghettos, barrios, and the American city*. New York: Russell Sage.

Lafer, Gordon. (2002). *The job training charade*. Ithaca, NY: Cornell University Press.

Lardner, James. (1998, March 16). Too old to write code? *U.S. News & World Report*. Cited in Lafer, 2002 (p. 250).

Mishel, Lawrence, Bernstein, Jared, and Boushey, Heather. (2003). *The state of working America: 2002/2003*. Ithaca, NY: Cornell University Press.

Mishel, Lawrence, Bernstein, Jared, and Schmitt, John. (2001). *The state of working America: 2000/2001*. Ithaca, NY: Cornell University Press.

Moss, Philip, and Tilly, Chris. (2001). *Stories employers tell: Race, skill, and hiring in America*. New York: Russell Sage.

Murnane, Richard, and Levy, Frank. (1996). *Teaching the new basic skills: Principles for educating children to thrive in a changing economy*. New York: Free Press.

Orfield, Myron. (1997). *Metropolitics: A regional agenda for community and stability*. Washington, DC: Brookings Institute.

Osterman, Paul. (2001). *Working in America: A blueprint for the new labor market*. Cambridge, MA: MIT Press.

Pigeon, Marc-Andre, and Wray, Randall. (1999). Down and out in the United States: An inside look at the out of the labor force population. Public Policy Brief No. 54. Annandale-on-Hudson, NY: The Jerome Levy Economics Institute of Bard College.

Short, Kathleen, Iceland, John, and Garner, Thesia. (1999). *Experimental poverty measures*. Washington, DC: U.S. Census Bureau.

Waldman, Amy. (1999, Oct. 20). Long line in the Bronx, but for jobs, not the Yankees. *New York Times*.

A Practice Sequence: Analyzing the Appeals in a Text

1 Make a list of the major premises that inform Anyon's argument, and examine the evidence she uses to support them. To what extent do you find her evidence credible? Do you generally agree or disagree with the conclusions she draws? Be prepared to explain your responses to your class or peer group.

2 Note instances where Anyon appeals to ethos, pathos, and logos. How would you describe the ways she makes these three types of appeals? How does she present herself? What does she seem to assume? How does she help you understand the chain of reasoning by which she moves from premises to conclusion?

3 Working in groups of three or four, compose a letter to Anyon in which you take issue with her argument. This does not mean your group has to disagree with her entire argument, although of course you may. Rather, present your group's own contribution to the conversation in which she is participating. You may want to

ask her to further explain one or more of her points, or suggest what she might be leaving out, or add your own take or evidence to her argument. As a group, you will have to agree on your focus. In the letter, include a summary of Anyon's argument or the part of it on which your group is focusing. Pay close attention to your own strategies for appealing to her — how you present yourselves, how you appeal to her values and emotions, and how you present your reasons for your own premises and conclusion.

9

From Introductions to Conclusions: Drafting an Essay

In this chapter, we describe strategies for crafting introductions that set up your argument. We then describe the characteristics of well-formulated paragraphs that will help you build your argument. Finally, we provide you with some strategies for writing conclusions that reinforce what is new about your argument, what is at stake, and what readers should do with the knowledge you convey.

DRAFTING INTRODUCTIONS

The introduction is where you set up your argument. It's where you identify a widely held assumption, challenge that assumption, and state your thesis. Writers use a number of strategies to set up their arguments. In this section we look at five of them:

- Moving from a general topic to a specific thesis (inverted-triangle introduction)
- Introducing the topic with a story (narrative introduction)
- Beginning with a question (interrogative introduction)
- Capturing readers' attention with something unexpected (paradoxical introduction)
- Identifying a gap in knowledge (minding-the-gap introduction)

Remember that an introduction need not be limited to a single paragraph. It may take several paragraphs to effectively set up your argument.

Keep in mind that you have to make these strategies your own. That is, we can suggest models, but you must make them work for your own argument. You must imagine your readers and what will engage them. What tone do you want to take? Playful? Serious? Formal? Urgent? The attitude you want to convey will depend on your purpose, your argument, and the needs of your audience.

■ The Inverted-Triangle Introduction

An **inverted-triangle introduction**, like an upside-down triangle, is broad at the top and pointed at the base. It begins with a general statement of the topic and then narrows its focus, ending with the point of the paragraph (and the triangle), the writer's thesis. We can see this strategy at work in the introduction from a student's essay below. The student writer (1) begins with a broad description of the problem she will address, (2) then focuses on a set of widely held but troublesome assumptions, and (3) finally, responding to what she sees as a pervasive problem, presents her thesis.

The student begins with a general set of assumptions about education that she believes people readily accept.

In today's world, many believe that education's sole purpose is to communicate information for students to store and draw on as necessary. By storing this information, students hope to perform well on tests. Good test scores assure good grades. Good grades eventually lead to acceptances into good colleges, which ultimately guarantee good jobs. Many teachers and students, convinced that education exists as a tool to secure good jobs, rely on

She then cites author bell hooks, to identify an approach that makes use of these assumptions — the "banking system" of education, a term hooks borrows from educator Paulo Freire.

the banking system. In her essay "Teaching to Transgress," bell hooks defines the banking system as an "approach to learning that is rooted in the notion that all students need to do is consume information fed to them by a professor and be able to memorize and store it" (185). Through the banking system, students focus solely on facts, missing the important themes and life lessons available in classes and school materials. The banking system misdirects the fundamental goals of education. Education's

The student then points to the banking system as the problem. This sets up her thesis about the "true purpose" of education.

true purpose is to prepare students for the real world by allowing them access to pertinent life knowledge available in their studies. Education should then entice students to apply this pertinent life knowledge to daily life struggles through praxis. In addition to her definition of the banking system, hooks offers the idea of praxis from the work of Paulo Freire. When incorporated into education, praxis, or "action and reflection upon the world in order to change it" (185), offers an advantageous educational tool that enhances the true purpose of education and overcomes the banking system.

The strategy of writing an introduction as an inverted triangle entails first identifying an idea, argument, or concept that people appear to accept as true; next, pointing out the problems with that idea, argument, or concept; and then, in a few sentences, setting out a thesis — how those problems can be resolved.

■ The Narrative Introduction

Opening with a short **narrative**, or story, is a strategy many writers use successfully to draw readers into a topic. A narrative introduction relates a sequence of events and can be especially effective if you think you need to coax indifferent or reluctant readers into taking an interest in the topic. Of course, a narrative introduction delays the declaration of your argument, so it's wise to choose a short story that clearly connects to your argument, and get to the thesis as quickly as possible (within a few paragraphs) before your readers start wondering "What's the point of this story?"

Notice how the student writer uses a narrative introduction to her argument in her essay titled "Throwing a Punch at Gender Roles: How Women's Boxing at Notre Dame Empowers Women."

The student's entire first paragraph is a narrative that takes us into the world of women's boxing and foreshadows her thesis.

Glancing at my watch, I ran into the gym, noting to myself that being late to the first day of boxing practice was not the right way to make a good first impression. I flew down the stairs into the basement, to the room the boxers have lovingly dubbed "The Pit." What greeted me when I got there was more than I could ever have imagined. Picture a room filled with boxing gloves of all sizes covering an entire wall, a mirror covering another, a boxing ring in a corner, and an awesome collection of framed newspaper and magazine articles chronicling the boxers whose pictures were hanging on every wall. Now picture that room with seventy-plus girls on the floor doing push-ups, sweat dripping down their faces. I was immediately struck by the discipline this sport would take from me, but I had no idea I would take so much more from it.

With her narrative as a backdrop, the student identifies a problem, using the transition word yet to mark her challenge to the conditions she observes in the university's women's boxing program.

The university offers the only nonmilitary-based college-level women's boxing program in America, and it also offers women the chance to push their physical limits in a regulated environment. Yet the program is plagued with disappointments. I have experienced for myself the stereotypes female boxers face and have dealt with the harsh reality that boxing is still widely recognized as only a men's sport. This paper will show that the women's boxing program at ND serves as a much-needed outlet for females to come face-to-face with aspects of themselves they would not typically get a chance to explore. It will

The writer then states her thesis (what her paper "will show"): Despite the problems of stereotyping, women's boxing offers women significant opportunities for growth.

also examine how viewing this sport as a positive opportunity for women at ND indicates that there is growing hope that very soon more activities similar to women's boxing may be better received by society in general. I will accomplish these goals by analyzing scholarly journals, old Observer [the school newspaper] articles, and survey questions answered by the captains of the 2003 women's boxing team of ND.

The student writer uses a visually descriptive narrative to introduce us to the world of women's college boxing; then, in the second paragraph, she steers us toward the purpose of the paper and the methods she will use to develop her argument about what women's boxing offers to young women and to the changing world of sports.

■ The Interrogative Introduction

An **interrogative introduction** invites readers into the conversation of your essay by asking one or more questions, which the essay goes on to answer. You want to think of a question that will pique your readers' interest, enticing them to read on to discover how your insights shed light on the issue. Notice the question Daphne Spain, a professor of urban and environmental planning, uses to open her essay "Spatial Segregation and Gender Stratification in the Workplace."

Spain sets up her argument by asking a question and then tentatively answering it with a reference to a published study.

In the third sentence she states her thesis — that men and women have very little contact in the workplace.

Finally, she outlines the effects that this lack of contact has on women.

To what extent do women and men who work in different occupations also work in different space? Baran and Teegarden propose that occupational segregation in the insurance industry is "tantamount to spatial segregation by gender" since managers are overwhelmingly male and clerical staff are predominantly female. This essay examines the spatial conditions of women's work and men's work and proposes that working women and men come into daily contact with one another very infrequently. Further, women's jobs can be classified as "open floor," but men's jobs are more likely to be "closed door." That is, women work in a more public environment with less control of their space than men. This lack of spatial control both reflects and contributes to women's lower occupational status by limiting opportunities for the transfer of knowledge from men to women.

By the end of this introductory paragraph, Spain has explained some of the terms she will use in her essay (*open floor* and *closed door*) and has offered in her final sentence a clear statement of her thesis.

In "Harry Potter and the Technology of Magic," literature scholar Elizabeth Teare begins by contextualizing the Harry Potter publishing phenomenon. Then she raises a question about what is fueling this success story.

In her first four sentences, Teare describes something she is curious about and she hopes readers will be curious about — the growing popularity of the Harry Potter books.

The July/August 2001 issue of *Book* lists J. K. Rowling as one of the ten most influential people in publishing. She shares space on this list with John Grisham and Oprah Winfrey, along with less famous but equally powerful insiders in the book industry. What these industry leaders have in common is an almost magical power to make books succeed in the marketplace, and this magic, in addition to that performed with wands, Rowling's novels appear to practice. Opening weekend sales charted like those of a blockbuster movie (not to mention the blockbuster movie itself), the reconstruction of the venerable *New York Times* bestseller lists, the creation of a new nation's worth of web sites in the territory of cyberspace, and of course the legendary inspiration of tens of millions of child readers — the Harry Potter books have transformed both the technologies of reading and the way we

In the fifth sentence, Teare asks the question she will try to answer in the rest of the essay.

understand those technologies. What is it that makes these books — about a lonely boy whose first act on learning he is a wizard is to go shopping for a wand — not only an international phenomenon among children and parents and teachers but also a topic of compelling interest to literary, social,

Finally, in the last sentence, Teare offers a partial answer to her question — her thesis.

and cultural critics? I will argue that the stories the books tell, as well as the stories we're telling about them, enact both our fantasies and our fears of children's literature and publishing in the context of twenty-first-century commercial and technological culture.

In the final two sentences of the introduction, Teare raises her question about the root of this "international phenomenon" and then offers her thesis. By the end of the opening paragraph, then, the reader knows exactly what question is driving Teare's essay and the answer she proposes to explain throughout the essay.

■ The Paradoxical Introduction

A **paradoxical introduction** appeals to readers' curiosity by pointing out an aspect of the topic that runs counter to their expectations. Just as an interrogative introduction draws readers in by asking a question, a paradoxical introduction draws readers in by saying, in effect, "Here's something completely surprising and unlikely about this issue, but my essay will go on to show you how it is true." In this passage from "'Holding Back': Negotiating a Glass Ceiling on Women's Muscular

Strength," sociologist Shari L. Dworkin points to a paradox in our commonsense understanding of bodies as the product of biology, not culture.

In the first sentence, Dworkin quotes from a study to identify the thinking that she is going to challenge.

Notice how Dworkin signals her own position (however) relative to commonly held assumptions.

Dworkin ends by stating her thesis, noting a paradox that will surprise readers.

Current work in gender studies points to how "when examined closely, much of what we take for granted about gender and its causes and effects either does not hold up, or can be explained differently." These arguments become especially contentious when confronting nature/culture debates on gendered *bodies*. After all, "common sense" frequently tells us that flesh and blood bodies are about biology. However, bodies are also shaped and constrained through cumulative social practices, structures of opportunity, wider cultural meanings, and more. Paradoxically, then, when we think that we are "really seeing" naturally sexed bodies, perhaps we are seeing the effect of internalizing gender ideologies — carrying out social practices — and this constructs our vision of "sexed" bodies.

Dworkin's strategy in the first three sentences is to describe common practice, the understanding that bodies are biological. Then, in the sentences beginning "However" and "Paradoxically," she advances the surprising idea that our bodies — not just the clothes we wear, for example — carry cultural gender markers. Her essay then goes on to examine women's weight lifting, and the complex motives driving many women to create a body that is perceived as muscular but not masculine.

■ The Minding-the-Gap Introduction

This type of introduction takes its name from the British train system, the voice on the loudspeaker that intones "Mind the gap!" at every stop, to call riders' attention to the gap between the train car and the platform. In a **minding-the-gap introduction**, a writer calls readers' attention to a gap in the research on an issue, and then uses the rest of the essay to fill in the "gap." A minding-the-gap introduction says, in effect, "Wait a minute. There's something missing from this conversation, and my research and ideas will fill in this gap."

For example, in the introductory paragraphs to their book *Men's Lives*, Michael S. Kimmel and Michael A. Messner explain how the book is different from other books that discuss men's lives, and how it serves a different purpose.

The authors begin with an assumption and then challenge it. A transition word (but) signals the challenge.

This is a book about men. But, unlike other books about men, which line countless library shelves, this is a book about men as men. It is a book in which men's experiences are not taken for granted as we explore the "real" and significant accomplishments of men, but a book in which those experiences are treated as significant and important in themselves.

The authors follow with a question that provokes readers' interest and points to the gap they summarize in the last sentence.

But what does it mean to examine men "as men"? Most courses in a college curriculum are about men, aren't they? But these courses routinely deal with men only in their public roles, so we come to know and understand men as scientists, politicians, military figures, writers, and philosophers. Rarely, if ever, are men understood through the prism of gender.

Kimmel and Messner use these opening paragraphs to highlight both what they find problematic about the existing literature on men and to introduce readers to their own approach.

Strategies for Drafting Introductions

1 **Use an inverted triangle.** Begin with a broad situation, concept, or idea, and narrow the focus to your thesis.

2 **Begin with a narrative.** Capture readers' imagination and interest with a story that sets the stage for your argument.

3 **Ask a question that you will answer.** Provoke readers' interest with a question, and then use your thesis to answer the question.

4 **Present a paradox.** Begin with an assumption that readers accept as true and formulate a thesis that not only challenges that assumption but may very well seem paradoxical.

5 **Mind the gap.** Identify what readers know and then what they don't know (or what you believe they need to know).

A Practice Sequence: Drafting an Introduction

1 Write or rewrite your introduction (which, as you've seen, may involve more than one paragraph), using one of the strategies described above. Then share your introduction with one of your peers and ask the following questions:

- To what extent did the strategy compel you to want to read further?

- To what extent is my thesis clear?

- How effectively do I draw a distinction between what I believe others assume to be true and my own approach?

- Is there another way that I might have made my introduction more compelling?

After listening to the responses, try a second strategy and then ask your peer which introduction is more effective.

2 If you do not have your own introduction to work on, revise the introduction below from one of our students' essays, combining two of the strategies we describe above.

> News correspondent Pauline Frederick once commented, "When a man gets up to speak people listen then look. When a woman gets up, people look; then, if they like what they see, they listen." Ironically, the harsh reality of this statement is given life by the ongoing controversy over America's most recognizable and sometimes notorious toy, Barbie. Celebrating her 40th birthday this year, Barbie has become this nation's most beleaguered soldier (a woman no less) of idolatry who has been to the front lines and back more times than the average "Joe." This doll, a piece of plastic, a toy, incurs both criticism and praise spanning both ends of the ideological spectrum. Barbie's curvaceous and basically unrealistic body piques the ire of both liberals and conservatives, each contending that Barbie stands for the distinct view of the other. One hundred and eighty degrees south, others praise Barbie's (curves and all) ability to unlock youthful imagination and potential. M. G. Lord explains Barbie best: "To study Barbie, one sometimes has to hold seemingly contradictory ideas in one's head at the same time. . . . The doll functions like a Rorschach test: people project wildly dissimilar and often opposing meanings on it. . . . And her meaning, like her face, has not been static over time." In spite of the extreme polarity, a sole unconscious consensus manifests itself about Barbie. Barbie is "the icon" of womanhood and the twentieth century. She is the American dream. Barbie is "us." The question is always the same: What message does Barbie send? Barbie is a toy. She is the image of what we see.

DEVELOPING PARAGRAPHS

In your introduction, you set forth your thesis. Then, in subsequent paragraphs, you have to develop your argument. Remember our metaphor: If your thesis, or main claim, is the skewer that runs through each paragraph in your essay, then these paragraphs are the "meat" of your argument. The paragraphs that follow your introduction carry the burden of evidence in your argument. After all, a claim cannot stand on its own without supporting evidence. Generally speaking, each paragraph should include a topic sentence that brings the main idea of the paragraph into focus, be unified around the main idea of the topic sentence, and adequately develop the idea. At the same time, a paragraph does not stand on its own; as part of your overall argument, it can refer to what you've said earlier, gesture toward where you are heading, and connect to the larger conversation to which you are contributing.

We now ask you to read an excerpt from "Reinventing 'America': Call for a New National Identity," by Elizabeth Martínez, and answer some questions about how you think the author develops her argument, paragraph by paragraph. Then we discuss her work in the context of the three key elements of paragraphs: *topic sentences*, *unity*, and *adequate development*. As you read, pay attention to how, sentence by sentence, Martínez develops her paragraphs. We also ask that you consider how she makes her argument provocative, impassioned, and urgent for her audience.

ABOUT THE READING

Elizabeth Martínez is a Chicana activist who since 1960 has worked in and documented different movements for change, including the civil rights, women's, and Chicano movements. She is the author of six books and numerous articles. Her best-known work is *500 Years of Chicano History in Pictures* (1991), which became the basis of a two-part video she scripted and codirected. Her latest book is *De Colores Means All of Us: Latina Views for a Multi-Colored Century* (1998). In "Reinventing 'America,'" Martínez argues that Americans' willingness to accept a "myth" as "the basis for [the] nation's self-defined identity" has brought the country to a crisis.

ELIZABETH MARTÍNEZ

From Reinventing "America": Call for a New National Identity

For some fifteen years, starting in 1940, 85 percent of all U.S. elementary schools used the Dick and Jane series to teach children how to read. The series starred Dick, Jane, their white middle-class parents, their dog Spot and their life together in a home with a white picket fence. *1*

"Look, Jane, look! See Spot run!" chirped the two kids. It was a house full of glorious family values, where Mom cooked while Daddy went to work in a suit and mowed the lawn on weekends. The Dick and Jane books also taught that you should do your job and help others. All this affirmed an equation of middle-class whiteness with virtue. *2*

In the mid-1990s, museums, libraries and eighty Public Broadcasting Service (PBS) stations across the country had exhibits and programs commemorating the series. At one museum, an attendant commented, "When you hear someone crying, you know they are looking at the Dick *3* and Jane books." It seems nostalgia runs rampant among many Euro-Americans: a nostalgia for the days of unchallenged White Supremacy — both moral and material — when life was "simple."

We've seen that nostalgia before in the nation's history. But today it sig- 4
nifies a problem reaching a new intensity. It suggests a national identity crisis that promises to bring in its wake an unprecedented nervous break-down for the dominant society's psyche.

Nowhere is this more apparent than in California, which has long been 5
on the cutting edge of the nation's present and future reality. Warning sirens have sounded repeatedly in the 1990s, such as the fierce battle over new history textbooks for public schools, Proposition 187's ugly denial of human rights to immigrants, the 1996 assault on affirmative action that culminated in Proposition 209, and the 1997 move to abolish bilingual education. Attempts to copycat these reactionary measures have been seen in other states.

The attack on affirmative action isn't really about affirmative action. 6
Essentially it is another tactic in today's war on the gains of the 1960s, a tactic rooted in Anglo resentment and fear. A major source of that fear: the fact that California will almost surely have a majority of people of color in 20 to 30 years at most, with the nation as a whole not far behind.

Check out the February 3, 1992, issue of *Sports Illustrated* with its 7
double-spread ad for *Time* magazine. The ad showed hundreds of new-born babies in their hospital cribs, all of them Black or brown except for a rare white face here and there. The headline says, "Hey, whitey! It's your turn at the back of the bus!" The ad then tells you, read *Time* magazine to keep up with today's hot issues. That manipulative image could have been published today; its implication of shifting power appears to be the recur-rent nightmare of too many potential Anglo allies.

Euro-American anxiety often focuses on the sense of a vanishing 8
national identity. Behind the attacks on immigrants, affirmative action and multiculturalism, behind the demand for "English Only" laws and the rejection of bilingual education, lies the question: with all these new people, languages and cultures, what will it mean to be an American? If that question once seemed, to many people, to have an obvious, univer-sally applicable answer, today new definitions must be found. But too often Americans, with supposed scholars in the lead, refuse to face that need and instead nurse a nostalgia for some bygone clarity. They remain trapped in denial.

An array of such ostriches, heads in the sand, began flapping their 9
feathers noisily with the publication of Allan Bloom's 1987 best-selling book, *The Closing of the American Mind*. Bloom bemoaned the decline of our "common values" as a society, meaning the decline of Euro-American cultural centricity (shall we just call it cultural imperialism?). Since then we have seen constant sniping at "diversity" goals across the land. The assault has often focused on how U.S. history is taught. And with reason,

for this country's identity rests on a particular narrative about the historical origins of the United States as a nation.

The Great White Origin Myth

Every society has an origin narrative that explains that society to itself   *10*
and the world with a set of stories and symbols. The origin myth, as
scholar-activist Roxanne Dunbar Ortiz has termed it, defines how a society understands its place in the world and its history. The myth provides
the basis for a nation's self-defined identity. Most origin narratives can be
called myths because they usually present only the most flattering view of
a nation's history; they are not distinguished by honesty.

Ours begins with Columbus "discovering" a hemisphere where some 80   *11*
million people already lived but didn't really count (in what became the
United States, they were just buffalo-chasing "savages" with no grasp of
real estate values and therefore doomed to perish). It continues with the
brave Pilgrims, a revolution by independence-loving colonists against a
decadent English aristocracy and the birth of an energetic young republic
that promised democracy and equality (that is, to white male landowners).
In the 1840s, the new nation expanded its size by almost one-third, thanks
to a victory over that backward land of little brown people called Mexico.
Such has been the basic account of how the nation called the United
States of America came into being as presently configured.

The myth's omissions are grotesque. It ignores three major pillars of   *12*
our nationhood: genocide, enslavement and imperialist expansion (such
nasty words, who wants to hear them? — but that's the problem). The
massive extermination of indigenous peoples provided our land base;
the enslavement of African labor made our economic growth possible;
and the seizure of half of Mexico by war (or threat of renewed war)
extended this nation's boundaries north to the Pacific and south to the
Rio Grande. Such are the foundation stones of the United States, within
an economic system that made this country the first in world history to
be born capitalist. . . .

Racism as Linchpin of the U.S. National Identity

A crucial embellishment of the origin myth and key element of the   *13*
national identity has been the myth of the frontier, analyzed in Richard
Slotkin's *Gunfighter Nation,* the last volume of a fascinating trilogy. He
describes Theodore Roosevelt's belief that the West was won thanks to
American arms, "the means by which progress and nationality will be
achieved." That success, Roosevelt continued, "depends on the heroism
of men who impose on the course of events the latent virtues of their

'race.' " Roosevelt saw conflict on the frontier producing a series of virile "fighters and breeders" who would eventually generate a new leadership class. Militarism thus went hand in hand with the racialization of history's protagonists. . . .

The frontier myth embodied the nineteenth-century concept of Manifest Destiny, a doctrine that served to justify expansionist violence by means of intrinsic racial superiority. Manifest Destiny was Yankee conquest as the inevitable result of a confrontation between enterprise and progress (white) versus passivity and backwardness (Indian, Mexican). "Manifest" meant "God-given," and the whole doctrine is profoundly rooted in religious conviction going back to the earliest colonial times. In his short, powerful book *Manifest Destiny: American Expansion and the Empire of Right,* Professor Anders Stephanson tells how the Puritans reinvented the Jewish notion of chosenness and applied it to this hemisphere so that territorial expansion became God's will. . . . *14*

Manifest Destiny Dies Hard

The concept of Manifest Destiny, with its assertion of racial superiority sustained by military power, has defined U.S. identity for 150 years. . . . *15*

Today's origin myth and the resulting concept of national identity make for an intellectual prison where it is dangerous to ask big questions about this society's superiority. When otherwise decent people are trapped in such a powerful desire not to feel guilty, self-deception becomes unavoidable. To cease our present falsification of collective memory should, and could, open the doors of that prison. When together we cease equating whiteness with Americanness, a new day can dawn. As David Roediger, the social historian, has said, "[Whiteness] is the empty and therefore terrifying attempt to build an identity on what one isn't, and on whom one can hold back." *16*

Redefining the U.S. origin narrative, and with it this country's national identity, could prove liberating for our collective psyche. It does not mean Euro-Americans should wallow individually in guilt. It does mean accepting collective responsibility to deal with the implications of our real origin. A few apologies, for example, might be a step in the right direction. In 1997, the idea was floated in Congress to apologize for slavery; it encountered opposition from all sides. But to reject the notion because corrective action, not an apology, is needed misses the point. Having defined itself as the all-time best country in the world, the United States fiercely denies the need to make a serious official apology for anything. . . . To press for any serious, official apology does imply a new origin narrative, a new self-image, an ideological sea-change. *17*

Accepting the implications of a different narrative could also shed light on today's struggles. In the affirmative-action struggle, for example, *18* opponents have said that that policy is no longer needed because racism ended with the Civil Rights Movement. But if we look at slavery as a fundamental pillar of this nation, going back centuries, it becomes obvious that racism could not have been ended by 30 years of mild reforms. If we see how the myth of the frontier idealized the white male adventurer as the central hero of national history, with the woman as sunbonneted helpmate, then we might better understand the dehumanized ways in which women have continued to be treated. A more truthful origin narrative could also help break down divisions among peoples of color by revealing common experiences and histories of cooperation.

For Analysis and Discussion

1. To what extent does the narrative Martínez begins with make you want to read further?
2. How does she connect this narrative to the rest of her argument?
3. How does she use repetition to create unity in her essay?
4. What assumptions does Martínez challenge?
5. How does she use questions to engage her readers?

■ Use Topic Sentences to Focus Your Paragraphs

The **topic sentence** states the main point of a paragraph. It should

- provide a partial answer to the question motivating the writer.
- act as an extension of the writer's thesis and the question motivating the writer's argument.
- serve as a guidepost, telling readers what the paragraph is about.
- help create unity and coherence both within the paragraph and within the essay.

Elizabeth Martínez begins by describing how elementary schools in the 1940s and 1950s used the Dick and Jane series not only to teach reading but also to foster a particular set of values — values that she believes do not serve all children enrolled in America's schools. In paragraph 4, she states her thesis, explaining that nostalgia in the United States has created "a national identity crisis that promises to bring in its wake an unprecedented nervous breakdown for the dominant society's psyche." This is a point that builds on an observation she makes in paragraph 3: "It seems nostalgia runs rampant among many Euro-Americans: a nostalgia for the days of unchallenged White Supremacy — both moral and material — when life was 'simple.'" Martínez often returns to this notion of nostalgia for a past that seems "simple" to explain what she sees as an impending crisis.

Consider the first sentence of paragraph 5 as a topic sentence. With Martínez's key points in mind, notice how she uses the sentence to make her thesis more specific. Notice too, how she ties in the crisis and break-down she alludes to in paragraph 4. Essentially, Martínez tells her readers that they can see these problems at play in California, an indicator of the "nation's present and future reality."

> *Nowhere is this more apparent than in California, which has long been on the cutting edge of the nation's present and future reality.* Warning sirens have sounded repeatedly in the 1990s, such as the fierce battle over new history textbooks for public schools, Proposition 187's ugly denial of human rights to immigrants, the 1996 assault on affirmative action that culminated in Proposition 209, and the 1997 move to abolish bilingual education. *Attempts to copycat these reactionary measures have been seen in other states.*

The final sentence of paragraph 5 sets up the remainder of the essay.

As readers, we expect each subsequent paragraph to respond in some way to the issue Martínez has raised. She meets that expectation by formulating a topic sentence that appears at the beginning of the paragraph. The topic sentence is what helps create unity and coherence in the essay.

▪ Create Unity in Your Paragraphs

Each paragraph in an essay should focus on the subject suggested by the topic sentence. If a paragraph begins with one focus or major point of discussion, it should not end with another. Several strategies can contribute to the unity of each paragraph:

Use details that follow logically from your topic sentence and maintain a single focus — a focus that is clearly an extension of your thesis. For example, in paragraph 5, Martínez's topic sentence ("Nowhere is this more apparent than in California, which has long been on the cutting edge of the nation's present and future reality") helps to create unity because it refers back to her thesis (*this* refers to the "national identity crisis" mentioned in paragraph 4) and limits the focus of what she includes in the paragraph to "the fierce battle over new history textbooks" and recent pieces of legislation in California that follow directly from and support the claim of the topic sentence.

Repeat key words to guide your readers.   A second strategy for creating unity is to repeat (or use synonyms for) key words within a given paragraph. You can see this at work in paragraph 12 (notice the words we've underscored), where Martínez explains that America's origin narrative omits significant details:

> The myth's omissions are grotesque. It ignores three major pillars of our nationhood: <u>genocide</u>, <u>enslavement</u> and <u>imperialist expansion</u> (such nasty words, who wants to hear them? — but that's the problem). The massive <u>extermination</u> of indigenous peoples provided our land base; the <u>enslavement</u> of African labor made our economic growth possible; and

the seizure of half of Mexico by war (or threat of renewed war) extended this nation's boundaries north to the Pacific and south to the Rio Grande. Such are the foundation stones of the United States, within an economic system that made this country the first in world history to be born capitalist. . . .

Specifically, Martínez tells us that the origin narrative ignores "three major pillars of our nationhood: genocide, enslavement and imperialist expansion." She then substitutes *extermination* for "genocide," repeats *enslavement,* and substitutes *seizure* for "imperialist expansionist." By connecting words in a paragraph, as Martínez does here, you help readers understand that the details you provide are all relevant to the point you want to make.

Use transition words to link ideas from different sentences.   A third strategy for creating unity within paragraphs is to establish a clear relationship among different ideas by using **transition words** or phrases. Transition words or phrases signal to your readers the direction your ideas are taking. Table 9.1 lists common transition words and phrases grouped by function — that is, for adding a new idea, presenting a contrasting idea, or drawing a conclusion about an idea.

Martínez uses transition words and phrases throughout the excerpt here. In several places, she uses the word *but* to make a contrast — to draw a distinction between an idea that many people accept as true and an alternative idea that she wants to pursue. Notice in paragraph 17 how she signals the importance of an official apology for slavery — and by implication genocide and the seizure of land from Mexico:

> . . . A few apologies, for example, might be a step in the right direction. In 1997, the idea was floated in Congress to apologize for slavery; it encountered opposition from all sides. But to reject the notion because corrective action, not an apology, is needed misses the point. Having defined itself as the all-time best country in the world, the United States fiercely denies the need to make a serious official apology for anything. . . . To press for any serious, official apology does imply a new origin narrative, a new self-image, an ideological sea-change.

TABLE 9.1   Common Transition Words and Phrases

ADDING AN IDEA	PRESENTING A CONTRASTING IDEA	DRAWING A LOGICAL CONCLUSION
also, and, further, moreover, in addition to, in support of, similarly	although, alternatively, as an alternative, but, by way of contrast, despite, even though, however, in contrast to, nevertheless, nonetheless, rather than, yet	as a result, because of, consequently, finally, in sum, in the end, subsequently, therefore, thus

Similarly, in the last paragraph, Martínez counters the argument that affirmative action is not necessary because racism no longer exists:

> . . . In the affirmative-action struggle, for example, opponents have said that that policy is no longer needed because racism ended with the Civil Rights Movement. But if we look at slavery as a fundamental pillar of this nation, going back centuries, it becomes obvious that racism could not have been ended by 30 years of mild reforms. . . .

There are a number of ways to rephrase what Martínez is saying in paragraph 18. We could substitute *however* for "but." Or, we could combine the two sentences into one to point to the relationship between the two competing ideas: *Although some people oppose affirmative action, believing that racism no longer exists, I would argue that racism remains a fundamental pillar of this nation.* Or we could pull together Martínez's different points to draw a logical conclusion using a transition word like *therefore.* Martínez observes that our country is in crisis as a result of increased immigration. *Therefore, we need to reassess our conceptions of national identity to account for the diversity that increased immigration has created.* We can substitute any of the transition words in Table 9.1 for drawing a logical conclusion.

The list of transition words and phrases in Table 9.1 is hardly exhaustive, but it gives you a sense of the ways to connect ideas so that readers understand how the ideas you write about are related. Are they similar ideas? Do they build on or support one another? Are you challenging accepted ideas? Or are you drawing a logical connection from a number of different ideas?

■ Use Critical Strategies to Develop Your Paragraphs

To develop a paragraph, you can use a range of strategies, depending on what you want to accomplish and what you believe your readers will need to be persuaded by what you argue. Among these strategies are using examples and illustrations; citing data (facts, statistics, evidence, details); analyzing texts; telling a story or anecdote; defining terms; making comparisons; and examining causes and evaluating consequences.

Use examples and illustrations.   Examples make abstract ideas concrete through illustration. Using examples is probably the most common way to develop a piece of writing. Of course, Martínez's essay is full of examples. In fact she begins with an example of a series of books — the Dick and Jane books — to show how a generation of school children were exposed to white middle-class values. She also uses examples in paragraph 5, where she lists several pieces of legislation (Propositions 187 and 209) to develop the claim in her topic sentence.

Cite data.   **Data** are factual pieces of information. They function in an essay as the bases of propositions. In the first few paragraphs of the excerpt, Martínez cites statistics ("85 percent of all U.S. elementary schools used the Dick and Jane series to teach children how to read") and facts ("In the mid-1990s, museums, libraries and eighty Public Broadcasting Service . . . stations across the country had exhibits and programs commemorating the series") to back up her claim about the popularity of the Dick and Jane series and the nostalgia the books evoke.

Analyze texts.   Analysis is the process of breaking something down into its elements to understand how they work together. When you analyze a text, you point out parts of the text that have particular significance to your argument and explain what they mean. By *texts,* we mean both verbal and visual texts. In paragraph 7, Martínez analyzes a visual text, an advertisement that appeared in *Sports Illustrated,* to reveal "its implication of shifting power" — a demographic power shift from Anglos to people of color.

Tell narratives or anecdotes.   Put simply, a narrative is an account of something that happened. More technically, a narrative relates a sequence of events that are connected in time; and an **anecdote** is a short narrative that recounts a particular incident. An anecdote, like an example, can bring an abstraction into focus. Consider Martínez's third paragraph, where the anecdote about the museum attendant brings her point about racially charged nostalgia among white Americans into memorable focus: The tears of the museum-goers indicate just how profound their nostalgia is. By contrast, a longer narrative, in setting out its sequence of events, often opens up possibilities for analysis. Why did these events occur? Why did they occur in this sequence? What might they lead to? What are the implications? What is missing? In paragraph 11, for example, Martínez relates several key events in the origin myth of America. Then, in the next paragraph, she explains what is omitted from the myth, or narrative, and builds her argument about the implications and consequences of those omissions.

Define terms.   A definition is an explanation of what something is and, by implication, what it is not. The simplest kind of definition is a synonym, but for the purpose of developing your argument, a one-word definition is rarely enough. When you define your terms, you are setting forth meanings that you want your readers to agree on, so that you can continue to build your argument on the foundation of that agreement. You may have to stipulate that your definition is part of a larger whole to develop your argument. For example: "Nostalgia is a bittersweet longing for things of the past; but for the purposes of my essay, I focus on white middle-class nostalgia, which combines a longing for a past that never existed with a hostile anxiety about the present."

In paragraph 10, Martínez defines the term *origin narrative* — a myth that explains "how a society understands its place in the world and its history . . . the basis for a nation's self-defined identity." The "Great White

Origin Myth" is an important concept in her developing argument about a national crisis of identity.

Make comparisons.   Technically, a **comparison** shows the similarities between two or more things, and a **contrast** shows the differences. In practice, however, it is very difficult, if not impossible, to develop a comparison that does not make use of contrast. Therefore, we use the term *comparison* to describe the strategy of comparing *and* contrasting. Doubtless you have written paragraphs or even whole essays that take as a starting point a version of this sentence: "X and Y are similar in some respects and different in others." This neutral formulation is seldom helpful when you are developing an argument. Usually, in making your comparison — in setting forth the points of similarity and difference — you have to take an evaluative or argumentative stance. Consider the comparison in this passage:

> Although there are similarities between the current nostalgias for Dick and Jane books and for rhythm and blues music of the same era — in both cases, the object of nostalgia can move people to tears — the nostalgias spring from emotional responses that are quite different and even contradictory. I will argue that the Dick and Jane books evoke a longing for a past that is colored by a fear of the present, a time when white middle-class values were dominant and unquestioned as they no longer are. By contrast, the nostalgia for R&B music may indicate a yearning for a past when multicultural musicians provided a sweaty release on the dance floor from those very same white-bread values of the time.

The writer does more than list similarities and differences; he offers an analysis of what they mean and is prepared to argue for his interpretation.

Certainly Elizabeth Martínez takes an evaluative stance when she compares versions of American history in paragraphs 11 and 12. In paragraph 11, she angrily relates the sanitized story of American history, setting up a contrast in paragraph 12 with the story that does not appear in history textbooks, a story of "genocide, enslavement and imperialist expansion." Her evaluative stance comes through clearly: She finds the first version repugnant and harmful, its omissions "grotesque."

Examine causes and evaluate consequences.   In any academic discipline, questions of cause and consequence are central. Whether you are analyzing the latest election results in a political science course, reading about the causes of the Vietnam War in a history course, or speculating about the long-term consequences of global warming in a science course, questions of why things happened, happen, or will happen are inescapable. Examining causes and consequences usually involves identifying a phenomenon and asking questions about it until you gather enough information to begin analyzing the relationships among its parts and deciding which are most significant. You can then begin to set forth your own analysis of what happened and why.

Of course, this kind of analysis is rarely straightforward, and any phenomenon worthy of academic study is bound to generate a variety of conversations about its causes and consequences. In your own thinking and research, avoid jumping to conclusions and continue to sift evidence until plausible connections present themselves. Be prepared to revise your thinking — perhaps several times — in light of new evidence.

In your writing, you also want to avoid oversimplifying. A claim like this — "The answer to curbing unemployment in the United States is to restrict immigration" — does not take into account corporate outsourcing of jobs overseas or the many other possible causes of unemployment. At the very least, you may need to explain the basis and specifics of your analysis, and qualify your claim: "Recent studies of patterns of immigration and unemployment in the United States suggest that unrestricted immigration is a major factor in the loss of blue-collar job opportunities in the Southwest." Certainly this sentence is less forceful and provocative than the other one, but it does suggest that you have done significant and focused research and respect the complexity of the issue.

Throughout her essay, Martínez analyzes causes and consequences. In paragraph 8, for example, she speculates that the *cause* of "attacks on immigrants, affirmative action and multiculturalism" is "Euro-American anxiety," "the sense of a vanishing national identity." In paragraph 13, she concludes that a *consequence* of Theodore Roosevelt's beliefs about race and war was a "militarism [that] went hand in hand with the racialization of history's protagonists." In paragraph 16, the topic sentence itself is a statement about causes and consequences: "Today's origin myth and the resulting concept of national identity make for an intellectual prison where it is dangerous to ask big questions about this society's superiority."

Having shown where and how Martínez uses critical strategies to develop her paragraphs, we must hasten to add that these critical strategies usually work in combination. Although you can easily develop an entire paragraph (or even an entire essay) using comparison, it is almost impossible to do so without relying on one or more of the other strategies. What if you need to tell an anecdote about the two authors you are comparing? What if you have to cite data about different rates of economic growth to clarify the main claim of your comparison? What if you are comparing different causes and consequences? Our point is that the strategies described here are methods for exploring your issue in writing. How you make use of them, individually or in combination, depends on which can help you best communicate your argument to your readers.

Steps to Developing Paragraphs

1 Use topic sentences to focus your paragraphs. Remember that a topic sentence partially answers the question motivating you to write; acts as an extension of your thesis; indicates to your readers what the paragraph is about; and helps create unity both within the paragraph and within the essay.

2 **Create unity in your paragraphs.** The details in your paragraph should follow logically from your topic sentence and maintain a single focus, one tied clearly to your thesis. Repetition and transition words also help create unity in paragraphs.

3 **Use critical strategies to develop your paragraphs.** Use examples and illustrations; cite data; analyze texts; tell stories or anecdotes; define terms; make comparisons; and examine causes and evaluate consequences.

A Practice Sequence: Working with Paragraphs

We would like you to work in pairs on paragraphing. The objective of this exercise is to gauge the effectiveness of your topic sentences and the degree to which your paragraphs are unified and fully developed.

Make a copy of your essay and cut it up into paragraphs. Shuffle the paragraphs to be sure they are no longer in the original order, and then exchange cut-up drafts with your partner. The challenge is to put your partner's essay back together again. When you both have finished, compare your reorderings with the original drafts. Were you able to reproduce the original organization exactly? If not, do the variations make sense? If one or the other of you had trouble putting the essay back together, talk about the adequacy of your topic sentences, ways to revise topic sentences in keeping with the details in a given paragraph, and strategies for making paragraphs more unified and coherent.

DRAFTING CONCLUSIONS

In writing a conclusion to your essay, you are making a final appeal to your audience. You want to convince readers that what you have written is a relevant, meaningful interpretation of a shared issue. You also want to remind them that your argument is reasonable. Rather than summarize all of the points you've made in the essay — assume your readers have carefully read what you've written — pull together the key components of your argument in the service of answering the question "So what?" Establish why your argument is important: What will happen if things stay the same? What will happen if things change? How effective your conclusion is depends on whether or not readers feel you have adequately addressed "So what?" — that you have made clear what is significant and of value.

In building on the specific details of your argument, you can also place what you have written in a broader context. What are the sociological implications of your argument? How far reaching are they? Are there political implications? Economic implications? Finally, explain again how your ideas contribute something new to the conversation by building on, extending, or even challenging what others have argued.

In her concluding paragraph, Elizabeth Martínez brings together her main points, puts her essay in a broader context, indicates what's new in her argument, and answers the question "So what?":

> Accepting the implications of a different narrative could also shed light on today's struggles. In the affirmative-action struggle, for example, opponents have said that that policy is no longer needed because racism ended with the Civil Rights Movement. But if we look at slavery as a fundamental pillar of this nation, going back centuries, it becomes obvious that racism could not have been ended by 30 years of mild reforms. If we see how the myth of the frontier idealized the white male adventurer as the central hero of national history, with the woman as sunbonneted helpmate, then we might better understand the dehumanized ways in which women have continued to be treated. A more truthful origin narrative could also help break down divisions among peoples of color by revealing common experiences and histories of cooperation.

Although Martínez refers back to important events and ideas she has discussed, she does not merely summarize. Instead, she suggests the implications of those important events and ideas in her first sentence (the topic sentence), which crystallizes the main point of her essay: Americans need a different origin narrative. Then she puts those implications in the broader context of contemporary racial and gender issues. She signals what's new in her argument with the word *if* (if we look at slavery in a new way, if we look at the frontier myth in a new way). Finally, her answers to "So what?" — important new insights into racial and gender issues — culminate in the last sentence, which also connects and extends the claim of her topic sentence, by asserting that a "more truthful origin narrative" could help heal divisions among peoples of color who have been misrepresented by the old origin myth. Clearly, she believes the implications of her argument matter: A new national identity has the potential to heal a country in crisis, a country on the verge of a "nervous breakdown" (para. 4).

Martínez also does something else in the last sentence of the concluding paragraph: She looks to the future, suggesting what the future implications of her argument could be. Looking to the future is one of five strategies for shaping a conclusion. The others we discuss are echoing the introduction, challenging the reader, posing questions, and concluding with a quotation. Each of these strategies appeals to readers in different ways; therefore, we suggest you try them all out in writing your own conclusions. Also, remember that some of these strategies can be combined. For example, you can write an introduction that challenges readers, poses a question, looks to the future, and ends with a quotation.

■ Echo the Introduction

Echoing the introduction in your conclusion helps readers come full circle. It helps them see how you have developed your idea from beginning to end. In the example below, the student writer begins with a voice speaking from behind an Islamic veil, revealing the ways that Western culture misunderstands the symbolic value of wearing the veil. The writer repeats this visual image in her conclusion, quoting from the Koran: "Speak to them from behind a curtain."

Notice that the author begins with "a voice from behind the shrouds of an Islamic veil" and then echoes this quotation in her conclusion: "Speak to them from behind a curtain."

Introduction: A voice from behind the shrouds of an Islamic veil exclaims: "I often wonder whether people see me as a radical, fundamentalist Muslim terrorist packing an AK-47 assault rifle inside my jean jacket. Or maybe they see me as the poster girl for oppressed womanhood everywhere." In American culture where shameless public exposure, particularly of females, epitomizes ultimate freedom, the head-to-toe covering of a Muslim woman seems inherently oppressive. Driven by an autonomous national attitude, the inhabitants of the "land of the free" are quick to equate the veil with indisputable persecution. Yet Muslim women reveal the enslaving hijab as a symbolic display of the Islamic ideals — honor, modesty, and stability. Because of an unfair American assessment, the aura of hijab mystery cannot be removed until the customs and ethics of Muslim culture are genuinely explored. It is this form of enigmatic seclusion that forms the feminist controversy between Western liberals, who perceive the veil as an inhibiting factor against free will, and Islamic disciples, who conceptualize the veil as a sacred symbol of utmost morality.

Conclusion: By improperly judging an alien religion, the veil becomes a symbol of oppression and devastation, instead of a representation of pride and piety. Despite Western images, the hijab is a daily revitalization and reminder of the Islamic societal and religious ideals, thereby upholding the conduct and attitudes of the Muslim community. Americans share these ideals yet fail to recognize them in the context of a different culture. By sincerely exploring the custom of Islamic veiling, one will realize the vital role the hijab plays in shaping Muslim culture by sheltering women, and consequently society, from the perils that erupt from indecency. The principles implored in the Koran of modesty, honor, and stability construct a unifying and moral view of the Islamic Middle Eastern society when properly investigated. As it was transcribed from Allah, "Speak to them from behind a curtain. This is purer for your hearts and their hearts."

Notice how the conclusion echoes the introduction in its reference to a voice speaking from behind a curtain.

■ Challenge the Reader

By issuing a challenge to your readers, you create a sense of urgency, provoking them to act to change the status quo. In this example, the student writer explains the unacceptable consequences of preventing young women from educating themselves about AIDS and the spread of a disease that has already reached epidemic proportions.

Here the author cites a final piece of research to emphasize the extent of the problem.

Here she begins her explicit challenge to readers about what they have to do to protect themselves or their students from infection.

The changes in AIDS education that I am suggesting are necessary and relatively simple to make. Although the current curriculum in high school health classes is helpful and informative, it simply does not pertain to young women as much as it should. AIDS is killing women at an alarming rate, and many people do not realize this. According to Daniel DeNoon, AIDS is one of the six leading causes of death among women aged 18–45, and women "bear the brunt of the worldwide AIDS epidemic." For this reason, DeNoon argues, women are one of the most important new populations that are contracting HIV at a high rate. I challenge young women to be more well-informed about AIDS and their link to the disease; otherwise, many new cases may develop. As the epidemic continues to spread, women need to realize that they can stop the spread of the disease and protect themselves from infection and a number of related complications. It is the responsibility of health educators to present this to young women and inform them of the powerful choices that they can make.

■ Look to the Future

Looking to the future is particularly relevant when you are asking readers to take action. To move readers to action, you must establish the persistence of a problem and the consequences of letting a situation continue unchanged. In the concluding paragraph below, the student author points out a number of things that teachers need to do to involve parents in their children's education. She identifies a range of options before identifying what she believes is perhaps the most important action teachers can take.

The second through fifth sentences present an array of options.

First and foremost, teachers must recognize the ways in which some parents are positively contributing to their children's academic endeavors. Teachers must recognize nontraditional methods of participation as legitimate and work toward supporting parents in these tasks. For instance, teachers might send home suggestions for local after-school tutoring programs. Teachers must also try to make urban parents feel welcome and respected in their school. Teachers might call parents to ask their opinion about a certain difficulty their child is having, or invite them to talk about something of interest to them. One parent, for instance, spoke highly of the previous superintendent who had let him use his work as a film producer to help with a show for students during homeroom. If teachers can develop innovative ways to utilize parents' talents and interests rather than just inviting them to be passively involved in an already-in-place curriculum, more parents might respond. Perhaps, most importantly, if teachers want parents to be involved in their students' educations, they must make the parents feel as though their opinions and concerns have real

In the last two sentences, the writer looks to the future with her recommendations.

weight. When parents such as those interviewed for this study voice concerns and questions over their child's progress, it is imperative that teachers acknowledge and answer them.

■ Pose Questions

Posing questions stimulates readers to think about the implications of your argument and to apply what you argue to other situations. This is the case in the paragraph below, in which the student writer focuses on immigration and then shifts readers' attention to racism and the possibility of hate crimes. It's useful to extrapolate from your argument, to raise questions that test whether what you write can be applied to different situations. These questions can help readers understand what is at issue.

The first question.

Also, my research may apply to a broader spectrum of sociological topics. There has been recent discussion about the increasing trend of immigration. Much of this discussion has involved the distribution of resources to immigrants. Should immigrants have equal access to certain economic and educational resources in America? The decision is split. But, it will be interesting to see how this debate will play out. If immigrants are granted more

Other speculative questions follow from possible responses to the writer's first question.

resources, will certain Americans mobilize against the distribution of these resources? Will we see another rise in racist groups such as the Ku Klux Klan in order to prevent immigrants from obtaining more resources? My research can also be used to understand global conflict or war. In general, groups mobilize when their established resources are threatened by an external force. Moreover, groups use framing processes to justify their collective action to others.

■ Conclude with a Quotation

A quotation can add authority to your argument, indicating that others in positions of power and prestige support your stance. A quotation also can add poignancy to your argument, as it does in the excerpt below, in which the quotation amplifies the idea that people use Barbie to advance their own interests.

> The question still remains, what does Barbie mean? Is she the spokeswoman for the empowerment of women or rather is she performing the dirty work of conservative patriarchy? I do not think we will ever know the answer. Rather, Barbie is the undeniable "American Icon." She is a toy, and she is what we want her to be. A test performed by Albert M. Magro at Fairmont State College titled "Why Barbie Is Perceived as Beautiful" shows that Barbie is the epitome of what we as humans find beautiful. The test sought to find human preferences on evolutionary changes in the human body. Subjects were shown a series of photos comparing different human body parts, such as the size and shape of the eyes, and asked to decide which feature they preferred: the primitive or derived (more evolved traits). The test revealed that the subjects preferred the derived body traits. Ironically, it is these preferred evolutionary features that are utilized on the body of Barbie. Barbie is truly an extension of what we are and what we perceive.

The writer quotes an authority to amplify the idea that individually and collectively, we project significance on toys.

> Juel Best concludes his discourse on Barbie with these words: "Toys do not embody violence or sexism or occult meanings. People must assign toys their meanings." Barbie is whoever we make her out to be. Barbie grabs hold of our imaginations and lets us go wild.

Steps to Drafting Conclusions

1 **Pull together the main claims of your essay.** Don't simply repeat points you make in the paper. Instead, show readers how the points you make fit together.

2 **Answer the question "So What?"** Show your readers why your stand on the issue is significant.

3 **Place your argument in a larger context.** Discuss the specifics of your argument, but also indicate its broader implications.

4 **Show readers what is new.** As you synthesize the key points of your argument, explain how what you argue builds on, extends, or challenges the thinking of others.

5 **Decide on the best strategy for writing your conclusion.** Will you echo the introduction? Challenge the reader? Look to the future? Pose questions? Conclude with a quotation? Choose the best strategy or strategies to appeal to your readers.

A Practice Sequence: Drafting a Conclusion

1 Write your conclusion, using one of the strategies described in this section. Then share your conclusion with a classmate. Ask this person to address the following questions:

- Did I pull together the key points of the argument?
- Did I answer "So what?" adequately?
- Are the implications I want readers to draw from the essay clear?

After listening to the responses, try a second strategy, and then ask your classmate which conclusion is more effective.

2 If you do not have a conclusion of your own, analyze each example conclusion above to see how well each appears to (1) pull together the main claim of the essay, (2) answer "So what?" (3) place the argument in a larger context, and (4) show readers what is new.

10

From Revising to Editing: Working with Peer Groups

Academic writing is a collaborative enterprise. By reading and commenting on your drafts, your peers can support your work as a writer. And you can support the work of your peers by reading their drafts with a critical but constructive eye. As a critical reader of your peers' writing, you bring your knowledge, experiences, and interests to bear on what you read, and your responses to their texts can help other writers continue the conversations they have joined. The questions you raise may reveal what is missing from a writer's argument, motivating the writer to revise his or her work. It is easier to see problems in other people's writing than in our own because we have a critical distance from their work that we don't have from our own. At the same time, as you read other work critically, you will begin to internalize the questions that will help you revise your own arguments.

In this chapter, we set out the differences between revising and editing, discuss the peer editing process in terms of the composition pyramid, present a model peer editing session, and then explain the writer's and reader's responsibilities through early drafts, later drafts, and final drafts, providing opportunities for you to practice peer response on three drafts of a student paper.

REVISING VERSUS EDITING

We make a distinction between revising and editing. By **revising**, we mean making changes to a paper to reflect new thinking or conceptualizing. If a reader finds that the real focus of your essay comes at the end of your draft, you need to revise the paper with this new focus in mind. Revising differs from **editing**, which involves minor changes to what will be the final draft of a paper — replacing a word here and there, correcting misspellings, or substituting dashes for commas to create emphasis, for example. When you're reading a first or second draft, the niceties of style, spelling, and punctuation are not priorities. After all, if the writer had to change the focus of his or her argument, significant changes to words, phrases, and punctuation would be inevitable. Concentrating on editing errors early on, when the writer is still trying to develop an argument with evidence, organize information logically, and anticipate counterarguments, is inefficient and even counterproductive.

Here are some characteristics of revising and editing that can guide how you read your own writing and the comments you offer to other writers:

REVISING	EDITING
Treats writing as a work in progress	Treats writing as an almost-finished product
Focuses on new possibilities both within and beyond the text	Addresses obvious errors and deficiencies
Focuses on new questions or goals	Focuses on the text alone
Considers both purpose and readers' needs	Considers grammar, punctuation, spelling, and style
Encourages further discovery	Polishes up the essay

You should understand that writing is a process, and that revising is an integral part of that process. Your best writing will happen in the context of real readers' responding to your drafts. Look at the acknowledgments in any academic book, and you will see many people credited with having improved the book through their reading and discussion of drafts and ideas. All academic writers rely on conversations with others to strengthen their work.

THE PEER EDITING PROCESS

In sharing writing with others, you need to be clear about your responsibilities. You may find that you assume one role when you read a peer's early draft, trying to encourage and support the writer to find ways to strengthen his or her argument. Although you will need to be critical, asking probing questions, you also will need to be sure that your conversation is constructive, that you encourage your peer to continue writing. You play a very different role when the writer tells you, "This is it. It's finished."

We emphasize that the different stages of writing — early, later, and final — call for different work from both readers and writers because writers' needs vary with each successive draft. These stages correspond to what has been called the composition pyramid (Figure 10.1).* The

*We thank Susannah Brietz-Monta and Anthony Monta for this idea.

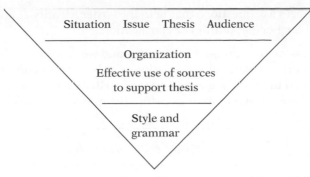

Figure 10.1   The Composition Pyramid

composition pyramid represents elements of writing that can help you decide what to pay attention to at different stages of writing.

The top of this inverted pyramid corresponds to the early stages of writing. At this point, members of the writing group should identify the situation the writer is responding to (for example, homelessness, inequality, or air pollution), the issue the writer has defined (for example, the economic versus the social costs of homelessness), the thesis or argument the writer advances, and the extent to which the writer addresses a given audience appropriately. The middle portion of the pyramid corresponds to a later stage of the writing process, the point at which members of the group should move on to discuss the extent to which the writer has organized the argument logically and used sources effectively to support the thesis. Has the writer integrated quotations smoothly into the paper? Is the evidence relevant, recent, and credible? Finally, the bottom of the pyramid corresponds to the final stages of drafting. As the writer's focus shifts to grammar and style, so should the group's. Questions to ask: Is this specific language appropriate to the intended audience? Has the writer presented the argument in ways that will compel readers — even those who disagree — to listen?

Steps in the Peer Editing Process

1 The writer distributes copies of the draft to each member of the writing group. (Ideally, the group should not exceed four students.)

2 The writer distributes a cover letter, setting an agenda for each member of the group.

3 The members read the cover letter.

4 The writer then reads the draft aloud, while members follow along, underlining passages and making notes to prepare themselves to discuss the draft.

5 Members ask questions that help the writer identify concepts that need further elaboration or clarification.

6 Discussion focuses on the strengths and weaknesses of the draft appropriate to the stage of writing and the writer's concerns. (Even in the early stage, readers and writer should sustain discussion for at least ten minutes before the next student takes a turn as writer.)

PEER GROUPS IN ACTION: A SAMPLE SESSION

Let's take a look at one writing group in action to see the potential of this approach to writing. One student, Brett Preacher, worked collaboratively with three other students for several weeks on plans for and drafts of his paper. The assignment was to argue whether the movie *Million Dollar Baby* accurately portrays poverty. Brett explained to his group that he had struggled to find ways to advance his argument at the same time that he was trying to synthesize different authors' points of view. Moreover, he was worried that he didn't do the assignment:

> BRETT: That was the assignment, to argue whether the movie portrays poverty justly or unjustly. That was the assignment, what we were supposed to do, and I didn't do that at all.
>
> CAITLIN: Well, I didn't do that either, but I used hooks's "Seeing and Making Culture: Representing the Poor" and Freedman's *From Cradle to Grave: The Human Face of Poverty in America*.
>
> BRETT: Yeah, well, I kind of quit. I strayed off the movie at the end. I basically quit talking about the movie about halfway through the paper, so the whole second half of my paper, so basically the whole second half of my paper is the weak part. I just kind of quit talking about *Million Dollar Baby*.

Brett restated his understanding of the assignment before reading his draft aloud. This is a valuable starting point because a writer's interpretation of the assignment — the task, the purpose, the audience — helps the peer readers understand why the writer is taking a particular approach. If the readers disagree with the writer's interpretation, they should discuss their differences before the writer shares the draft, to determine an appropriate response to the assignment.

As you read the excerpt Brett shared with his group, we would like you to analyze the extent to which he formulated an argument that synthesizes his reading:

- Highlight Brett's key claim(s).
- Note the connections he makes to different readings.
- Decide what those connections mean.

Preacher 1

Brett Preacher
Professor Tindall
English 200
October 10, 20--

Representing Poverty in <u>Million Dollar Baby</u>

In "Seeing and Making Culture: Representing the Poor," bell hooks discusses the extent to which the media describes the poor as all nihilistic and longing for material worth. This image is slightly expressed in the movie <u>Million Dollar Baby</u> through Maggie's family. In the only scenes her family makes an appearance, they present themselves as white trash by worrying that their welfare will be taken away and trying to make an easy dollar off a crippled Maggie. Jonathan Friedman, however, seems to capture the essence of the movie much more accurately in a chapter out of his book, <u>From Cradle to Grave</u>, called "The Human Face of Poverty in America." In this chapter, Freedman presents many stories that support his argument that perseverance can help people rise from a life of poverty. This argument is portrayed perfectly by Maggie throughout the movie.

In the movie, Maggie strives to become a professional boxer to support herself rather than succumb to a life of poverty as her family did. Through drive and determination, Maggie strives to rise out of poverty despite all the doubt and negativity directed towards her. With nothing more than her wages and tips from her waitressing job, she saves her money, sacrificing much along the way to pay for her trainer. Her family, however, represents the other side of the spectrum and looks for nothing more than an easy way out of their welfare sustained lifestyle. Rather than working to better themselves, they depend on welfare, and after putting Maggie down repeatedly about her career, they try to sign her savings over to themselves when she gets injured. Through her hard work and determination, Maggie achieves her dream in the end, helping to support the argument Friedman makes. Jonathan Freedman catches the face of poverty precisely by arguing that perseverance can put anyone out of a life of poverty. Most people, however, cannot fathom this idea until they have witnessed something similar.

Preacher 2

3

In her essay, hooks describes the generalizations that the media have of the poor, which convey stereotypes. Friedman observes that it takes money, organization, and laws to maintain a social structure, but none of it works if there are not opportunities for people to meet and help each other along the way. For example, he tells the story of about Nitza, a young homeless mother with four children. She is forced to put her children into foster care for three years until she works her way out of poverty and can support her family. Friedman's point is that that there is not enough opportunity to maintain the social structure that we desire. At the same time, we see that Nitza succeeds because she is motivated to change her circumstances.

Unable to identify Brett's key claim, his writing group members asked a number of questions that they hoped would guide Brett toward making an explicit claim about whether or not the film *Million Dollar Baby* represents poverty in a fair way:

> CAITLIN: So what you are saying is that the film does and doesn't support hooks's argument that the media misrepresent the poor?
> MEGHAN: You give a lot of examples here, like about Maggie. You could expand those into a paper. But what point do you want to make?
> BRETT: Yeah, each example could be in a different paragraph.
> CAITLIN: Those could be your main points, you know?

Caitlin believed that Brett's point may have been more implicit than explicit, that the film *Million Dollar Baby* "does and doesn't support hooks's argument that the media misrepresent the poor." Caitlin's suggestion underscores the complexity of what Brett was trying to argue — that the film does and doesn't represent poverty in a fair way — and poses a challenge that Meghan appeared to understand. Meghan suggested to Brett that he formulate different paragraphs to advance the point that *Million Dollar Baby* offers a contradictory image of poverty that is at once realistic and unrealistic. Caitlin agreed when she said that "those could be your main points." (Actually, that's just one key claim.)

However, Daimon, the fourth member of the group, recognized that Brett was going to have to develop his discussion of *Million Dollar Baby* before it became clear whether or not the film offers two conflicting images of poverty:

> DAIMON: It's just you don't talk about *Million Dollar Baby* enough, and I think that's what the essay is supposed to be about. Not so much about the other two. You can use the other two, but not so much as you did.
>
> BRETT: Just tie in *Million Dollar Baby* a little more, you think?
>
> CAITLIN: Well, because you talk a lot, it does fit with your paper, but it doesn't . . . it's supposed to be about *Million Dollar Baby*. . . . Do you think the film portrays poverty in a realistic way?
>
> MEGHAN: Yeah, give examples of the way the film describes Maggie's family. It's like they depend on her to get themselves out of poverty.

And then Caitlin steered Brett back to the point she made earlier — that Brett could revise his paper to address the complicated way the film represents poverty:

> CAITLIN: That could be the issue. There are contradictory images of poverty and how people deal.
>
> BRETT: Yeah, well, I don't know. I'm going to have to think about that.

Brett's draft reflects his first attempt to get his ideas down. It's fine for a first draft to be exploratory. When writers formulate a working thesis or when they fail to formulate a thesis, readers in a peer group can offer support, noting strengths or pointing to places of greatest interest in an effort to sustain the writer's energy for writing. Caitlin helped Brett generate a plan for taking the next step by pointing out how he could define the issue — "There are contradictory images of poverty and how people deal."

A peer group can also ask questions to help a writer set new goals. A good strategy is to paraphrase particular parts of the draft so that the writer can hear how you, the reader, have understood what he or she is trying to say. This is what Caitlin did when she said, "So what you are saying is that the film does and doesn't support hooks's argument that the media misrepresent the poor?"

WORKING WITH EARLY DRAFTS

■ Consider the Writer's Responsibilities

When you present an early draft of your essay to your writing group, you want the group to focus on top-level pyramid concerns — situation, purpose, issue, thesis, and audience. You should explain this and any other concerns you have in a cover letter. Use the template in Figure 10.2 as a model for what needs explaining in the letter to your readers.

During the session it's important to be open to suggestions. Although you don't have to incorporate every suggestion your group makes when you revise your draft, be sure you at least understand the members' comments and concerns. If you don't understand what the members are saying about your draft, ask them to clarify or give you an example.

Finally, if you decide not to take someone's suggestion, have a good reason for doing so. It's fine to say no to a suggested change in the purpose or intended audience of your essay if that change means you won't be addressing the terms of the assignment or that you would no longer be interested in the issue.

FIGURE 10.2　　The Writer's Cover Letter: Early Drafts

1. What is your question (or assignment)?
2. What is the issue motivating you to write?
3. How have published writers addressed the issue about which you are writing?
4. What is your working thesis?
5. Who is your audience, and what kind of response do you want from your readers?
6. What do you think is working best?
7. What specific aspect of the essay are you least satisfied with at this time?
8. What kind of feedback do you especially want today?

■ Consider the Reader's Responsibilities

Your task as a reader is to follow along as the early draft is read, paying special attention to the concerns the writer has explained in the cover letter and focusing on the top of the pyramid: situation, issue, thesis, and audience. Take notes directly on the draft copy, circling or underlining sections you find confusing or have questions about, so that you can refer to them specifically in the discussion.

When it's your turn to talk, have a conversation about your reactions to the draft — where the draft amused, confused, or persuaded you, for example. Don't just jump in and start telling the writer what he or she should be doing in the paper. Your role as a reader is to give the writer a live audience: Your responses can help the writer decide what parts of the paper are working and what parts need serious revision. There are times, however, when you should play the role of *deferring reader*, putting off certain comments. You don't want to overwhelm the writer with problems no matter how many questions the essay raises.

Offer both positive and negative remarks. Start by pointing out what is working well in the paper, so the writer knows where he or she is on the right track. This also leaves the writer more open to constructive criticism. But don't shy away from telling the writer what should be working better. It's your job as a reader to offer honest and specific responses to the draft, so the writer can develop it into an effective piece of writing. Figure 10.3 lists key questions you should ask as a reader of an early draft.

FIGURE 10.3   A Reader's Questions: Early Drafts

1. Are the questions and issues that motivate the writer clear?
2. Has the writer effectively related the conversation that published writers are engaged in?
3. What is at issue?
4. What is the writer's thesis?
5. Is the writer addressing the audience's concerns effectively?
6. What passages of the draft are most effective?
7. What passages of the draft are least effective?

■ Analyze an Early Draft

Keep these questions in mind as you read the following excerpt from a student's early draft. After reading a number of scholarly articles on the civil rights movement, Tasha Taylor decided to address what she sees as the difference between scholars' understanding of the movement and more popular treatments in textbooks and photographs. She also tries to tie in the larger question of historical memory to her analysis of southern blacks' struggle for equality — what people remember about the past and what they forget. In fact, she begins her essay with a quotation she believes summarizes what she wants to argue ("The struggle of man against power is the struggle of memory against forgetting").

As you read Taylor's essay, take detailed notes, and underline passages that concern you. Then write a paragraph or two explaining what she could do to strengthen the draft. Keep in mind that this is an early draft, so focus on the top level of the pyramid: the situation or assignment; the issue; the thesis; and the audience.

Taylor 1

Tasha Taylor
Professor Winters
English 111
October 23, 20--

Memory Through Photography

The struggle of man against power is the struggle of memory against forgetting.

—Milan Kundera

Ask the average American what the key components of the civil rights movement are, and most people will probably recall Martin Luther

King, Jr. speaking of a dream in front of the Lincoln Memorial, Rosa Parks riding a bus, a few court decisions, and perhaps a photograph of Elizabeth Eckford cowering before an angry mob in front of Central High School in Little Rock. Few people are aware A. Philip Randolph planned the march on Washington. Few could describe Rosa Parks's connection to the civil rights movement (for example, the fact that she had been a member of the NAACP since 1943) before her legendary refusal to give up her seat in December 1955, which led to the Montgomery Bus Boycott. Few recognize the years of struggle that existed between the Brown v. Board of Education decision and the actual desegregation of schools. Few consider the fate of Elizabeth Eckford after the federal troops were sent to protect her and the other members of the Little Rock Nine had left Central High or the months of abuse (physical and emotional) that they endured in the name of integration. What most people know is limited to textbooks they read in school or the captions under photographs that describe where a particular event occurred.

Why is it that textbooks exclusively feature the stories of larger than life figures like Martin Luther King? Why is it that we remember things the way we do? Historical events "have little meaning without human interpretation, without our speaking about them within the contexts of our lives and our culture, without giving them names and meanings" (Kolker xix). Each person experiencing the exact same event will carry a different memory from that event. Trying to decipher what memories reveal about each person is a fascinating yet difficult endeavor, because each retelling of a memory and each additional memory alters existing ones.

The story that photographs and textbooks tell us does not even begin to describe the depth of the movement or the thousands who risked their lives and the lives of their families to make equality a reality. Embracing this selective memory as a nation prevents understanding and acknowledgement of the harsh reality of other images from the civil rights movement (demonstrators being plowed down by fire hoses, beatings, and the charred bodies of bombing victims) which are key aspects of understanding who we are as a society. The question therefore is why. Why is it that textbook writers and

> Taylor 3
>
> publishers have allowed so much of this history to be skewed and forgotten? How can it be that barely 50 years after these events so many have been forgotten or diluted?

For Analysis and Discussion

1. What is working well in Taylor's draft?
2. What is Taylor's thesis or argument?
3. To what extent does she connect her analysis of the civil rights movement and historical memory?
4. What parts of her analysis could Taylor explain further? (What do you still need to know?)
5. What would you suggest Taylor do next?

WORKING WITH LATER DRAFTS

■ Consider the Writer's Responsibilities

At a later stage, after you've had the opportunity to take readers' suggestions and do further research, you should be able to state your thesis more definitively than you did in your earlier draft. You also should be able to support your thesis with evidence, anticipating possible counterarguments. Ideally, your readers will still provide constructive criticism, offering their support, as in the first draft, but they will also question and challenge more than before.

Here, too, you want to help readers focus on your main concerns, which you should explain in a cover letter. You may still need to work on one or two top-level pyramid concerns; but your focus will likely be midlevel concerns — organization and the effective use of sources. Use the list of questions in Figure 10.4 to help you write your cover letter.

FIGURE 10.4   The Writer's Cover Letter: Later Drafts

1. What is your research question?
2. What is the issue motivating you to write?
3. What is your thesis?
4. How do you go about identifying a gap in readers' knowledge, modifying others' ideas, or trying to correct readers' misunderstandings?

(*continued on next page*)

FIGURE 10.4   (Continued)

5. To what extent do you distinguish your argument from the information you quote, summarize, or paraphrase from the sources you have read?

6. To what extent have you organized your ideas in ways that will help readers follow the logic of your argument?

7. To what extent have you anticipated potential counterarguments to your thesis?

8. What do you think is working best?

9. What specific aspect of the essay are you least satisfied with at this time?

■ Consider the Reader's Responsibilities

In a later draft, your focus as reader should be on midlevel concerns in the composition pyramid: places in the writer's text that are confusing, that require better transitions, or that could use sources more effectively. You can challenge writers at this stage of the composing process, perhaps playing the role of *naive reader*, suggesting places in the draft where the writer has left something out or isn't clear. The naive reader's comments tend to take the form of questions: "Do you mean to suggest that everyone who learns to write well succeeds in life? What kind of success are you talking about?" Closely related to the naive reader is the *devil's advocate reader*. This reader's comments also challenge the writer, often taking the form of a question like this: "But why couldn't this be attributed to the effects of socialization rather than heredity?" Figure 10.5 offers questions for reading later drafts.

FIGURE 10.5   A Reader's Questions: Later Drafts

1. To what extent is it clear what questions and issues motivate the writer?

2. What is the writer's thesis?

3. How effectively does the writer establish the conversation — identity a gap in people's knowledge, attempt to modify an existing argument, or try to correct some misunderstanding?

4. How effectively does the writer distinguish between his or her ideas and the ideas he or she summarizes, paraphrases, or quotes?

5. How well does the writer help you follow the logic of his or her argument?

6. To what extent are you persuaded by the writer's argument?

7. To what extent does the writer anticipate possible counterarguments?

8. To what extent does the writer make clear how he or she wants readers to respond?

9. What do you think is working best? Explain by pointing to specific passages in the writer's draft.

10. What specific aspect of the draft is least effective? Explain by pointing to a specific passage in the writer's draft.

■ Analyze a Later Draft

Now read the following excerpt from Taylor's second draft. You will see that she begins with her discussion of historical memory. She also has included an analysis of a book of photographs that Nobel Prize–winning author Toni Morrison compiled. Take notes as you read the draft and write a paragraph in which you describe what you see as some of the strengths of what Taylor has written and what she can do to make other elements stronger. In particular, focus on the middle level of the composition pyramid — on organization and the effective use of sources and evidence to support her thesis.

Taylor 1

Tasha Taylor
Professor Winters
English 111
November 14, 20--

Memory Through Photography

The struggle of man against power is the struggle of memory against forgetting.

–Milan Kundera

Memory is such an integral part of what it is to be human, yet is something so often taken for granted: people assume that their memories are accurate to protect themselves from the harsh realities of the atrocities committed by ordinary people. Even the pictures used to represent the much-celebrated civil rights movement give us a false sense of security and innocence. For example, the Ku Klux Klan is most often depicted by covered faces and burning crosses; the masks allow us to remove ourselves from responsibility. Few could describe Rosa Parks's connection to the civil rights movement (for example, the fact that she had been a member of the NAACP since 1943) before her legendary refusal to give up her seat in December 1955, which led to the Montgomery Bus Boycott. Few recognize the years of struggle that existed between the Brown v. Board of Education decision and the actual desegregation of schools. Few consider the fate of Elizabeth Eckford after the federal troops were sent to protect her and the other members of the Little Rock Nine had left Central High or the months of abuse (physical and emotional) that they endured in the name of integration. What most people know is limited to textbooks they read in school or the captions under photographs that describe where a particular event occurred.

_1_

Taylor 2

It is important, therefore, to analyze what is remembered and even more importantly to recognize what it is forgotten: to question why it is that it is forgotten, what that says about society today, how far it has come and how much it has unwittingly fallen back into old patterns such as prejudice and ignorance. The discrepancies in cultural memory are due more to a society's desire to remember itself in the best light and protect itself from the reality of its brutality and responsibility. Such selective memory only temporarily heals the wounds of society; lack of awareness does not cause healing. Although there have been many recent moves to increase awareness, they are tainted by unavoidable biases and therefore continue to perpetuate a distorted memory.

Images play a central role in the formation of cultural memory because people can point to photographs and claim them as concrete evidence: "Images entrance us because they provide a powerful illusion of owning reality. If we can photograph reality or paint or copy it, we have exercised an important kind of power" (Kolker 3). A picture of black and white children sitting at a table together is used to reinforce the cultural perception that the problems of racism are over, that it has all been fixed.

In her book Remember, Toni Morrison strives to revitalize the memory of school integration through photographs. The book is dedicated to Denise McNair, Carole Robertson, Addie Mae Collins, and Cynthia Wesley, the four girls killed in the 16th Street Baptist Church bombing in 1963. Morrison writes, "Things are better now. Much, much better. But remember why and please remember us" (Morrison 72). The pictures are of black and white children happily eating together, solemnly saluting the flag together, and holding hands. The photographs of the four murdered girls show them peacefully and innocently smiling as if everything really is better now. In reality, according to the Bureau of Alcohol, Tobacco and Firearms, between 1995 and 1997 there were 162 incidents of arson or bombing in African American houses of worship (ATF Online). There are a few images of people protesting integration, but they are also consistent with the cultural memory (protesters are shown simply holding signs and yelling, not beating and killing innocent children). Finally, the captions are written in a child's voice. Yet it is not a child's voice at all it is merely a top down view of children that serves to perpetuate a distorted cultural memory.

Taylor 3

The photographs used to suggest how things are much, much
better now are misleading. For example, the last photograph is of a
black girl and a white girl holding hands through a bus window,
which was transporting them to an integrated school. The caption
reads: "Anything can happen. Anything at all. See?" (71). It is a very
powerful image of how the evil of Jim Crow and segregation exist in a
distant past and the nation has come together and healed. However,
Morrison neglects to point out that the picture was taken in Boston,
Massachusetts, not the deep south, the heart of racism. Children
holding hands in Boston is much less significant than if they were in
Birmingham where that action would be concrete evidence of how far
we as a nation have come.

Morrison also glorifies of Martin Luther King, Jr. and Rosa Parks
pointing to them as epitomizing the movement. Unfortunately, she
perpetuates the story that one needs to be special or somehow larger
than life to affect change. Paul Rogat Loeb writes in Soul of a Citizen:

> Once we enshrine our heroes, it becomes hard for mere mortals to
> measure up in our eyes . . . in our collective amnesia we lose the
> mechanisms through which grassroots social movements of the
> past successfully shifted public sentiment and challenged
> entrenched institutional power. Equally lost are the means by
> which their participants managed to keep on, sustaining their
> hope and eventually prevailing in circumstances at least as diffi-
> cult as those we face today. (Loeb 38/36)

Placing a select few on pedestals and claiming them as next to divine
heroes of the movement does society a disservice; people fail to realize that ordinary people can serve as agents of change.

Morrison's book ignores the thousand of ordinary people who
risked their lives for the cause to bring about equality. The caption
besides the picture of Rosa Parks in Remember reads "because if I ever
feel helpless or lonely I just have to remember that all it takes is one
person" (Morrison 62). Ironically, Morrison gives credit for the Montgomery Bus Boycott to one person, ignoring the months of planning
and involved dozens of planners. Even the photograph presents Rosa
Parks in a position of power. It is a low-angle shot up at Parks that
makes her appear larger than life and authoritative. The photographs
of Martin Luther King, Jr. also further the impression of power with a

5

6

7

Taylor 4

close up shot of his face as he stands above thousands of participants in the March on Washington. Although these photographs were selected to perpetuate the hero illusion, it is more inspiring to remember the ordinary people who took a stand and were able to accomplish extraordinary feats because of their dedication and persistence rather than glorify extraordinary people who were destined for greatness.

For Discussion and Analysis

1. What is Taylor's thesis or argument?
2. How well does she help you follow the logic of her argument with transitions?
3. How effectively does she distinguish between her ideas and the ideas she summarizes, paraphrases, or quotes?
4. To what extent are you persuaded by her argument?
5. What should Taylor do next?

WORKING WITH FINAL DRAFTS

▪ Consider the Writer's Responsibilities

Your final draft should require editing, not revising. At this stage, readers should focus on errors in style and grammar in the text, not on the substance of your work. Here, too, indicate your main concerns in a cover letter (Figure 10.6).

FIGURE 10.6   The Writer's Cover Letter: Final Drafts

1. What is your unique perspective on your issue?
2. To what extent do the words and phrases you use reflect who you believe your readers are?
3. Does your style of citation reflect accepted conventions for academic writing?
4. What do you think is working best?
5. What specific aspect of the essay are you least satisfied with at this time?

▪ Consider the Reader's Responsibilities

Once a writer's ideas are developed and in place, readers should turn their attention to the bottom level of the composition pyramid, to matters of style and grammar. At this stage, details are important: Is this the best word to use? Would this sentence be easier to follow if it was broken into two sentences? Which spelling is correct — *Freedman* or *Friedman*? Are citations handled consistently? Should this question mark precede or follow the quotation mark? The *grammatically correct reader* evaluates and makes judgments about the writer's work. This reader may simply indicate with a mark of some sort that there's a problem in a sentence or paragraph, or may even correct the writer's work. Figure 10.7 is a list of questions a reader should ask of a final draft.

FIGURE 10.7   A Reader's Questions: Final Drafts

1. How does the writer go about contributing a unique perspective on the issue?
2. To what extent does the writer use words and phrases that are appropriate for the intended audience?
3. To what extent does the style of citation reflect accepted conventions for academic writing?
4. What do you think is working best?
5. What specific aspect of the essay are you least satisfied with at this time?

■ Analyze a Near-Final Draft

Now read Taylor's near-final draft and write a paragraph detailing what she can do to strengthen it. Again, you will see that Taylor has made substantial changes. She compares Morrison's book of photographs to a Spike Lee documentary that she watched with her class. As you read the essay, focus on the bottom level of the composition pyramid: Does the writer use appropriate language? Does she adhere to appropriate conventions for using and citing sources? (See Chapter 7 for information on MLA and APA formats.)

Taylor 1

Tasha Taylor
Professor Winters
English 111
December 5, 20--

Memory Through Photography

Memory is such an integral part of what it is to be human, yet it is something so often taken for granted: people assume that their memories are accurate to protect themselves from the harsh realities of the atrocities committed by ordinary people. Even the pictures

1

Taylor 2

used to represent the much-celebrated civil rights movement give us a false sense of security and innocence. For example, the Ku Klux Klan is most often depicted by covered faces and burning crosses; the masks allow us to remove ourselves from responsibility. Few could describe Rosa Parks's connection to the civil rights movement before her legendary refusal to give up her seat in December 1955, which led to the Montgomery Bus Boycott (for example, the fact that she had been a member of the NAACP since 1943). Few recognize the years of struggle that existed between the 1954 Brown v. Board of Education decision and the actual desegregation of schools. Few consider the fate of Elizabeth Eckford after the federal troops sent to protect her and the other members of the Little Rock Nine had left Central High or the months of abuse (physical and emotional) that they endured in the name of integration. What most people know is limited to the textbooks they read in school or the captions under photographs that describe where a particular event occurred.

It is important, then, to analyze what is remembered, and even more important to recognize what is forgotten: to question why it is that it is forgotten, what that says about society today, how far it has come and how much it has unwittingly fallen back into old patterns of prejudice and ignorance. The discrepancies in cultural memory are due more to society's desire to remember itself in the best light and protect itself from the reality of its brutality and responsibility. Such selective memory only temporarily heals the wounds of society; lack of awareness does not cause healing. Although there have been many recent moves to increase awareness, they are tainted by unavoidable biases and therefore continue to perpetuate a distorted memory.

Images play a central role in the formation of cultural memory because people can point to photographs and claim them as concrete evidence: "Images entrance us because they provide a powerful illusion of owning reality. If we can photograph reality or paint or copy it, we have exercised an important kind of power" (Kolker 3). A picture of black and white children sitting at a table together is used to reinforce the cultural perception that the problems of racism are over, that they have all been fixed.

In her book Remember, Toni Morrison strives to revitalize the memory of school integration through photographs. The book is dedicated to Denise McNair, Carole Robertson, Addie Mae Collins, and Cynthia Wesley, the four girls killed in the 16th Street Baptist Church bombing in 1963. Morrison writes: "Things are better now. Much, much better. But remember why and please remember us" (72). The pictures are of black and white children happily eating together, solemnly saluting the flag together, and holding hands. The photographs of the four murdered girls show them peacefully and innocently smiling as if everything really is better now. In reality, according to the Bureau of Alcohol, Tobacco, Firearms and Explosives, between 1995 and 1997 there were 162 incidents of arson or bombing in African American houses of worship (ATF Online). There are a few images of people protesting integration, but they are also consistent with the cultural memory (protesters are shown simply holding signs and yelling, not beating and killing innocent children). Finally, the captions are written in a child's voice. Yet it is not a child's voice at all; it is merely a top-down view of children that serves to perpetuate a distorted cultural memory.

The photographs used to suggest how things are much, much better now are misleading. For example, the last photograph, taken through a bus window, is of a black girl and a white girl holding hands; the bus was transporting them to an integrated school. The caption reads. "Anything can happen. Anything at all. See?" (71). It is a very powerful image of how the evil of Jim Crow and segregation exist in a distant past and the nation has come together and healed. However, Morrison neglects to point out that the picture was taken in Boston, not in the Deep South, the heart of racism. Children holding hands in Boston is much less significant than if they were in Birmingham, where that action would be concrete evidence of how far we as a nation have come.

Morrison also glorifies Martin Luther King Jr. and Rosa Parks, pointing to them as epitomizing the movement. Unfortunately, she perpetuates the story that one needs to be special or somehow larger than life to effect change. Paul Rogat Loeb writes in Soul of a Citizen:

> Once we enshrine our heroes, it becomes hard for mere mortals
> to measure up in our eyes. . . . In our collective amnesia we lose
> the mechanisms through which grassroots social movements of
> the past successfully shifted public sentiment and challenged
> entrenched institutional power. Equally lost are the means by

Taylor 4

which their participants managed to keep on, sustaining their hope and eventually prevailing in circumstances at least as difficult as those we face today. (38/36)

Placing a select few on pedestals and claiming them as next-to-divine heroes of the movement does society a disservice; people fail to realize that ordinary people can serve as agents of change.

Morrison's book ignores the thousands of ordinary people who risked their lives for the cause to bring about equality. The caption beside the picture of Rosa Parks in Remember reads "Because if I ever feel helpless or lonely I just have to remember that all it takes is one person" (Morrison 62). Ironically, Morrison gives credit for the Montgomery Bus Boycott to one person, ignoring the months of planning that involved dozens of planners. Even the photograph presents Rosa Parks in a position of power. It is a low-angle shot up at Parks that makes her appear larger than life and authoritative. The photographs of Martin Luther King Jr. also further the impression of power with a close-up shot of his face as he stands above thousands of participants in the March on Washington. Although these photographs were selected to perpetuate the hero illusion, it is more inspiring to remember the ordinary people who took a stand and were able to accomplish extraordinary feats because of their dedication and persistence rather than to glorify extraordinary people who were destined for greatness.

In contrast, Spike Lee's 1998 documentary titled 4 Little Girls is a stirring depiction of the lives and deaths of the girls who died in the 1963 16th Street Baptist Church bombing. In his film, Spike Lee looks behind what some would call "societal amnesia" to disclose the harsh realities of the civil rights movement. Lee interviews family members and friends of the murdered girls, revealing the pain and anger that they grapple with more than forty years after the tragedy. Lee not only includes images of the bombed church but also the charred and nearly unrecognizable bodies of the murdered girls. These disturbing images underscore the reality of their deaths without appearing sensationalist. The film does an exceptional job of reminding the viewer of the suffering and mindless hate that were prevalent during the civil rights movement.

However, the documentary is also biased. For instance, the girls were not little; they were fourteen, not really little girls. Lee chose to describe them as little to elicit emotion and sympathy for their tragic

7

8

9

Taylor 5

deaths. They were victims. They had not marched through the streets demanding equality; instead, Denise McNair, Carole Robertson, Addie Mae Collins, and Cynthia Wesley were simply attending Sunday school and were ruthlessly murdered. Victimizing Denise, Carole, Addie Mae, and Cynthia is not detrimental to the cultural memory in and of itself. The problem is that the victimization of the four girls is expanded to encompass the entire black community, undermining the power and achievement of the average black citizen. We need to remember the people who struggled to gain employment for blacks in the labor movement of the 1940s and 1950s that initiated the civil rights movement.

One can argue that despite the presence of misleading images in Spike Lee's film and Toni Morrison's book, at least some of the story is preserved. Still, it is easy to fall victim to the cliché: those who do not remember history are doomed to repeat it. Just because a portion of the story is remembered, it does not mean that society is immune to falling back into its old habits. This cultural amnesia not only perpetuates the injustices of the time but leaves open the possibility that these atrocities can occur again. If people believe the government can simply grant black equality, then they may believe that it can also take it away. In essence memory is about power: "The struggle of man against power is the struggle of memory against forgetting." Those who are remembered hold power over the forgotten. Their legacy is lost and so is their ability to inspire future generations through their memory.

10

Taylor 6

Works Cited

ATF Online. Bureau of Alcohol, Tobacco, Firearms and Explosives, U.S. Department of Justice. Dec. 2004. <http://www.atf.treas.gov/ aexis2/brkd_hw.html>.

Kolker, Robert. Film, Form, and Culture. New York: McGraw Hill, 1998.

Kundera, Milan. The Columbia World of Quotations. New York: Columbia University Press, 1996. Dec. 2004. <www.bartleby.com/66/>.

Loeb, Paul Rogat. Soul of a Citizen. New York: St. Martin's/Griffin, 1999.

Morrison, Toni. Remember. Boston: Houghton Mifflin, 2004.

For Analysis and Discussion

1. What would you say is Taylor's argument?
2. To what extent does she provide transitions to help you understand how her analysis supports her argument?
3. To what extent does she integrate quotations appropriately into the text of her argument?
4. To what extent does the style of citation reflect accepted conventions for academic writing?
5. If Taylor had more time to revise, what would you suggest she do?

FURTHER SUGGESTIONS FOR PEER EDITING GROUPS

Monitoring your own writing group can help ensure that the group is both providing and receiving the kinds of responses the members need. Here is a list of questions you might ask of one another after a session:

- What topics were discussed?
- Were most questions and comments directed at the level of ideas? Structure? Language?
- Were topics always brought up with a question or a comment?
- Who initiated talk more frequently — the writer or the readers?
- What roles did different group members play?
- Did each author open with specific questions or concerns?
- Did the readers begin by giving specific reactions?

After answering these questions, identify two things that are working well in your group. Then identify two things that you could improve. How would you go about making those improvements?

When we asked our students what they thought contributed to effective conversation in their writing groups, here is what they told us:

- Honest and spontaneous expression
- Free interaction among members
- High levels of personal involvement
- Members' commitment to insight and change
- The sense that self-disclosure is safe and highly valued
- Members' willingness to take responsibility for the group's effectiveness
- Members' belief that the group is important
- Members' belief that they are primary agents of help for one another
- Members' focus on communication within the group over other discussions

11

Other Methods of Inquiry: Interviews and Focus Groups

Sometimes to advance your argument you may need to do original research. By **original research**, we mean using primary sources of evidence you gather yourself. (Another common term for this type of investigation is *field research*.) Remember that primary sources of evidence include firsthand or eyewitness accounts like those found in letters or newspapers, or in research reports in which the researcher explains his or her impressions of a particular phenomenon — for example, gender relations in classroom interactions. (In contrast, a secondary source is an analysis of information contained in primary sources.)

The type of original research we discuss in this chapter relies on people — interviewees and members of focus groups — as primary sources of information. To inquire into gender dynamics in college science classrooms, then, you might conduct interviews with young women to understand their perceptions of how gender affects teaching. Or you might convene a focus group to put a variety of perspectives into play on questions about gendered teaching practices. The pages that follow present strategies for conducting interviews and setting up focus groups that can generate multiple responses to your research questions.

When you conduct research, keep in mind that you are not setting out to prove anything; instead, the process of inquiry will enable you to answer the questions *you* ask, address problems, and move readers to rethink their positions. Good critical readers know that the arguments they produce as writers are influenced by what they choose to discuss and how they construe the evidence they provide.

Although there is really no way to avoid the limitations of writing from one point of view, writers can provide readers with multiple sources of information, so that they can make their own judgments about what to believe or not believe. In fact, this is the argument we make above in studying inequities in education. Relying on a single source of data will inevitably limit your field of vision. Multiple sources of information add complexity and texture to your analysis, conveying to readers the thoroughness of your approach.

WHY DO ORIGINAL RESEARCH?

We can think of four reasons (all of which overlap to some extent) why you might do original research for a writing class.

To Increase Your Ability to Read Critically.   When you do original research, you learn, at a basic and pragmatic level, how the studies you consult in a researched argument come into being — you're on the ground floor of knowledge making. As a critical reader, you know it's important to ask questions like these: What is the source of the author's claim? Why should I believe the author? What is the source of the author's authority? What are the possible counterarguments? When you are doing original research, you are in the position of that author, with a real stake in establishing your own authority. By coming to understand what it takes to establish your own authority, you are in a better position to evaluate how effectively other researchers establish theirs.

Let's say your research question concerns gender differences in math education. You might read a study that asserts that girls and young women are being shortchanged in math classes, impeding their ability to go into math-related fields. You would want to ask about the nature of the data used to support this claim. If the author of the study states that 56 percent of the female students interviewed said they were discouraged from going into math-related fields, you might wonder where the figure of 56 percent came from. How many girls and young women were interviewed? How was this sample selected? What were the students asked? Questions like these inform your own use of interviews and focus groups.

To Increase Your Own Research Skills.   Doing original research broadens your own range of research methods. By developing a repertoire of research methods, you will be better able to explore questions that may be too complex to answer by examining texts alone. One scholar put it this way: "I couldn't see what a text was doing without looking at the worlds in which these texts served as significant activities."* After all, it is one thing to read a research report and understand its purpose, its intended

---

*Bazerman, C. (1988). *Shaping written knowledge: The genre and activity of the scientific article in science.* Madison: University of Wisconsin Press, p. 4.

audience, the nature of its claims, and the like. But it is quite another to watch scientists at work and begin to understand how they have come to know what they know. The discovery of DNA, for example, was the result of an arduous process that involved much risk, collaboration, chance, error, and competition. The neat structure of a scientific report could mislead you into thinking that science is a linear process that begins with a question, moves on to an experiment, and ends with an answer. Real research is messier than that. Original research takes us behind the words we read, introducing levels of complexity.

To Broaden Your Scope of Inquiry.   Doing original research may also broaden the scope of your inquiry. First, it is useful to use different research methods than the ones you are accustomed to using. Learning to interview and run focus groups, at the very least, can give you insight and practice for nonacademic applications — market research, for example. Second, it can make you aware of how people outside your field address the questions you raise. Consider, for example, the different perspectives an educator, a sociologist, and an economist would bring to the question of educational inequities. An educator might study educational inequities as a curricular problem, and so analyze the content of different curricula within and across schools. A sociologist might visit students' homes, noting the presence or absence of books or asking parents how they go about preparing their children for school. An economist might examine income levels in both wealthy and impoverished neighborhoods. The point is that each field brings its own perspective to a problem, adding complexity and richness to your own discussion of that problem.

To Make a Unique Contribution to a Conversation of Ideas.   Finally, doing original research affords you the opportunity to make a unique contribution to a conversation of ideas. Instead of relying exclusively on texts others have written as evidence for your claims, you can offer your own data to address a question or problem, data that others do not have available. For instance, if you wanted to examine claims that primary school teachers pay more attention to boys in class than to girls, you could review the relevant literature and then add to that literature a study that systematically analyzes the ways in which teachers in different classrooms treat boys and girls.

GETTING STARTED: WRITING A PROPOSAL

A **proposal** is a formal plan that outlines your objectives for conducting a research project, specifies the methods you intend to use, and describes what you expect the implications of the work to be. The proposal is a tool that helps guide you through various stages of the project. The most immediate benefit of writing a proposal is that through the act of writing — by setting forth an outline of your project — your thinking will become more precise.

At a minimum, a research proposal should include three sections: purpose, method, and discussion and implications. You may also want to include additional sections with materials that provide concrete support for your proposal — some of the tools that will help you get the job done. You should arrange your plan and use headings so that readers can find information quickly.

■ Describe Your Purpose

In the purpose section of your proposal, formulate the question that is motivating your study. Inquiry begins with a good question.

• A good question can help you think through the issue you want to write about.

• It is specific enough to guide your inquiry and to be answered with the tools and resources you have available and have decided to use.

• It does not limit the answer to yes, no, or either/or.

• It asks how, why, should, or the extent to which.

• It conveys a clear idea of who you are answering the question for — your audience.

In your purpose section (usually the introduction), you should summarize the issue and explain how it has led to the question driving your research. You also should explain why you are interested in this issue area, why it is important, and what is at stake. Ask yourself why others should be interested in your effort to answer the question.

■ Define Your Method

In the method section, you list and describe the tools and strategies you will use to conduct your research. Some of the tools and strategies of original research are

• conducting interviews or focus groups,

• taking notes,

• recording on audio- or videotape a particular activity or activities,

• doing background, historical, or archival work,

• observing and coming to terms with your own impressions.

In addition to identifying your method, you need to discuss the appropriateness of your tools and strategies, why they are the best means for answering your research question. Given the objectives you have set for yourself and the constraints of doing the research, are some methods better than others?

- ## Discuss Your Implications

It may seem a little premature to talk about what you hope to find in your study, but it is important to address "So what?" — to explain what you believe is the significance of your study. Place your argument in the context of the conversation you want to join and explain how your study can contribute to that conversation. Write about how your study will build on, challenge, or extend other studies in your area of research. And, finally, identify what you believe is going to be new about your findings.

- ## Include Additional Materials That Support Your Research

Depending on your instructor and the level of formality of your proposal, you may be asked to include additional materials that reveal other dimensions of your research. Those materials may include (1) an annotated bibliography, (2) scripts of the questions you are planning to ask in interviews and focus groups, and (3) the consent forms you will ask interviewees or participants in your focus groups to sign.

Annotated bibliography.   An **annotated bibliography** is a list of sources (arranged alphabetically by author) that you plan to consult and make use of in your research paper. Typically you provide a citation (author, date, title of source, and publication information) and a short summary of the source. You can present all your sources in one long list or organize them by type of source (books, journals, and so forth). An excerpt from a student's annotated bibliography is shown in Figure 11.1.

FIGURE 11.1   An Excerpt from a Student's Annotated Bibliography

Bibliography

Books

Dupper, D. R. (2003). *School social work: Skills and interventions for effective practice.* Hoboken, NJ: John Wiley & Sons.

> This book provides a general overview of the duties and responsibilities of school social workers. It explains various social problems that many students encounter, and evaluates intervention and prevention programs.

Kryder-Coe, J. H., Salamon, L. H., & Molnar, J. M. (Eds.). (1991). *Homeless children and youth: A new American dilemma.* New Brunswick, NJ: Transaction.

> This book examines the impact of child homelessness on society, the causes of child homelessness, and society's

---

(*continued on next page*)

FIGURE 11.1   (Continued)

response to child homelessness. Part of the book focuses on
the developmental and educational consequences of homelessness on children.

Vostanis, P., & Cumella, S. (Eds.). (1999). *Homeless children:*
Problems and needs. London: Jessica Kingsley.

This book is a collection of articles examining the various
aspects of life for homeless children. One article focuses
specifically on problems surrounding education for homeless
youth.

Journal Articles

All of the following journal articles focus on the educational and
developmental needs of homeless youth. They relate this issue to the
effectiveness of the McKinney-Vento Homeless Assistance Act (1987),
to the current and future work of school counselors and social workers, and to the development of community programs.

Markward, M. J., & Biros, E. (2001, July). McKinney revisited: Implications for school social work. *Children & Schools, 23*(3).
Retrieved September 28, 2004, from
http://web11.epnet.com.lib-proxy.nd.edu/

This article examines the extent to which the McKinney-Vento
Act has affected homeless children and youth. It discusses
the implications the act has had for school social work.

Moroz, K. J., & Segal, E. A. (1990, January). Homeless children:
Intervention strategies for school social workers. *Social Work in*
Education, 12(2). Retrieved September 28, 2004, from
http://web11.epnet.com.lib-proxy.nd.edu/

This article investigates the various effects of homelessness
on children. The authors propose a model for intervention for
school social workers that would connect them with community services.

Questions You Plan to Ask.   Including a list (or lists) of the questions
you expect to ask those you plan to interview or survey will help you focus
your thinking. What personal information do you need to know? What
information about your issue? What opinions and recommendations
would be helpful? Each list should include at least five good questions, but
can include many more. A sample set of questions to ask the parents of
homeless children appears in Figure 11.2.

FIGURE 11.2   Sample Interview Questions

Parent(s)

1. a. Describe your current living and family situation (parents, siblings, how long homeless, where living, where child attends school).

    b. Describe your child.

    c. Describe your relationship with your child.

2. a. Do you think homelessness is affecting your child's schooling?

    b. If so, tell me how (grades, friends, attendance, transportation).

3. Tell me about enrolling your child in school. What was the process like? Were there any problems? Conditions? Challenges?

4. a. Do you feel that your child's right to an education has been recognized?

    b. Why or why not? What experiences can you point to to support your answer?

5. Describe the relationship between your child and his or her teachers.

6. a. What types of support services is your child currently being offered in school and in the community?

    b. How effective are those services?

    c. How supportive of your child's educational and developmental growth do you feel your child's school has been?

    d. What about the Center for the Homeless?

    e. Do you have any recommendations for these sources of help or requests for other types of help or services for your child that are not currently offered?

7. How do you envision your child's future?

Consent Forms.   Whenever you plan to solicit information in an interview or focus group, you need to get the interviewee's or participants' permission to make use of that information in your research paper. We have included a sample consent form for an interview in Figure 11.3.

FIGURE 11.3   Sample Interview Consent Form

You are invited to participate in a study of homelessness and education conducted by Mary Ronan, an undergraduate at the University of Notre Dame, during the next few months. If you decide to participate, you will

1. provide up to two interviews with the researcher,

2. allow the researcher to use excerpts from the interviews in publications about research with the understanding that your identity will not be revealed at any time.

   Participation is completely voluntary. You may choose to stop participating at any time prior to completion of the project. Should you have any questions at any time, you are welcome to contact the researcher by phone or e-mail. Your decision to participate will have no effect on or prejudice your future relationship with the University of Notre Dame. One possible benefit of participating in the

---

(*continued on next page*)

FIGURE 11.3   (Continued)

study is that you will have the opportunity to learn about the implications of homelessness on education.

If you are willing to participate in this research, please read and sign the consent form below. You will be given a copy of this form to keep.

CONSENT FORM

I agree to participate in all of the procedures above. I understand that my identity will be protected during the study and that others will not have access to the interviews I provide. I also understand that my name will not be revealed when data from the research are presented in publications. I have read the above and give the researcher, Mary Ronan, permission to use excerpts from transcripts of tapes without identifying me as the writer or speaker.

_____

Date

_____

Signature

_____

Signature of Researcher
[Telephone number]/[E-mail address]

■ Establish a Timeline

To write a proposal, you'll need to draw up a schedule for your research. This timeline should include the dates when you expect to finish the proposal, when you will conduct interviews and focus groups, when you hope to have a draft, and when you will complete the project. As you develop your timeline, you need to be realistic about when you can actually complete the different stages of collecting your data and writing. You can anticipate that events will prevent everything from going as planned. People cannot always meet you when you would like them to, and you may have to change your own schedule. Therefore, be sure to contact participants well in advance of the time you would like to speak with them in interviews or focus groups.

Steps to Writing a Proposal

1 Describe your purpose. Summarize your issue, describing how it has led you to the question motivating your research.

2 Define your method. What tools and strategies are you planning to use? Why are they appropriate and sufficient for your purposes?

3 Discuss your implications. What is the context of the conversation you are entering? What significant information do you expect your study to uncover?

4 Include additional materials that support your research. These may include an annotated bibliography, a series of interview questions, and blank consent forms.

ANALYZING A PROPOSAL

Our student Mary Ronan submitted a formal proposal for a study of the education of a homeless child. Ronan's proposal was exceptionally well prepared, thorough, and thoughtful; and she included a number of additional materials — an annotated bibliography; sample questions for the teachers, students, and parents she planned to interview; and sample consent forms. We reprint only the main part of her proposal, the part that includes her purpose, methods, and discussion and implications sections, for you to consider as a model for proposal writing. Notice how Ronan summarizes her issue and explains how it led to her research, and how she makes her readers understand why her research is important.

Ronan 1

Research Paper Proposal:
A Case Study of One Homeless Child's Education and Lifestyle
Mary Ronan

In 2000, the Urban Institute estimated that 1.35 million children experience homelessness over the course of a year (Urban Institute, 2000). The U.S. Department of Education estimated that the number of children and youth in homeless situations increased from approximately 841,700 to 930,000 in 2000 (U.S. Department of Education, 2000). It also determined that preschool and elementary-aged children make up the largest numbers of children experiencing homelessness (U.S. Department of Education, 2000). Homelessness as experienced by school-aged children is clearly increasing.   *1*

Homeless children and youth are defined as "those individuals who lack a fixed, regular, and adequate nighttime residence" (McKinney-Vento Homeless Assistance Act, 1987). This includes children who live in shelters, cars, motels, and numerous other inadequate housing situations. The McKinney-Vento Act states that each child of a homeless individual and each homeless youth must have equal access to the same free, appropriate public education as provided to other children. It states specifically that homelessness alone is not a sufficient reason to separate these students from the mainstream school environment.   *2*

Homelessness has serious implications for children's developmental and academic growth. Developmental problems include   *3*

Ronan 2

withdrawal, aggression, short attention span, sleep disorders, speech delays, regressive behaviors, immature motor behavior, immature peer interaction, and inappropriate social interaction with adults (Baumohl, 1996; Pawlas, 1994). These developmental problems lead to academic problems, which are especially evident in reading and math. The majority of homeless students read below grade level and score below grade level in mathematics (Pawlas, 1994; Stormont-Spurgin & De Reus, 1995; Walsh & Buckley, 1994; Ziesemer & Marcoux, 1992). Homeless students have higher rates of school transfer, special education services, and grade retention (Baumohl, 1996; Walsh & Buckley, 1994). Homeless students face barriers to school enrollment and attendance. These students often do not have the documents required for school enrollment; as a result, many children are turned away from attending school until this issue is resolved (U.S. Department of Education, 2000). Transportation to and from school is the biggest problem for homeless youth (U.S. Department of Education, 2000). These barriers directly and negatively affect the success of homeless students in school.

　　A stable lifestyle for these children is crucial to their mental, emotional, physical, and social well-being. "Stability is central to children's growth and development, and times of transition are times of risk" (Baumohl, 1996, p. 118). Homelessness creates great risks for the developmental and academic growth of youth; these risks need to be confronted. "Children who have lost their homes live the experience of having, as they describe it, 'nowhere to go'" (Walsh & Buckley, 1994, p. 2). _4_

　　Communities need to examine how they are reacting and responding to the struggles and needs of homeless students. Despite the obstacles that homeless students face, schools are an ideal setting for developing and organizing the educational and social services they need (Wall, 1996). Comprehensive services including both educators and social workers can be done both within and outside the school system (Wall, 1996). If these homeless children's lives are to improve, they will require the help of schools and social agencies, both working as parts of a community that is sensitive and responsive to these students' needs. It is clear that society understands the importance of caring for homeless students, but to what extent have schools and social service agencies carried out their suggestions or plans? _5_

Ronan 3

The McKinney-Vento Homeless Assistance Act defines homeless youth and explains the rights of students facing homelessness. It
provides specific guidelines for how schools and social service agencies are to care for homeless students' educational needs. Yet,
Congress has not adequately funded state or local efforts to implement this legislation. In 2003, Congress appropriated $55 million for
educational programs under the McKinney-Vento Act. However, this is
$15 million less than the authorized amount of $70 million (National
Coalition for the Homeless, 2004). Is the country doing everything it
can to ensure the rights of homeless children as stated in the
McKinney-Vento Homeless Assistance Act?

6

The question this research is attempting to answer is "To
what extent are schools and social service agencies, working as
parts of larger communities, creating a stable lifestyle that will
improve homeless students' developmental and educational growth?"
There has not been much research examining how effectively schools
and social service agencies are creating stability in homeless students' lives. In order to better the lives of these children, research
must be done investigating and evaluating the current services
offered.

7

The developmental and academic lives of students are threatened by the lack of stability resulting from homelessness. This issue
is a very important one as the numbers of homeless children continue
to increase each year. Answering this question will provide valuable
information to both schools and social agencies about how to better
care for the specific needs and rights of homeless students. Moreover,
this research will lead to a greater sense of community caring for
those who live in poverty. It may inspire future research and the
creation of programs that better aid homeless students.

8

Methods

I will take a case study approach in order to better understand this issue and attempt to answer my research question. My
case study will focus on one child from the South Bend Center for the
Homeless. I will interview the child, his or her parents, teacher,
school social worker, and others who play a role in creating stability
in this child's life. I will take notes as well as audio-record the interviews. These interviews will allow me to explore the connections

9

Ronan 4

between homelessness and education as explained by the voices of those who witness or are affected by homelessness every day.

I will also be using archival information, including both journal articles and books, from the library. I will explore what other researchers have contributed to this issue and what they are currently saying about it. I will also examine present-day statistics involving homelessness, youth, and education, and will study the plans of various government and community programs and policies, particularly the McKinney-Vento Homeless Assistance Act. This will help me to further develop and answer my own questions about homelessness and education. *10*

Utilizing these various methods will provide me with a broad range of information and resources that will aid me in completing my research. Directly discussing this education issue with participants will hopefully lead to an honest and realistic perspective. It is the true stories of those who are faced with the issue of homelessness on a daily basis that will bring this important issue to the surface. *11*

Discussion and Implications

In America, over 800,000 children are homeless. In South Bend, over 300 children live in one of three homeless shelters. It is believed that 50 percent of these local children will grow up to be homeless. Many homeless children do not attend school regularly. Studies have found that those who do attend school do not perform as well as their peers and have difficulties socializing with others. A school should be a permanent safe-haven for these students. A school should be one place that these students might be able to consider their home. Why then do problems involving homeless youth and education continue to exist? *12*

Homelessness traps the young in a vicious cycle from which they may never be able to escape. If they are continuously moving from shelter to shelter, they are continuously moving from school to school. As a result, their attendance may drop; their performance may not be at grade level; they may be stereotyped and labeled by others based on their temporary lifestyle. Without the psychological, social, and mental benefits a strong formal education imparts, the homeless child seems to be left to the fate of his or her parents. The cycle of homelessness continues for another generation. *13*

Ronan 5

Clearly, this issue is an important one. When we think of the   *14*
homeless, we might imagine a disheveled man sleeping on the street
or a woman holding a cardboard sign begging for food. But what
about the children who, instead of going home to a three-bedroom
house in a residential neighborhood, go to a large dormitory at a
shelter? The issue of homelessness and its effects on education need
to be examined.

The need for school social workers is great. It seems that   *15*
much more can be offered to those students who face such grave
realities every day. Communities need to work with both schools and
social agencies to ensure that these children are cared for. Homelessness impairs the ability of the individual to receive a good education,
something to which every child has a right.

Perhaps as a result of this study there will be more community   *16*
and school action and involvement to support homeless students.
Perhaps there will be better busing systems so that these students
can remain enrolled in the same school for longer periods. Perhaps
school social workers can work toward finding more permanent living
arrangements for their homeless students. Perhaps more mentoring
and tutoring programs can be formed to aid homeless students. Much
can be done and should be done to better the lives of these students.

For Analysis and Discussion

1. How would you describe the conversation Ronan wants to contribute to in her study of homeless children?
2. What is the gap or issue that she identifies?
3. What is at stake in addressing this problem?
4. To what extent do you think Ronan's proposed research is compelling?
5. To what extent do you think the author can answer her question by using the research methods she describes?

INTERVIEWING

An **interview** is a face-to-face conversation in which you ask questions to collect information or opinions that relate to your research question. It's certainly possible to conduct an interview by phone, especially if the interviewee is not local, but a face-to-face conversation, in which you can note physical details and body language, is preferable.

The ways writers incorporate interviews into their writing appears almost seamless; but keep in mind that a finished text hides the process involved in conducting a successful interview. What you don't see is the planning that occurs. Writers have to make appointments with each of the people they interview; they have to develop a script, or list of questions, before actually conducting the interview; and they have to test the questions to be sure they work — that is, that the answers give them the information they are looking for. In other words, the key to a successful interview is preparation. The following information should help you plan for your interview and prepare you for writing down your results.

■ Plan the Interview

You'll want to do some preliminary research to identify people who can help you understand more about your subject: What kind of expertise or experience do they have? Then you have to contact them to find out if they are willing to be interviewed. Begin by explaining your project and why you want to interview them (you may want to send them a copy of your proposal). Let them know about how much of their time you are requesting: Half an hour? An hour? (More than an hour is probably excessive.) If you are planning to record the interview — always a wise idea — make sure the person consents to being recorded. Then make the necessary arrangements. For example, you may need to reserve a room where you can conduct your interview without being disturbed.

Obviously it is crucial to find out in your first contact whether your candidates actually have expertise in an area relevant to your study. If they lack that expertise, consider asking if they can recommend someone who has it.

It's important to set up appointments with people early on. To keep on schedule, list the names of people who have agreed to be interviewed:

Interviewee 1: _____ Contacted? _____(y/n)

Interviewee 2: _____ Contacted? _____(y/n)

■ Prepare Your Script

You should now begin to work on your script in earnest. If you submitted a series of questions with your proposal, you may have received some response to them from your instructor or classmates. Perhaps they suggested refinements or proposed additional questions. If you agree with their suggestions, now is the time to incorporate them. As you work on your script, keep the following points in mind:

Try to Establish Common Ground.   In any conversation, you want to establish common ground, and an interview is no different. Do you have any interests in common with the person that may ease you into the inter-view? Order your questions so that you begin by establishing common ground and then move on to the issues you want to learn more about.

Start with Nonthreatening Questions.   For example, "How long have you been working at the homeless shelter?" "What prompted you to work at a homeless shelter?" "What role do you play with the children at the homeless shelter?"

Ask Filter Questions.   Filter questions help you determine what the person you are interviewing knows or has experienced. For instance, you might ask a worker at a homeless shelter if he or she works with children. If not, does he or she work with parents? Of course, if you've done your homework, you will know where to start the interview.

Beware of Yes/No Questions.   Try not to ask questions that encourage simple yes or no responses. Work on rephrasing yes/no questions in your script so that you're more likely to get an enlightening answer. For example, don't ask "Do you think that the children at the homeless shelter can overcome the obstacles they face?" Instead, ask something like this: "How do you think children at the homeless shelter can overcome the obstacles they face?"

Try Funneling.   *Funneling* means moving from more-general questions — "What challenges have you faced as an educator in the homeless shelter?" — to more-specific ones — "How did you respond to those challenges?"

Rehearse and Then Revise the Script.   After you've reworked your script, rehearse it with your writing group or some friends to see how it works. You want to develop a sense of how an interviewee is going to respond to your questions. Is the wording clear? Are you getting the information you need? If not, what other questions should you ask? How did the order and pacing of the questions make your stand-in interviewees feel? How long did the interview take? After the rehearsal, revise the script to improve the content, order, and pacing of your questions.

■ Conduct the Interview

On the day of an interview, contact your interviewee again to make sure he or she remembers the time of the interview and knows how to find the location where it will take place. See to it that your tape recorder or video camera is charged and functioning, and has sufficient recording capacity for the interview. Be on time. Start by having the person sign a simple consent form (see Figure 11.3). It should specify how you will use the material and should indicate that the interviewee knows you will be recording the interview and agrees to let you use quotes from the interview in your paper.

Once you begin asking questions, if at all possible, take notes and record the conversation. Be flexible with the script as you go. Pursue new questions that are raised by what the interviewee tells you. If the interviewee's answers are vague, evasive, or misdirected, try rephrasing your questions to be more specific about the information you need. If you think the interviewee is implying something that is of special interest to you, ask for clarification. This kind of reflective query may shake loose some interesting new material.

Toward the end of the interview, check your script for important questions you may have forgotten to ask. If there are several, try to ask only the most important ones in the time remaining.

■ Make Sense of the Interview

Conducting an interview is only part of the challenge; you then have to make sense of what was said. That process involves four steps:

1. *Familiarize yourself with the conversation.* If you recorded the interview, listen to or watch it a couple of times to become really familiar with what was said. Read through your notes several times too.

2. *Transcribe the interview.* Being familiar with the conversation will make it easier to transcribe. Keep in mind that transcription takes more time than you think, and plan accordingly. An hour interview usually takes about three hours to transcribe.

3. *Analyze the interview.* Read through the interview again. Look for answers to the questions motivating your research, and look for recurring patterns or themes. Make a list of those ideas relevant to the issues you intend to focus on, especially evidence that might support your argument.

4. *Find one good source.* Using the themes you identify in your analysis as a guide, find one good source that relates to your interview in some way. Maybe your subject's story fits into an educational debate (for example, public versus private education). Or maybe your subject's story counters a common conception about education (that inner-city schools are hopelessly inadequate). You're looking for a source you can link to your interview in an interesting and effective way.

■ Turn Your Interview into an Essay

Try to lay out on paper, in paragraphs, the material you've collected that pertains to the focus of your paper. In a first draft, you might take these steps:

1. State your argument, or the purpose of your essay. What do you want to teach your readers?

2. Begin writing your supporting evidence for your thesis. What examples from your reading, observations, or interviews do you want to offer your readers? How do those examples illuminate your claim?

3. Place quotations from more than one source in as many paragraphs as you can, so that you can play the quotations off against one another. What is significant about the ways you see specific quotations "in conversation" with one another? How do these conversations between quotations help you build your own point?

4. Consider possible counterarguments to the point you want to make.

5. Help readers understand what is at stake in adopting your position.

Steps to Interviewing

1 Plan the interview. After you've identified candidates through research, contact them to explain your project and set up appointments if they are willing to participate.

2 Prepare your script. Draft your questions, rehearse them with your classmates or friends, and then make revisions based on their responses.

3 Conduct the interview. Be flexible with your script as you go, making sure to take good notes even if you are recording the interview.

4 Make sense of the interview. Review the recording and your notes of the interview, transcribe the interview, analyze the transcript, and connect the conversation to at least one good source.

5 Turn your interview into an essay. State your argument, organize your evidence, use quotes to make your point, consider counterarguments, and help your readers understand what's at stake.

USING FOCUS GROUPS

Focus groups can provide you with an original source of evidence to complement (or complicate, contradict, or extend) the evidence you find in books and articles. Conducting a focus group is much like conducting an interview. According to Bruce L. Berg, in *Qualitative Research Methods for the Social Sciences,* a **focus group** "may be defined as an interview style designed for small groups . . . addressing a particular topic of interest or relevance to the group and the researcher." College administrators often speak with groups of students to understand the nature of a problem — for instance, whether writing instruction is as effective as it should be beyond a first-year writing course, or whether technology is used to best effect in classes across the curriculum. One advantage of a focus group, as opposed to an interview, is that once one person starts talking, others join in. It is generally easier to get a conversation going in a focus group than to get an interview started with a single person.

A typical focus group session is guided by a facilitator, or moderator. The moderator's job is much like the interviewer's: to draw out information from the participants on topics of importance to a given investigation. The informal atmosphere of the focus group is intended to encourage participants to speak freely and completely about their behaviors, attitudes, and opinions. Interaction among group members often takes the form of brainstorming, generating a larger number of ideas, issues, topics, and even solutions to problems than could be produced through individual conversations.

What follow are several basic tasks necessary to orchestrating a focus group.

■ Select Participants for the Focus Group

Focus groups should consist of five to seven participants, in addition to you, the moderator. Think carefully about the range of participants you'll need to gather the information you're hoping to gather. Depending on your issue, you might choose participants based on gender, ethnicity, major, year in school, living situation, or some other factor. Do you want a wide range of participants? Or do you want to control the focus of the conversation by looking at just one particular group of people? For instance, if you wanted to find out if technology is serving students' needs, would you talk only to people in the sciences? Or would you want a cross-section of disciplines represented? Or if your question is whether colleges and universities should take race and ethnicity into consideration when selecting students from the applicant pool, would you limit participation to the admissions staff? Where should you look for input on the purpose of giving preference to minority students or the advantages of a diverse campus?

■ Plan the Focus Group

Planning is as important for a focus group as it is for an interview. Make specific arrangements with participants about the time and place of the focus group session, and be clear about how much time it will take, usually 30 minutes. You should tape-record or videotape the session, in addition to any notes you take. Jot down important information during the session, and allow yourself time to make more extensive notes as soon as it is over. You will need to get permission from respondents to use the information they give you and ensure their anonymity. (In your essay, you can refer to participants by letter, number, or some other designation.) Make a sheet with your signature that spells this out clearly, and make sure all your participants sign it before the session. You should include a statement pointing out that people have the right not to participate. We have included sample consent forms in Figures 11.4 and 11.5.

FIGURE 11.4   Sample Consent Form for a Focus Group

You are invited to participate in a study of academic writing at the university over the next four years. You were selected from a random sample of all first-year students. If you decide to participate, you will

1. provide the researcher with copies of the writing you complete for every class and the assignment, when available;

2. attend up to four focus group sessions during a given academic year;

3. allow the researcher to use excerpts from the writing you complete and the focus group sessions in publications about research with the understanding that your identity will not be revealed at any time.

In all, out-of-class participation will take no more than four hours during an academic year.

Participation is completely voluntary; you may stop participating at any time prior to completion of the project. Should you have any questions at any time, you are welcome to contact the researcher at the address below or via e-mail. Your decision to participate or not will have no effect on your grade in any course or prejudice your future relationship with the university. One benefit of participating in the study is that you will have the opportunity to learn important information about writing.

If you are willing to participate in this research, please read and sign the consent form below. You will be given a copy of this form to keep.

CONSENT FORM

I agree to participate in all of the procedures above. I understand that my identity will be protected during the study and that instructors will not have access to the statements I make in focus group sessions. I also understand that my name will not be revealed when data from the research are presented in publications. (Tapes from this study will be kept for five years and then destroyed.) I have read the above and give the researcher, Stuart Greene, and his coauthors permission to use excerpts from what I write or transcripts of tapes without identifying me as the writer or speaker.

_____   _____

Date   *Signature*

                                  _____

                                  Signature of Researcher
                                  [Telephone number]/[E-mail address]

■ Prepare Your Script

Many of the guidelines for designing interview questions (see p. 262) apply equally well to focus group questions. So, for example, you might start by establishing common ground or with a couple of nonthreatening questions. For variety, and to keep the discussion moving, use both open and closed (yes/no answer) questions. Consider asking participants for definitions,

---

FIGURE 11.5   Sample Consent Form for a Focus Group

Should colleges and universities take race and ethnicity into consideration when selecting new freshmen from the applicant pool? What is the purpose of giving preference to minority status in admissions? What does a diverse campus offer its students? These are some of the issues I want to discuss in today's focus group. But before we start, let me tell you about the assignment and your involvement.

The focus group is an interview style designed for small groups of five to seven participants. Focus group interviews are guided discussions that address a particular topic of interest or relevance to the group and the researcher. The informality of the focus group structure is intended to encourage participants to speak freely about their behaviors, attitudes, and opinions. For the purposes of my research, focus groups are a way to include multiple perspectives in my paper.

This session will be recorded so that I can prove my research. No names will be used in any drafts or in my final paper; instead, I will use letters (A, B, C) to identify different speakers. Two focus groups — one for minority students at Notre Dame and another for nonminority students — are being held so that I can obtain opinions and viewpoints from both sides of the issue and discuss their similarities and differences in my report. Some things to keep in mind during the session:

- Because I need to transcribe the dialogue, try not to talk over another person.
- Feel free to agree or disagree with a question, statement, or another person's answer.
- Focus on the discussion, not the question.
- Avoid going off on tangents.
- Be open and honest in all your responses.

Thank you for taking the time to be involved in my research. By signing below you give me permission to use the comments you provide for my paper. You understand that in no way will your identity be revealed, except by your minority or nonminority status. If you would like a copy of the results of the focus groups, please include your e-mail address, and the documents will be sent to you.

Name _____   Male Female (circle one)
Ethnicity _____   Class of _____
E-mail address _____

---

impressions, examples, their ideas of others' perceptions, and the like. Also, consider quoting from key passages in the scholarly research you will be using and asking for the group's responses to these "expert" theories. Not only will this be interesting; it also will help you organize and integrate your focus group evidence with evidence from library sources in your essay. Ask a wider range of questions than you think you might need, so that you can explore side issues if they arise.

■ Conduct the Focus Group

On the day you conduct the focus group, contact those who have agreed to participate to remind them of when and where it will happen. Show up ahead of time to make sure that your tape recorder or video camera is in good working order and that the room has sufficient seating for the participants. And don't forget your script. Here are three other guidelines:

Ask Questions That Draw People Out.   During the focus group, be ready to draw out participants with follow-up questions ("Can you offer an example?" "Where do you think this impression comes from?"). Encourage all participants to speak; don't allow one member to dominate the discussion. (You may need to ask a facilitating question like "Do the rest of you agree with X's statement?" or "How would you extend what X has said?" or "Has anyone had a different experience?")

Limit the Time of a Focus Group Session.   It's a good idea to limit the session to twenty to thirty minutes. When deciding how long the session should last, remember that it will take approximately three times longer to transcribe it. You must transcribe the session so that you can read through the participants' comments and quote them accurately.

Notice Nonverbal Interactions.   The tape recorder or video camera will give you a record of what was said, but be sure to notice nonverbal interactions and responses in your session, taking notes of body language, reluctance or eagerness to speak, and dynamics between group members that either open up or shut down conversation. These responses should be part of the data you analyze.

■ Interpret the Data from the Focus Group

Once you transcribe your focus group session, decide how you will refer anonymously to your participants. You then need to interpret the significance of the way participants talk about issues, as well as the information they relate. Interpret the nonverbal communication in the group as well as the verbal communication.

In making claims based on focus group data, remember that data from focus group interviews are not the same as data from individual interviews. They reflect collective thinking, ideas shared and negotiated by the group. Also, although you might speculate that data from a focus group are indicative of larger trends, be careful about the kinds of claims you make. One first-year student's idea is not necessarily every first-year student's idea.

The principal aim of doing original research is to make a contribution to a conversation using primary material as evidence to support your

Steps for Conducting Focus Groups

1 **Select participants for the focus group.** Identify the range of your five to seven participants. Are you looking for diverse perspectives or a more specialized group?

2 **Plan the focus group.** Make sure you have a specified time and place, and that your participants are willing to sign consent forms.

3 **Prepare your script.** Prepare a variety of open and closed questions; consider quoting research you are interested in using in your paper to get participants' responses; and try to rehearse and revise.

4 **Conduct the focus group.** Record the session; ask questions that draw people out; limit the time of the session; and notice nonverbal interactions. And don't forget the consent forms.

5 **Interpret the data from the focus group.** Transcribe and analyze the data, including nonverbal communications; draw conclusions, but be careful not to overgeneralize from your small sample.

argument. For instance, when you conduct interviews or focus group discussions, you are collecting information (or data) that can offer a unique perspective. And doing original research also can enable you to test others' claims or assumptions and broaden your scope of inquiry beyond secondary materials. An effective piece of original research still relies on secondary materials, particularly as you find ways to locate what you discover in the context of what other authors have observed and argued. Moreover, there is the value of using multiple sources of information to support your claims — using your observations and the findings of others to say something about your subject. Also important, the research method(s) you choose depends on the question you ask. A focus on the types of educational opportunities available to the homeless lends itself more to close observation, interviews, and perhaps focus groups.

Finally, we want to end with an ethical reminder: *Be fair to your sources.* Throughout this chapter, we have included a number of forms on which you can base your own consent forms when you conduct interviews and focus groups. When people give you their consent to use their words, it is incumbent on you — really it is essential — that you represent as faithfully as possible what people have said. As a researcher, you are given a kind of power over the people you interview and write about, using what they tell you for your own purposes. You cannot abuse the trust they place in you when they consent to be part of your research. It is important that they understand why you're doing the research, and how your theories and assumptions will likely figure into your interpretation of the information you gather. You must also be aware of how their words will be construed by those who read what you write.

(Acknowledgments continued from p. iv)

Barbara Ehrenreich. "Cultural Baggage." From *The New York Times Magazine*, April 5, 1992. Copyright © 1992 by Barbara Ehrenreich. Reprinted with permission.

E. D. Hirsch Jr. "Preface to *Cultural Literacy*." From *Cultural Literacy* by E. D. Hirsch Jr. Copyright © 1987 by Houghton Mifflin Company. Reprinted by permission of Houghton Mifflin Company. All rights reserved.

Ada María Isasi-Díaz. "Hispanic in America: Starting Points." Originally published in *Christianity in Crisis*, May 31, 1991. Copyright © 1991 Ada María Isasi-Díaz. Reprinted with permission of the author.

James W. Loewen. "The Land of Opportunity." From *Lies My Teacher Told Me: Everything Your American History Textbook Got Wrong* by James W. Loewen. Copyright © 1996 by James W. Loewen. Reprinted by permission of The New Press.

Elizabeth Martínez. "Reinventing 'America': Call for a New National Identity." From *De Colores Means All of Us: Latina Views for a Multi-Colored Century* by Elizabeth Martínez. Copyright © 1998 by Elizabeth Martínez. Reprinted by permission of South End Press.

Anna Quindlen. "No Place Like Home." From *Thinking Out Loud: On the Personal, the Politicians, the Public, and the Private* by Anna Quindlen. Copyright © 1993 by Anna Quindlen. Used with permission of Random House, Inc.

Myra Sadker and David Sadker. "Hidden Lessons." From *Failing at Fairness: How Our Schools Cheat Girls* from *The New York Times*. Copyright © 1994 by Myra Sadker and David Sadker. Reprinted with the permission of Scribner, an imprint of Simon & Schuster. All rights reserved.

Ronald Takaki. "Policies: Strategies and Solutions." From *Debating Diversity: Clashing Perspectives on Race and Ethnicity in America*, Third Edition, edited by Ronald Takaki. Copyright © 2002 by Oxford University Press, Inc. Reprinted with the permission of Oxford University Press, Inc.

Index of Authors, Titles, and Key Terms